CLOUGH
AND
WALKER

CLOUGH AND WALKER

FOREST'S GREATEST MANAGERS

DON WRIGHT

AMBERLEY

For Sam and Oliver, grandsons and 3G Foresters.

First published 2016

Amberley Publishing
The Hill, Stroud
Gloucestershire, GL5 4EP

www.amberley-books.com

British Library Cataloguing in Publication Data.
A catalogue record for this book is available from the British Library.

ISBN 978 1 4456 5971 8 (hardback)
ISBN 978 1 4456 5972 5 (ebook)

Origination by Amberley Publishing.
Printed in the UK.

Contents

Warm Up

What follows is an appreciation of Billy Walker and Brian Clough, the two longest-serving and best managers of Nottingham Forest Football Club, and a personal memoir by one fortunate enough to witness most of their seasons the south bank of the Trent. Despite contrasting personalities, there were striking similarities between the two and they shared an approach to the game that harmonised with the traditions of the Garibaldi Reds: the belief in passing and keeping possession of the ball. This had been the Forest way almost from the club's beginning. Most teams had relied on individual dribbling and forward rushes – you might say 'kick and rush' – but, after captaining Forest against Major Francis Marindin's famous Royal Engineers at Christmas in 1873, Sam Weller Widdowson adopted the military men's strategy of short passing combinations that became part of the Foresters' DNA. Welsh international Ivor Powell, manager of Bradford City in the early 1950s, once claimed: 'We have a wonderful harmonium in the dressing room.'

The first match Labour politician and journalist Roy Hattersley (Baron Hattersley since November 1997) saw involved Billy Walker's Forest. It was at Hillsborough against Sheffield Wednesday on 2 December 1944, just before his twelfth birthday. 'It was love at first sight' for Wednesday, Hattersley wrote, and he has remained a fan ever since. His father, Frederick, who took him to the game was a Forest supporter all his life. He had been a Roman Catholic priest in Shirebrook who left the church to run away with Enid, a local woman, and set up home in Sheffield, where Roy was born. 'We never left the ground before quarter past five,' Hattersley wrote. This was not to avoid the crush but waiting for the results of other matches to come up on the display boards. His father wouldn't leave before learning the Forest result. 'No ball ever flew in the air without him reminding me of an ancient Nottingham adage. "Only angels play up there," he used to say.' Clearly a continuing theme on Trentside. The match, which Wednesday won 2-1, was in the wartime League One North. The Forest team included goalkeeper Larry Platts, full-backs Bob McCall and Geoff Thomas, Bill Baxter and Ted Blagg in the half-back line and the Reds' goalscorer, left-winger Tommy Johnston.

'Warm up' and 'cool down' exercise routines are valued modern advances. In the eras of Walker and Clough, 'shooting in' was about the limit for players before kick-off. In the amateur game there wasn't always time for that. Once on Bennerley rec' at Cotmanhay we were kept hanging about because our opponents arrived late. Then we were told to run around the pitch. When the visitors, most of them young miners, turned up they apologised for the delay and for being covered in coal dust. They had just come off shift, they explained, and hadn't had time to shower at the spanking new post-nationalisation pithead baths. 'Don't believe a word of it,' our manager told us. 'They think that being pit black makes them look tough. Well, it doesn't frighten us. Not Cotmanhay lads. We've seen blue scars never mind dirt when our dads have stripped off in the scullery to get into a tin bath after coming home from the pit. They've got it cushy nowadays.' It worked like Clough's psychology. 'We'll show 'em,' we told ourselves.

They were the best of times for Forest supporters, the Walker and Clough eras. There is a statue of Brian Clough in the city centre, a sculpted bust in the reception area off Pavilion Road and a stand named in his honour. His assistant, Peter Taylor, also has a City Ground stand named after him. Across the river, a stand is named after Jimmy Sirrell, who managed Notts County for some twelve years in three spells, and outside the ground on Meadow Lane there is a statue of him sitting on the bench with his trainer, Jack Wheeler. I hope that readers of the following chapters will come to agree with me that the achievements of Billy Walker deserve proper recognition.

I

Dynamo Generation

Spring 1935 was a significant season of the year for the three of us: Billy Walker, Brian Clough and me. I was born on 4 April, Clough a fortnight earlier and at the end of the month Walker, then thirty-seven, won his first silverware as a manager, guiding Sheffield Wednesday to a 4-2 victory over favourites West Bromwich Albion in the FA Cup Final at Wembley. The official programme, priced at sixpence, omitted to mention the competing clubs on the front cover. On 6 May, George V and Queen Mary were to celebrate their diamond jubilee and their majesties' anniversary was deemed by the Football Association more worthy of prominence. Details of the finalists were moved to inside pages.

A consumptive youngster whose father, a former professional with Wolves, warned his sickly son that he was too frail for football, Billy Walker grew into a sturdy six-footer and went on to captain Aston Villa and England. He signed professional forms in May 1919 and stayed with Villa for the whole of his playing career, remaining the club's all-time record goalscorer with 244 goals in 531 appearances. Walker scored both goals in his first-team debut, a 2-1 FA Cup victory against Queen's Park Rangers on 10 January 1920, and in the same season collected an FA Cup winner's medal when Villa beat Huddersfield 1-0 in the final at Stamford Bridge.

Walker also scored on his international debut, a 2-0 defeat of Ireland at Roker Park, Sunderland, on 23 October 1920. He was capped eighteen times, scoring nine goals – including England's first at the new Empire Stadium, Wembley, on 12 April 1924, equalising against Scotland with a precise left-footed shot. He captained England against France, Scotland and in his final international in 1932 – a 4-3 victory over Austria's renowned 'Wunderteam' at Stamford Bridge.

After retiring as a player in December 1933, the thirty-six-year-old Walker became manager of Sheffield Wednesday just before Christmas, when the side was struggling near the foot of the First Division. He turned their fortunes around. Wednesday finished third behind champions Arsenal. Disappointment followed the FA Cup triumph and Walker resigned in November 1937 after an angry confrontation.

Non-league Chelmsford City gave him the chance to rebuild his reputation and in March 1939 he was appointed manager of Nottingham Forest, then a struggling Second Division club. It was the beginning of a remarkable twenty-five-year relationship. Walker kept the club going through the Second World War with one of the game's first youth development policies, and in a golden decade during the 1950s led them from the Third Division South to the First Division, which culminated in a glorious 2-1 FA Cup triumph against Luton Town at Wembley in 1959, when Forest played with ten men for two-thirds of the game after Roy Dwight was taken to hospital with a broken leg – no substitutes were allowed in those days.

Billy Walker retired after twenty-one years as manager in July 1960. He stayed on at the City Ground as a member of the club's committee until his death in November 1964.

I first saw a Billy Walker Forest team play in 1945 and a Brian Clough Reds' team in 1975. Clough's unmatchable reign at the City Ground lasted eighteen years. Another England international forward as a player, he was Forest's most successful and second longest-serving manager.

Clough and I were at junior school during the war years. For both of us, a ball was our constant companion. He had a park to play on a short walk from his home in Middlesbrough and had brothers to join him in games. I played on my own in our backyard or else in the street with my friends. Brian's father, Joe, had seen active service during the First World War with the King's Own Yorkshire Light Infantry. My father was one of the first to be called up in 1940 when the Second World War began in earnest. He was in the Grenadier Guards and, being a motorcycle enthusiast, joined as a despatch rider with the Guards Armoured Brigade. Both our dads were left with limps as a memento of their service.

Victory in Europe was celebrated in the UK on 8 May 1945. Still in the army, my father was unenthusiastic about the celebratory street parties and reluctant to fly a flag from our bedroom window. By the time he had relented, the British, Commonwealth and American banners had gone and all the Ilkeston Co-operative Society store had left on their counters were a few Soviet flags. Well, Russia had been an important ally so the Hammer and Sickle adorned our house. Later, in the winter, the whole country was excited by a short visit from the Moscow Dynamo football team.

But first, for me, on the 26 May there was a match to see at the Manor Ground between an Ilkeston and District XI and a Nottingham Forest side brought by Billy Walker to support the armed forces charity SSAFA (Soldiers, Sailors, Airmen and Families Association). On Friday 1 June the *Ilkeston Advertiser* reported that:

> After a keen and interesting game, Ilkeston won by 4 goals to 1. Mr Walker, manager of the Forest team, came to watch several of the players and was keenly interested in two of the Ilkeston players. Also the name of an Ilkeston schoolboy was given to Mr Walker and it is understood that this boy will go for a series of trials in the near future.

After the match, the teams and friends enjoyed a social evening in Holy Trinity church hall. Billy Walker was impressed by the standard of the local players, the enthusiasm and number of spectators and the facilities at the Manor Ground. The time was ripe for a new town club to be formed and, now the war was over, there was no good reason for it not to happen.

Billy Walker's challenge was taken up almost immediately and at the beginning of August an *Advertiser* headline announced, 'New Ilkeston Town Football Club'. On Saturday 18 August I took myself off to see twenty-eight players take part in a trial match and heard that Town would play in the Notts and Derbyshire Senior League against teams from Forest, Leicester City, Derby County and Notts County, as well as local sides. Turnstile operators and kit cleaners were needed and eight boys between the ages of twelve and fourteen were wanted as ball boys – unfortunately, I was two years too young. It was announced that admission charges would be nine pence (boys four pence) and season tickets would cost ten shillings each. It was also the club's intention to organise supporters' buses for away matches 'now that motor fuel restrictions had been relaxed'. When a Forest team came to the Manor Ground for a league match on 22 September they showed 'greater understanding and cohesion' in winning 3-1. The 'Walker way' was already winning me over.

In late autumn news came to lift the spirits of a war-weary Britain hit by shortages that even football had to deal with – bananas were back. The papers reported that the first cargoes were on their way from the West Indies. But there was a leather shortage and clubs used the same ball for many matches. Rationing affected everyone. It took 158 clothing coupons to outfit a football team – five for a pair of boots, four per shirt, three for a pair of shorts, two per pair of socks and eight for the goalkeeper's jersey. Smaller clubs found it hard to put together enough coupons and some appealed to supporters for help. When former Derby County defender veteran Jack Webb joined Ilkeston Town he gave the club his spare clothing coupons to buy kit. His gift was not enough to secure his place after the club suffered a record 11-1 defeat in the FA Cup on 1 November 1947. Ilkeston, then in the Central Alliance, had beaten Ransome and Marles (Newark) and Boston United, both of the higher Midland League, in the first two qualifying rounds, attracting a crowd of 7,200 to the Manor Ground for the latter match. So on 1 November the team and 2,000 travelling supporters (making up a third of the gate) went to Grantham's London Road ground in high spirits. They were outclassed and Webb's lack of pace was exposed by his immediate opponent centre-forward Jack McCartney, who scored six.

The spirits of the Town contingent remained high. On the way home, the players' coach, on which I was fortunate enough to travel, stopped at a village pub and such a good time was had that the landlord commented, 'If that's what you're like when you've lost 11-1, I'd like to see you when you've won.' A week previously, Ilkeston had scored ten goals to two against Bolsover Colliery in the league. At the end of the season Town were runners-up to Billy Walker's Forest 'A' in the Alliance. Town were three points behind the young Reds but had scored 104 goals, twenty more than the champions.

The *Daily Worker* led the way in reporting that Soviet league champions Moscow Dynamo were to tour the UK. On Sunday 4 November two Lend-Lease Dakotas, their wing tips emblazoned with red stars, touched down at Croydon airport and the Russian players, coaches and trainers, officials, a doctor and interpreter, together with accompanying radio and print journalists, stepped out into the London sunshine and media glare.

The 1945/46 season was a transitional one and Forest played in the Football League South with teams like Arsenal, Chelsea, Tottenham Hotspur, Charlton Athletic, Fulham, Derby County, Aston Villa and Leicester City. Dynamo asked to play Arsenal and so the question was – who else would provide their opposition? Billy Walker was quick to issue an invitation to the City Ground. His former club, Sheffield Wednesday, were also eager prospective hosts. But a second London club, Chelsea, was chosen along with Cardiff City and Glasgow Rangers. Efforts to extend the tour were rebuffed by the Russians, who also rejected the opportunity to play an FA XI, much to the disappointment of Forest centre-half Bob Davies, whose selection had been urged by former Arsenal and England star Charles Buchan, then an influential football correspondent with the *News Chronicle*.

Tuesday 13 November was a cold and overcast day but crowds, including servicemen, had been queuing in front of the Stamford Bridge turnstiles from 8 a.m. By kick-off the stands and terraces were packed with 85,000 spectators. Somewhat against the run of play, Chelsea were two goals up at half-time with Tommy Lawton leading the attack, Dynamo having missed from the penalty spot. Raymond Glendenning's radio commentary for the BBC did not begin until the second half. Ten-year-old Brian Clough and I were impatient listeners. The Russians were fighting back and with fifteen minutes left were level. Then we heard the excitement in Glendenning's voice as Lawton soared above two defenders to head a glorious goal. Tiring Chelsea struggled to hold on to their lead and in the 85th minute, inside-left Bobrov drove home a cross from the right wing to equalise. So honours were even at the final whistle when the commentator described how the crowd invaded the pitch and carried Bobrov shoulder-high from the field.

Bobrov became a hero for Brian and me, too. I like to think it was because he was a great player but perhaps also the fact that his name was the easiest for ten-year-olds to pronounce and remember had something to do with it. Some forty-five years later we were still talking about him and the Dynamo tour. The topic came up during a conversation at the City Ground when Forest manager Brian Clough, chairman Geoffrey Macpherson, secretary Ken Smales and I, then editor of the *Newark Advertiser*, met in the chairman's office ostensibly to discuss my newspaper's coverage of the club. After the second successive European Cup triumph at the end of May, City Ground attendances were falling alarmingly. Manchester United attracted nearly 30,000 at the beginning of October but there were only 17,000 at the next home match against Brighton. The *Advertiser* already carried a column by John Lawson, Forest's press officer, so we agreed to supplement this with exclusive features on the Reds. By a happy coincidence gates did pick up, helped by an excellent run in the FA Cup that was halted by Ipswich after a sixth-round replay.

The main issue having been settled, I reminded Geoffrey of his 1950 parliamentary battle in the Ilkeston constituency. He had stood as a Liberal candidate in a 'David and Goliath' contest against Labour's George Oliver, who was defending a 30,000 majority, the fourth largest in the country. I recalled that Geoffrey shaved a couple of thousand off that majority and took second place from the Conservatives. Brian, famously a socialist, had been attentive. Then he asked me, 'Exactly how old are you?' I replied, 'Just a fortnight younger than yourself.' He gave Geoffrey a mischievous look and commented, 'You look well. Your chairman must be more congenial than mine.'

On the Saturday after the Chelsea match, Moscow Dynamo played Cardiff City in front of 40,000 spectators at Ninian Park. Bobrov scored a hat-trick in a 10-1 victory. The Russians then returned to London to face Arsenal at Tottenham Hotspur's White Hart Lane (Highbury had suffered bomb damage) on Wednesday 21 November. Eyebrows were raised when the Arsenal team was announced and it was seen that 'guest' players (in the absence of the likes of Denis Compton and Bryn Jones on army service overseas) included Stanley Matthews of Stoke City and Stan Mortensen, Blackpool's rising star. There were claims that Dynamo was taking on an England XI. But Dynamo also had 'guests' playing, including our favourite, Bobrov, who, though we didn't know this at the time, was the star of the Red Army's Central House team.

White Hart Lane, with nearly 55,000 inside, was shrouded in fog when the teams emerged into the murky afternoon. Dynamo took the lead in the first minute but centre-forward Ronnie Rooke (then of Fulham) equalised. Arsenal took a 3-1 lead with two goals from Mortensen just before half-time, but the third goal in five minutes came from the Russians to cut the lead to 3-2. No sooner had Glendenning begun his commentary for the BBC than the teams were level again. Then Bobrov memorably shot home on the run from just outside the penalty area to score his second of the game – and Dynamo's winner. The last twenty minutes were dominated by the Russians with Glendenning lamenting that neither he nor the crowd could see through the fog.

Wednesday 28 November saw 90,000 spectators crammed into Ibrox for what turned out to be the last match of the tour. Once again, Dynamo took an early lead and they led 2-1 at the interval. The second half made the most exciting listening of all with Rangers adopting an 'up and at 'em' approach and the Russians holding on desperately to their slender lead. Then, in the last quarter of an hour, the English referee turned down a Rangers' penalty appeal but changed his mind after consulting a Scottish linesman. An earlier penalty had been missed but this time centre-half George Young stepped forward to take the kick and left the great goalkeeper 'Tiger' Khomich standing as the ball sped past him into the net. The match finished 2-2. The Russians declined further fixtures and returned home, to the disappointment of Billy Walker among others. The never-to-be-forgotten Vsevolod Bobrov, incidentally, was Dynamos' leading scorer with six of their nineteen goals. Back in Russia, he starred in the Central House team that won the league in three consecutive seasons. He also won Olympic gold as an ice hockey player. In 2016 Dynamos were relegated from the Russian Premier League.

An intelligent man, Walker was a progressive manager – a listener who absorbed ideas like a sponge. England's victory over the Austrian

'Wunderteam' in 1932 did not diminish his admiration for the along-the-ground passing style displayed by the visitors and he sought out their coaches to talk about teamwork, especially manager Hugo Meisl and Englishman Jimmy Hogan, who had been reappointed trainer specially for the London international. Lancashire-born Hogan was the most influential coach the Continent had ever known and was credited with the development of German, Dutch, French, Swiss and Hungarian football as well as his acclaimed work with the Austrians.

Turning down a job-for-life offer from Meisl, who was also general secretary of the Austrian FA, Hogan became manager of Aston Villa in November 1936, three years after Walker had taken charge of Sheffield Wednesday. They both parted company with their respective clubs as war approached. Hogan went back to Burnley but rejoined Villa as youth coach in 1953. He persuaded manager Eric Houghton to allow his youngsters to go to Wembley to watch England play Hungary. He promised the experience would open their eyes. Indeed it did, and all England saw the light as Hidegkuti, Puskas and the rest of the 'magical Magyars' inflicted a humiliating 6-3 defeat on the home nation. After the match the Hungarian manager-coach said, 'We played football as Jimmy Hogan taught us.' The following summer England were beaten 7-1 in Budapest.

That winter English champions Wolves took on first Moscow Spartak and then Puskas's Honved of Budapest under the new £30,000 Molineux floodlights. Brian Clough and I, both national servicemen in the RAF, watched the games in the NAAFI on BBC television. Spartak were holding out for a goalless draw but in the last ten minutes Wolves, captained by a determined Billy Wright, scored four goals. It was theatre as well as sport.

On 13 December 1954, Wolves, defending champions and leading the Football League by one point, faced Hungarian champions Honved, who went two goals ahead in the first quarter of an hour. At half-time Wolverhampton manager Stan Cullis ordered the club's staff to water the pitch to make it heavy going. Four minutes after the restart winger Johnny Hancocks scored from the penalty spot to pull a goal back. Then centre-forward Roy Swinbourne scored twice in two minutes for a 3-2 home victory. There were 55,000 at Molineux and the referee was Nottingham's Reg Leafe.

Cullis and sections of the press declared Wolves 'champions of the world'. His team had proven that 'English football was the genuine, original, unbeatable article'. Journalist Willy Meisl, younger brother of Hugo and a football writer for the British Olympic Association's magazine, *World Sports*, disagreed and condemned the pitch as a 'quagmire'. An Anglophile, he wanted England to reassert itself at the top of international football. He wrote a book, *Soccer Revolution*, which was published in 1955, that advocated a style of play he called 'the Whirl'. It was based on the coaching of his brother and Hogan with players able to interchange freely, full-backs attacking like wingers and forwards able to defend – the modern game, in fact.

Writing in the magazine *Sport* that year, Hogan himself claimed,

> I still maintain that we [England] have the best players but it is our style of playing the game that has gone wrong – not forgetting our training methods which are seriously at fault.

After all, despite the Hungarian defeats, England were still good enough to beat Scotland 7-2 – making Tommy Docherty, who had played for the Scots, appreciate what a fine side the Hungarians must have been. French journalist Gabriel Hanot, then editor of *L'Equipe*, the sports daily published in Paris, claimed Wolves were inferior to Real Madrid and AC Milan and suggested that 'a European championship be organised' to give clubs the opportunity to prove they were the best. Meeting in London on 8 May 1955, FIFA authorised the new European Cup club competition, providing that it was run by UEFA. Real Madrid won the first five finals, but in 1979 and 1980 it was the glory of Clough and Forest.

2

City Ground
to City Ground

From a very young age, Billy Walker had an inner compulsion to play football. Nothing else mattered.

'Fame, fortune – I never considered these,' he wrote in *Soccer in the Blood*, his 1960 autobiography. He was prepared to risk his health, his schooling and even his hopes of marriage. 'If you find this hard to believe then, simply, you haven't got it; I mean you haven't got the bug that eats at a man with as much virulence as the drink bug and the gambling bug eat at other men,' he said. 'If you've got it, you've got it, and that's an end of it. At least, that's how it is with me. It started as soon as I could stagger round the garden with a ball and now, at the age of sixty-two, I've still got it.'

The young Billy Walker played out in the street in all weather and was frequently soaked to the skin. Play was stopped when he was diagnosed with tuberculosis and ordered off to a sanatorium for three months. Back home, he slept in an open hut at the bottom of the garden. Rest, fresh air and injections, a hundred of them, were prescribed until finally he could get about. 'I'd make my move to wherever the nearest game of football was going on,' he said.

As a thirteen-year-old, he deliberately failed an examination so that he could continue to play schools' football. His sister sat the exam at the same time – and passed. His aim was to play for England Boys and a schoolboy 'cap' came the next year. Later, he admits, he was 'an erratic courtier' keeping his 'date' waiting because of playing football. The young lady, Sarah Brown, laid down the law. 'It's either football or me,' she said. He chose football. Older and wiser heads from both families told him this was plain foolishness and the couple were brought together again. They married at Walsall in March 1919. 'She came to tolerate and stayed to cheer,' Walker wrote. As for his wife, 'You will see her any Saturday in the Forest stand: and you will see my daughter (Marjorie) and her husband, my grand-daughter, Diane, when she is home from school and our son Michael. I didn't win. Football won.'

Walker was born at Wednesbury in the Black Country on 29 October 1897. His father, George Walker, was a professional footballer – a full-back with Wolverhampton Wanderers. As a toddler, Billy would wander off to the nearby Molineux ground and kick at the gate until someone came. 'I want m'dad,' he would say and, usually, he'd be allowed inside to watch the players at practice. 'That was the start of it, and there has been nothing else in my life ever since,' Walker wrote. His father didn't want him following in his footsteps and his parents tried to keep him in the house when Wolves were at home. 'They locked the door but no locks and bolts were going to keep me from seeing the Wolves and m'dad,' he went on. 'I made my way out through the cellar grate-opening and took my usual place behind the Wolves' goal bawling away in support. I was football mad.'

George Walker strongly opposed his son's desire to become a professional footballer but gradually recognised Billy's talent and finally gave his approval but with a warning: 'Hard work, hard knocks, harsh criticisms, no fortune and few good friends – that's football. Try farming, go to sea, drive a bus, anything but the College of Kicks,' was his parental advice. George had been the first footballer in the family. His own father, William Henry Walker, after whom Billy was named, was a Quaker. Billy's maternal grandfather, Tom Jacques, was a very different character. He was a hand-forger in the nut and bolt trade and came from the nearby town of Darlaston. He would send out to the public house for a quart of whisky, mull it with sugar, sit by the fireside all evening and drink it. Walker recalled, 'He was eighty when he died.'

Billy Walker's reputation as an outstanding schoolboy footballer was enhanced by a phenomenal record of scoring eighty goals for King's Hill in twenty-five Walsall Schools League matches. The scouts gathered. George Walker, then a colliery archer making wooden arch supports, was still not keen on his son becoming a pro but at the age of sixteen Billy jumped at the chance of signing amateur forms with Aston Villa – though he was slightly disappointed that his father's former club, Wolves, had shown no interest after impressing them with nine goals in forty minutes while playing for Wednesbury Old Athletic.

Villa had first call on his services but, with the family now living in Darlaston, Billy was snapped up as a 'guest' player by the town football club. He made his debut as a seventeen-year-old and was a regular in Darlaston's 1915/16 Walsall Combination championship team, scoring two goals against Hednesford Town on the final day of the season to clinch the league title. Darlaston were known as 'the Citizens' as back in 1900 they had changed the name of their Waverley Road home from the Wakes Ground to the City Ground, by which it is still known to this day. So Billy Walker's football career took him from the City Ground in the West Midlands to the City Ground in the East Midlands. At the tender age of fourteen, Walker played for Hednesford Town alongside his brother, George junior, making a total of thirty-four appearances for them in the 1911/12 season.

While still at Darlaston, Billy was called up by Villa for occasional wartime matches. He scored on his debut on Boxing Day 1916 but a West Bromwich Albion side, including England international full-back Jesse Pennington, hit five, and his first goal at Villa Park came in a 2-1 defeat by Birmingham City. Despite having four army medicals, Walker was rejected for military service because of his health record. As well as TB, he had suffered from rickets as a boy when his legs would simply collapse under him. 'No treatment had any effect but the condition cleared up by itself when I was about ten years of age,' he said. 'But all my playing days, and since, people have made affectionate fun of my knock-knees. And they were a gift to cartoonists.' He was nicknamed 'Knocky'. 'Opponents claimed they helped me to sell the dummy every way at once.' During the war he worked in a nut and bolt manufacturers just like his grandfather before him.

The Football League resumed on the last Saturday of August 1919. Walker had to wait until the departure of England international centre-forward 'Happy' Harry Hampton to take his place in the senior side. Hampton remains Villa's leading goalscorer in the league with 215 goals and added twenty-seven more in the FA Cup. Walker managed one fewer in league games but scored thirty in FA Cup ties, giving him the all-time Villa record goal tally by two goals. Walker started as he meant to go on, hitting both goals against Queen's Park Rangers on 10 January 1920 in a 2-1 FA Cup first-round victory. It was not until the 1925/26 season that leading clubs became exempt until the competition's third round.

A week later, he made the first of his 478 Football League appearances, all in the First Division for Villa, in a goalless draw at Burnley. His first league goal came in the next away game – a 1-1 draw against Everton at Goodison Park. Having gained his place, he was determined to keep it and became the regular first choice for the next thirteen years until his retirement.

Villa went to Old Trafford in the second round of the FA Cup and a Billy Walker goal helped them to a 2-1 victory. Sunderland at home and Tottenham Hotspur away were each beaten 1-0 and then Walker scored twice as Chelsea were eliminated 3-1 in the semi-final at Bramall Lane, Sheffield. The final was played in front of a crowd of 50,000 at Stamford Bridge, where Huddersfield Town conceded the only goal of the game ten minutes into extra time. A corner kick by Arthur Dorrell, Walker's left-wing partner for eight successive seasons, was headed home by powerful inside-right Billy Kirton, a converted full-back. It gave Villa the FA Cup for a then record sixth time, overtaking the trophy's first winners, Wanderers, as well as Blackburn Rovers. A famous London amateur side, Wanderers beat Royal Engineers in the first final in 1872. They had been formed, incidentally, as the Forest Football Club in 1859 but changed their name in 1864 – a year before the formation of Nottingham Forest FC.

Dorrell and Kirton, like Walker, were cup-winners in the first season with Villa. Another was the redoubtable centre-half Frank Barson, a rough-cut Sheffielder, described by Walker as a teammate and tutor 'whose presence on the field was worth all the tactical talks of a dozen coaches off it'. He recalled Barson bellowing from behind 'hit it!' then 'good lad' and a nudge in the ribs when the instruction had been followed. 'With a man like Barson you learned from almost every ball,' said Walker. 'He was the greatest captain of them all.'

Goalkeeper was England international Sam Hardy, who was in his first season back at Villa Park after 'guesting' for Nottingham Forest. Signing Hardy had been Forest secretary-manager Bob Marsters' master stroke. The club's golden jubilee year of 1915 had been a time of deep crisis. Players who had not already left for war service with the Footballers' Battalion accepted a 25 per cent pay cut. The Football League helped out with a £50 grant followed by £10 a week to the end of the season; £90 was raised from a public appeal, and the city council waived a quarter's ground rent of just over £36. Then the League drew up special regulations for wartime football, creating regional tournaments and permitting players not on active service to play for any club provided they did so for sport and were not paid. Marsters immediately grasped the possibilities. Money was no longer a problem in acquiring star performers; his persuasive powers were enough. Hardy's genius lay in uncanny sense of anticipation that meant he rarely needed to be spectacular. He played thirty-five of Forest's thirty-six competitive games in 1915/16 and the one he missed was a 4-1 defeat at Derby. He also played eight times at the beginning of the 1916/17 season before joining the Royal Navy.

Hardy returned to the Reds for the triumphant 1918/19 season and was joined at Christmas by England international and West Ham inside-forward Danny Shea, one of the best of all ball players, another 'guest' star. On a foggy day in east London in 1911, Shea's goals had knocked Forest out of the FA Cup 2-1. He later admitted taking full advantage of murky conditions to punch both goals into the net – a 'double Maradona'. He more than made up for it by, with Hardy, helping Forest win the major prize – the Victory Shield – when the war ended. Forest were regional champions in 1918/19 and Everton won the northern division. The sides met in a two-legged final played on a home and away basis. A crowd of 15,000 saw a goalless draw in the first match at the City Ground on 10 May 1919, when Forest's Noah Burton had a goal disallowed for offside and Everton's Gault missed a penalty trying to beat Hardy but shooting wide. Everton were always favourites and now the trophy seemed destined for Merseyside. A week later, Goodison Park was packed with 40,000 fans but this time Burton was not to be denied and got the only goal in the 42nd minute.

So Sam Hardy was a Victory Shield winner with Forest and when football returned to normal the following season, he helped Villa win the FA Cup. In the summer of 1921, Forest paid Aston Villa his highest transfer fee, £1,000, and it proved money well spent. The great goalkeeper, although thirty-eight, clearly had much to do with the Reds winning that season's Second Division championship for only thirty goals were conceded in forty-two games – a divisional record. He went on to make 110 League and Cup appearances, playing his last game on 4 October 1924 – a 1-1 First Division draw with Newcastle United watched by 22,000 at the City Ground. After his retirement from football he became a publican in the Chesterfield area. He died in England's World Cup-winning year, 1966. Billy Walker kept in touch with his former teammate, whom he regarded as 'the greatest goalkeeper I have ever seen'.

'One of the most amazing games I ever saw him play was in that Cup win against Tottenham at White Hart Lane,' he said. 'Unfortunately for Spurs' Tommy Clay, a Nottingham man, he sliced the ball into his own goal and that's how we got the one that mattered. After that it was Tottenham versus Sam Hardy for sixty minutes.' The home supporters berated their players again and again for shooting 'straight at him', but it was Hardy's uncanny anticipation that made it all look so easy.

Walker wrote,

I have one poignant personal recollection of his marvellous goalkeeping. In a practice game before the season started I was playing for the reserves against the first team. Towards the end of the first half I went through the defence and lifted my head up to see where to shoot. I saw Sam move towards his left-hand post and straight away I shot to the opposite post as hard as I could. When my head came up, there was Sam standing at that post just catching the ball. His husky voice came to me: 'Send a postcard, send a postcard.' At half-time I went to him and asked: 'What did you mean, Mr Hardy.' We youngsters called all the senior professionals Mister. 'Where was I when you picked your head up?' he asked. I said: 'At the left post, so I shot for the right post.' So Sam said: 'Why do you think I took up that position?' I caught on. He'd made me shoot where he wanted me to. I can tell you there was nothing spectacular about Sam but what a goalkeeper he was!

Mr and Mrs Walker were among the guests at the golden wedding anniversary celebration of Mr and Mrs Hardy in Chesterfield.

3

Clough's Hero

Like Billy Walker, Brian Clough failed an important school exam – in his case the eleven-plus. Unlike the former, he was less than happy about it, particularly as his siblings made it to grammar school: 'Bit of a let down to the family I was,' he said in a BBC interview. He subsequently became a prefect and head boy at his school but this failure still rankled fifty years later when he told a television interviewer, 'I don't have any O-levels, I don't have any A-levels, and when my children chastise me and give me stick about this I put my European Cup medals on the table, my championship medals, I've got a tableful – they're my O-levels and A-levels.' The perceived early disgrace may have made him driven to become one of the best centre-forwards of his time and then one of football's greatest managers. According to a contemporary, he was 'a bit of a bully' as a prefect. Clough himself admitted revelling in the responsibility: 'I actually enjoyed standing at the top of the stairs and warning the late arrivals,' he said. His headmaster considered him 'the best prefect the school's ever had'.

Joe Clough, Brian's father, served with the King's Own Yorkshire Light Infantry in the First World War and walked with a limp after being shot in the ankle. Brian was born on 21 March 1935, at No. 11 Valley Road, Middlesbrough, a garden estate of council houses built after the war. The family house had a large garden with a lawn, ideal for games of football with a small ball, as well as a vegetable patch and space for growing roses. Joe worked as a sugar-boiler and later manager at a sweet factory a quarter of a mile from Middlesbrough's Ayresome Park ground, where he was a terrace regular idolising the team's 'golden boy' – England inside-forward Wilf Mannion, who was awarded twenty-six caps between 1946 and 1951 and scored eleven international goals. Mannion, who died on

Teeside on 14 April 2000, aged eighty-one, played in the national side with Stanley Matthews, Tom Finney, Jackie Milburn, Stan Mortensen, Billy Wright and Alf Ramsey. Brian shared his father's admiration of the home-town player, who he said 'played football the way Fred Astaire danced'. Clough later found himself sharing a dressing room with the great inside-forward.

Clough's early memories were full of football talk; his dad was obsessed with the game and the players. Mannion and England captain full-back George Hardwick would visit Joe's factory and he would give them sweets. Football was a religion but Sundays belonged to his mam. She dragged the family off to the Anglican church, all of them in their Sunday best, and on the walk back home they were allowed ice creams. Monday was washing day and Brian, when he got home from school, was expected to help mangle the sheets. 'If ever I'm feeling a bit uppity, whenever I get on my high horse, I go and take another look at my dear mam's mangle that has pride of place at my home in Quarndon,' he began his autobiography. 'It had stood for a dozen years or so in our Joe's garage before being beautifully restored. Now it serves as a reminder of the days when I learned what life was all about. On top of it is the casket holding the scroll to my Freedom of the City of Nottingham. My whole life is there in one small part of one room.'

Author Harry Pearson, writing in the football periodical *The Blizzard* about 'Slaggy Island' – the local name for South Bank, a grim industrial area 3 miles east of Middlesbrough but a breeding ground for footballers, including Mannion – recalled a conversation about a cup-tie played there and a particular incident. A 'shiny-eyed teenage centre-forward' banged in a hat-trick and, at the final whistle, walked over to the opposing goalkeeper, tapped him on the shoulder and said, 'One day, when I'm playing for England, you'll brag to your mates about this. By the way, I'm Brian Clough.' Another who learned his football in such games was Leeds and England manager Don Revie, towards whom Clough developed a deep antipathy. Revie, eight years Clough's elder, grew up just a fifteen-minute walk from Valley Road in Bell Street near Ayresome Park.

As a young boy, Clough would watch from the bedroom window as matches were played on the Acklam steelworks ground a few yards beyond the back garden. He was the fifth surviving child of eight and had two sisters and five brothers. The brothers would take part in kickabouts on nearby Clairville Common. On school playing fields, Clough developed a reputation as a nimble but sturdily built boy who could score goals. As a fourteen-year-old he struck five second-half goals to win a game Grove Hill School had been losing 3-0 at half-time. Even then he was assertive on the pitch and his games master had to tell him to 'shut up and get on with it'. Argumentative he certainly was but, added the master, he was usually right.

Clough left school at fifteen and, guided by his mother Sally he joined ICI (Imperial Chemical Industries). On his first day he was put in charge of fellow apprentices. He tried out as a turner and fitter but, bored by the work, he failed the apprenticeship. Given another chance, he became a junior clerk at a cement works, an offshoot of ICI. But it was football he was best at – even though his team, Marton Grove Youth Club, lost one match 20-0 to South Park Rovers. His brother Bill was playing for a team at Great Broughton around 15 miles from Middlesbrough in the Cleveland hills. The team was managed by Nancy Goldsborough, who ran the village post office, and the pitch was marked out on a local farmer's field. Bill persuaded her to take on sixteen-year-old Brian and in the 1952/53 season there were four Clough brothers in the side – Joe, Des, Bill and Brian. Des went on to play at centre-half for Bishop Auckland and later captained Whitby Town. Brian insisted on wearing the No. 9 green shirt. Perhaps it was a nostalgic memory of that rather than Peter Shilton's goalkeeper's number one jersey that made him so fond of his familiar green sweater at Forest. His goalscoring reputation was boosted when, after helping to clear 3 inches of deep snow from the village pitch so that a cup tie against Skinningrove could be played, he found the net ten times in a 16-0 victory.

'Mrs Goldsbrough organised the matches, arranged referees and linesmen, and helped clear the sheep from the field,' Brian wrote in *Clough: The Autobiography* (1994). 'She didn't attempt to coach us or tell me how to put the ball in the net. No need. There were no showers and no bath. We arrived dirty, went home a lot dirtier, and enjoyed every single second.'

As well as the village team and Marten Grove, Clough turned out for Marske Rovers, Acklam steelworks, South Bank and played in interdepartmental matches at ICI, frequently amounting to six games a week. His boss warned him to put more effort into the job he was being paid for and less on the football field. Others recognised that a lad with his talent had the potential to make it in the professional game. Ray Grant, headmaster of Hugh Bell secondary school, helped to run Middlesbrough's junior side and recommended that a club scout take look at the youngster who had been banging in the goals for Great Broughton. Former England centre-forward George Camsell, who had scored a record 326 League goals for Middlesbrough before the Second World War, watched him play against Stokesley in a local cup tie but was unimpressed. Grant decided to see for himself. The sixteen-year-old was having a quiet game but, in the second half, a cross-field pass fell just behind him. Instinctively, Clough half-turned, flicked the ball over his shoulder, ran past a defender and fired into the roof of the net. This convinced Grant and Clough was signed as an amateur by the Second Division club in September 1952.

The episode was remarkably similar to the signing of another young centre-forward, Garry Birtles, by Brian Clough's Nottingham Forest some twenty-five years later. After a tip-off from scout Maurice Edwards, Clough's assistant Peter Taylor urged him to see the lad play for Long Eaton United at Enderby. There was a false rumour that Manchester United were interested in him. 'I've seen Birtles – and the Bovril was better than he was,' Clough famously reported on his return. Taylor decided to make his own assessment and persuaded Long Eaton manager Geoff Barrowcliffe to let Birtles join Forest on trial. Barrowcliffe himself had spent sixteen years and made 475 appearances as a Derby County full-back after joining the Rams from Ilkeston Town in 1950. Taylor went to watch him in a reserves match at Coventry. The dismal reports he had received from the coaching staff were being confirmed. He marked his card: No, no and no. Then it happened. 'Birtles evaded a defender's challenge by dummying to go one way, dragging the ball back with the sole of his left foot and changing direction in an instant,' the assistant manager wrote in his book *With Clough by Taylor*. 'He moved into the box, kept cool and shot. The ball flashed just outside the post.' Yes! It was enough. Forest paid Long Eaton £2,000 to sign a future European Cup hero. As Camsell had failed to spot Clough's burgeoning talent he also initially missed Birtles' qualities, preferring another youngster Steve Elliott, who was later transferred to Preston North End for £90,000.

The young Clough soon began playing regularly for Middlesbrough Juniors and towards the end of the 1952/53 season joined Northern League side Billingham Synthonia, who paid him £1 a match. He didn't declare it – not to cheat the Inland Revenue – but wrote, 'I suppose I regarded it as expenses and spent it on dubbin for my big old-fashioned boots.' In fact, he was a 'Synner' for only four matches, scoring three goals. The name Sythonia – 'sounds more like an orchestra,' said Clough – comes from a contraction of 'Synthetic Ammonia', a fertiliser produced by ICI. The 'Synners' are still members of the Northern League.

Turning seventeen, Clough signed professional forms with Middlesbrough, who paid him a £1-a-week retainer with a £7 match fee if he was able to play in any of their teams. In 1953 he was also called up for National Service. It was the coronation year of Queen Elizabeth II and all the armed services were preparing for the big day – 2 June – when the ceremony would take place at Westminster Abbey. Clough became an aircraftman second class and picked up a further 37s 6d from the Royal

Air Force. 'The first thing I remember about my days in the RAF is the uniform,' he wrote. 'I'd hated the thought of leaving home for two years but that uniform generated a strange sense of pride the moment I was kitted out and put it on. I suppose that, in one sense or another, I've been wearing a type of uniform all my life.'

Brian did his square-bashing at Padgate near Manchester. I did mine at the same time but at the Number 11 School of Recruit Training, RAF Hednesford, in the middle of the woodland at Cannock Chase, Staffordshire. After a period at the RAF Regiment's training camp, RAF Dumfries in south-west Scotland, he was posted to RAF Watchet in Somerset. The distance from Teeside limited his outings with Middlesbrough's reserves or third team but he got games for the station side. He was a touch miffed, however, at being ignored by the RAF's national selectors. He reached the rank of Leading Aircraftman. I went one better as a Senior Aircraftman but also only got to play for my station RAF Mildenhall, a Bomber Command group headquarters dominated by an airbase for the nuclear bombers of the American Strategic Air Command. Not reaching a higher rank bothered neither of us: 'The friendship, the strength of camaraderie among a group of young men reluctantly brought together, somehow produced a status far more meaningful,' Clough said. And it was in the RAF that he got the close-cropped crew-cut hairstyle he kept throughout his playing days.

Demobbed, twenty-year-old Clough returned to Middlesbrough to find himself lost in a crowd of more than thirty full-time players and was the fifth-choice centre-forward. In front of him were Charlie Wayman, a veteran who had played for Newcastle United, Southampton and Preston North End; Ken McPherson, bought from Notts County for a substantial £18,000 fee; Alan Peacock, a future England international, and Doug Cooper, although Cooper only got into the first team before Clough for only five matches. It was frustrating, irritating even. He felt down and needed a lift.

4

Wondrous Walker

Six months after gaining a Cup winner's medal with Villa, Billy Walker added a first England cap. He had scored fourteen goals in the club's first eleven League games of the 1920/21 season and was chosen to lead his country's attack against Ireland at Roker Park, Sunderland, on 23 October. For Cup Final captain Andy Ducat it was the last of six appearances in an England shirt. Walker scored in a 2-0 victory. He went on to gain eighteen caps, a Villa record until 1991, when it was surpassed by David Platt, who finished with sixty-two earned with various clubs. Walker's were spread over twelve seasons and would surely have totalled far more but for the limited number of international matches played in those days. Both players became England captains. And Platt, of course, also later managed Forest though briefly and much less successfully than Walker.

On Saturday 28 August, the opening day of the 1920/21 season, Walker scored four goals at Villa Park in a 5-0 victory over Arsenal. These were the first of thirty-two goals he was to score that season – a personal best. Villa completed a First Division 'double' with another Walker goal at Highbury. He had a career average of a goal every two games against the Gunners – fifteen in thirty-one fixtures. His four goals in one match was a first for a Villa player and he repeated the feat in a 5-1 home win against Sheffield United in December 1929. In all, Walker notched a dozen League and Cup hat-tricks. Uniquely, all three of his goals in a 7-1 trouncing of Bradford City at Villa Park in November 1921 came from penalties. The goalkeeper was Scottish international Jock Ewart who, fortunately, was noted for his sense of humour. He had already been beaten twice from the spot when, with City already five goals down, a third penalty kick was awarded.

'You can imagine his feelings as he faced up to the possibility of my establishing a record against him,' said Walker. 'Naturally, I wanted to complete the hat-trick but neither I nor anybody on the ground could foresee what was to come. I took the kick and – fired wide! The referee whistled and ordered me to take it again as a Bradford City man had stepped inside the area. The second time I shot over the bar and again the referee ordered the kick to be retaken, for another player had moved!' That was the last straw for big Jock Ewart. 'It looks as if this fella has got to score,' he complained to the ref. 'He can as far as I'm concerned.' With that, the goalkeeper deliberately stood by the right-hand goalpost and invited Walker to put the ball into the other side of the net. When it went in, Ewart had his last word, 'There you are, Ref! He's got his hat-trick. Are you satisfied now?'

Billy Walker scored England's first-ever goal at Wembley to earn a 1-1 draw with Scotland on 12 April 1924. It was then known as the Empire Stadium and had been completed a year earlier, having been built in 300 days at the cost of £750,000. It was ready only four days before the famous 'White Horse' Final between Bolton Wanderers and West Ham United. Police Constable George Scorey and his white horse Billy helped control the crowd, which had spilled onto the pitch and far exceeded the stadium's official 127,000 capacity. Taken by surprise, the Football Association had not considered admission by ticket only. Perhaps because of this fright, the recorded attendance for the first international a year later was just 37,250. Scotland went in front five minutes before half-time when inside-right William Cowan shot against the post and the ball rebounded off goalkeeper Ted Taylor into the net. Billy Walker's equaliser came in the 60th minute. The England side was captained for the first time by right-half Frank Moss of Villa and another teammate, Tommy Smart, was at right-back. Walker described Smart as a great full-back and even greater character. He recalled the player clashing with Villa's chairman Fred Rinder, just as strong a personality, after arriving late for the train to a match at Newcastle. Rinder ordered Smart back to Villa Park to play in the reserves. 'I'm picked against Newcastle and that's where I'm going,' the defiant defender retorted. 'You can please thissen.' The outcome? 'Tommy did play at Newcastle and he played a blinder as well,' reported Walker. Bolton's David Jack, a goalscorer in the 1923 Cup Final, was at inside-right and Charlie Buchan of Arsenal at inside-left for England. Later Jack was signed by manager Herbert Chapman to replace Buchan at Highbury.

Walker really earned his twelfth cap when he captained England to a 3-2 victory against France at the Stade Olympique de Colombes, Paris. He went in goal for the last fifteen minutes when goalkeeper Fred Fox was carried off after being accidentally kicked in the face. Walker also acted as Villa's emergency goalkeeper and appeared in Forest's goal six times in wartime football during his early years as manager. Arthur Dorrell, his left-wing partner at Villa, gained his third cap and scored one of England's goals.

After scoring his ninth goal for England in a drawn match with Wales at Wrexham on 12 February 1927, Walker was left out of the side and a succession of inside-lefts were tried before he was brought back and restored to the captaincy for the prestige match against the celebrated Austrian 'Wunderteam' at Stamford Bridge on 7 December 1932. They included Harry Burgess of Sheffield Wednesday, who later played under Walker's management at Hillsborough. Now the national selectors felt they needed to draw upon the experience and authority of the thirty-five-year-old Villa veteran for one last appearance on the international stage against the 'unofficial champions of Europe'. Austria had been unbeaten in eighteen matches, including a 5-0 humiliation of Scotland.

The England side included Sammy Crooks of Derby County at outside-right with Arsenal's David Jack as his inside partner. Villa supplied the left-wing pairing of Walker with Eric Houghton, who was to end his playing career at Notts County, then become Walker's chief scout at Forest before returning to Meadow Lane as manager in May 1949. Houghton's Magpies, inspired by the great Tommy Lawton, gained promotion as Third Division South champions and in 1953 he took over as manager of Aston Villa, with whom he had played for eighteen years, and led them to an FA Cup Final victory against Manchester United in 1957. Houghton packed a powerful shot and was an expert penalty taker with seventy of his 170 goals in 392 League and Cup games for Villa coming from spot-kicks.

The match against Austria was also Houghton's last in an England shirt and gave him his seventh cap. Blackpool centre-forward Jimmy Hampson scored after only a few minutes and again after Walker and Houghton combined before the half-hour. Instructions by manager Hugo Meisl and brilliant technical coach Jimmy Hogan inspired the Austrians to a second-half performance that reflected their huge reputation. Centre-forward Matthias Sindelar, tall, pale and so thin he was called 'the paper man', led the comeback with an astute pass for Karl Zischek to pull a goal back. With thirteen minutes remaining, Houghton restored England's two-goal advantage with a fierce free-kick awarded for handball. The excitement grew as Sindelar's clever footwork and baffling body swerve put him clear to score with a shot on the run in the 80th minute. Two minutes later Crooks made it 4-2 with a 15-yarder and, with just three minutes left, Zischek scored his second and Austria's third. Though given a scare, England, with Walker's influence crucial, held on to win.

Billy Walker also represented the Football League six times. He played in another FA Cup Final but this time was on the losing side against Newcastle United, who won 2-0 at Wembley. Aston Villa finished in the top half of the First Division in every one of Walker's thirteen full seasons as an automatic choice – the exception was in the 1924/25 season when they were fifteenth. Walker took over the captaincy in 1926 and led them to their most successful five-year spell in the League during his time at the club. They were never out of the top five and for two of those seasons were runners-up to Arsenal.

The Villa archives website describes him as 'Wondrous Walker'. To the ultimate question – who's the greatest claret and blue star of all time – editor Paul Brown answers, 'It's hard to look past the late, great Billy Walker.' Whenever he was asked who was lining up for Villa before the kick-off, club and international teammate full-back Tommy Smart would reply, 'Billy Walker … and ten others.' And the Villa Park fans would shout during every attack, 'Give it to Walker!' The *Aston Villa 2000* book comments, 'Walker had the most extravagant body swerve that literally left opponents on their behinds – and a thunderous shot.' John Lerwell's *Aston Villa Chronicles* suggests Walker was 'a whimsical fellow who could make a football do parlour tricks – and it would follow him if he whistled'.

Perhaps the most heartfelt tribute came from Jack Watts, a supporter for nine decades and a club stalwart who, until his death in March 2015, was match day host for American owner Randy Lerner. Counting Billy Walker as Villa's greatest-ever player, Jack told the website, 'It wasn't just his impressive statistics. Beautifully balanced, he was good with both feet and could head a ball superbly.' This was with a heavy ball on muddy pitches. 'An old-fashioned inside-left rather than a centre-forward, his skills rubbed off on the players around him. Tom "Pongo" Waring and Eric Houghton, the hardest kicker of a ball I've ever seen, were big stars in their own right. But, if they were around today, I'm sure they would tell you they became even better players through playing alongside Billy Walker.'

So Walker the footballer was outstanding. But what was he like as a person? Mr Watts recalled,

I remember the first time I met Billy properly. I was playing football with my mates in Perry Bar Park and the ball sailed over my head and down the path. 'Go and get it then,' they told me, so off I scampered. A man and a woman were strolling in the opposite direction, arm in arm. I shouted: 'Hey, mate, kick the ball here!' He was wearing a suit but he duly obliged. The classy manner in which he kicked the ball made me look again. Could he possibly be a professional footballer? He was. The man who passed the ball to me was my idol, Billy Walker. Well, I was awestruck. I simply didn't know what to say. I was eleven or twelve at the time and meeting my hero was something I never forgot.

If he was popular with the fans, Walker was also a hero to the players – especially during the General Strike of 1926. Villa could not afford to pay their players but Walker came to the rescue. He organised a match involving the professionals that attracted a 7,000 crowd and the gate receipts paid their wages.

An outstanding goalscorer who got into double figures in twelve consecutive seasons from 1919/20, he became more of a schemer and the brains behind the team as his long and distinguished playing career neared its end. Villa's form slumped after his final appearance – a 3-2 defeat at Portsmouth on 30 September 1933 – and at the end of the 1935/36 season the club was relegated for the first time.

Writing in *Soccer in the Blood*, Billy Walker vividly describes his poignant last day at Villa Park:

I remember as if it were yesterday going down to the ground on a Friday in January 1933. I had secured a job as secretary-manager with Sheffield Wednesday and, when I went to wish the lads goodbye I realised what I was doing and what it meant to me. I had the hardest task in the world to walk down towards those great Villa gates to the street after receiving their good wishes and hearing many of these lads say as I was leaving: 'Don't forget – if you ever want a player, we'll be available.' I felt like running back and telling them all: 'I don't want to leave.' In fact, I had been told not to leave by the secretary, Billy Smith, who said there was always a job at Villa Park for me. I longed to go back and say to Billy: 'Tell me what the job is and I will stay.' I confess that my eyes were misty and it was with a lump in my throat that I finally and slowly walked through the gates.

5

Enter Taylor

Freshly demobbed from the Royal Air Force, Brian Clough found himself confined to the reserves at Middlesbrough and had a brief falling-out with manager Bob Dennison, whom he saw as 'kindly but an old-school type slow to spot my potential'. Then along came 'streetwise Pete', the new reserve goalkeeper Peter Taylor, signed for £3,500 from Coventry City.

Born and bred in the Meadows, Nottingham, Taylor was six years older than Clough, a dad and experienced enough to know his way around. Taylor was the sixth of eight children, and his father, Tom, was an engineer at the Royal Ordnance gun factory near their Rutland Road home. According to his sister Joan, Peter always loved football. The Victoria Embankment by the River Trent was his playground and he always carried a ball. 'One day he got into trouble for rolling up his new coat to make a goalpost and then, forgetfully, leaving it behind after a game,' she said. Told to say a prayer before bed one night, he whispered, 'Please God, make me lucky.'

Billy Walker signed the young Taylor to play in goal for Forest Colts in 1942 and on 21 April 1945 he made his first team debut as a sixteen-year-old against Notts County at Meadow Lane. A Forest side including George Mee at centre-forward with Tom Johnston and Tot Leverton on the wings, Ted Blagg centre-half and the backs Bill Baxter and Bob McCall, were 3-1 victors. A week later, the young goalkeeper conceded five goals as the Magpies got their revenge, wininng 5-2. The matches were watched by 4,000 at Meadow Lane and 3,000 at the City Ground. Geoff Thomas played at right-back in the second match and Jack Edwards was at inside-left. Both Forest goals came from penalties.

At Coventry, manager Harry Storer had a profound influence on Taylor's thinking about football and management. He also got on well with Dennison, a Coventry man. 'It was difficult not to become friends with Peter Taylor,' Clough said. They first met at a Probables v. Possibles traditional pre-season fixture in 1955. 'I was impressed immediately by the way this crew-cut unknown shielded the ball and how cleanly he struck it,' wrote Taylor. 'Above all, I admired the arrogance of his play. But management and staff were blind to the diamond under their noses.' Scottish wing-half Jimmy Gordon, a coach at Ayresome Park, adversely reported, 'Doesn't work hard enough.' He was later to become a trusted trainer for Clough at Derby, Leeds and Forest. Clough and Taylor played together for the first time a week later in the Middlesbrough reserve side at Spennymoor. 'I decided to take the future of Brian Clough into my own hands,' wrote Peter Taylor.

He sought out Dennison to tell him what a fine prospect the young centre-forward was but the manager's failure to act on his recommendation was frustrating. So Taylor found the youngster. 'I don't know what's going on at this club,' he told him. 'You're better than anybody here.' Those were just the words of encouragement Clough needed to hear. 'Everybody needs somebody to confirm their own belief in themselves,' he wrote in his autobiography. It was the first recognition he'd ever had as a footballer. 'That was Peter. That was him throughout the rest of his life – instant judgment, taking little or no time, as long as it was based on what he considered to be solid evidence. He boosted me. I've tried to do the same for many players, even those like Trevor Francis in the million-pounds bracket. Irrespective of their ability, you'd be absolutely staggered at how much they need a reassuring little lift at various stages of their careers.'

Taylor did more than that. Impatience with Dennison made him pick up the phone and ring Harry Storer, then manager of Derby County, about 'the best young centre-forward I've ever seen'. Derby were playing at Hartlepools in the Third Division North in September and Taylor took Clough to the game. 'The staff at Middlesbrough reckon he's not mobile enough,' Taylor told Storer, adding Derby could have Clough 'for peanuts'. Storer had blown all his cash on two other players so nothing came of the suggestion, which was probably just as well as a deal in those circumstances would have breached FA regulations.

That same month, Brian Clough made his League debut for Middlesbrough against Barnsley at Oakwell. He didn't make much of an impression. 'I was eager to get out there and justify myself,' he wrote. But on the way out with his teammates, Dennison called to him, 'It's up to you now.' It was 'a downer'. He felt deflated. What the young Clough wanted to hear from his manager was, 'Good luck, son. I know you'll do well.' That would have put him at ease. Instead, he had 'fear in my heart'. It was a mistake Clough never made as a manager. 'When footballers go out onto the field they have to be relaxed not frightened,' he wrote. 'Sometimes that frame of mind is difficult to achieve but they simply have to relax. There was no point in my spending all week training and motivating players and then sending them into a match as tight as guitar strings.'

Clough scored his first League goal a week later when Middlesbrough recovered from 2-0 down to beat Leicester City 4-3. He scored the winner in a 2-1 victory over Lincoln but, after being dominated by experienced centre-half Ken Thomson in a 3-1 defeat to Stoke, was replaced by veteran Charlie Wayman for the visit to Hull, where Peter Taylor made his Middlesbrough debut. Clough's response to being dropped was to hit four goals in eleven minutes for the reserves in a 6-2 defeat of Gateshead reserves but it wasn't enough to earn him a first-team recall that season. He was picked for only nine games in 1955/56 and scored three goals. 'He didn't establish himself,' recalled Taylor. 'I played only six League games myself and the pair of us were regarded as no more than useful reserves.'

Clough's patience snapped and he banged in a transfer request. It was turned down. He didn't lose out altogether, selling the story to the *Middlesbrough Gazette* for £50. And he persuaded Dennison to up his basic wage from £9 to £11. 'No, it was not the kind of response I would have either encouraged or tolerated from a player once, years later, I had joined the managerial ranks,' he admitted. 'I quickly learned how to use the media. I didn't get my transfer but Dennison did later give me the captaincy. Some of the other players didn't like that and my appointment as skipper led to a bit of a bust-up and two "camps" in the squad. Talk about team spirit!'

Taylor and Clough soon became close friends. Together they coached schoolboys at Redcar and the headmaster paid them £1 4s each for an hour – a useful addition to their club wages – and 'the bonus was the pleasure of working with youngsters'. 'The pair of us were obsessed with football,' Taylor said. 'All our time went in training for it, playing it, watching it in the old Northeast Wednesday League and arguing about it.' Neither had many other friends. In the summer they went to Taylor's family home in Nottingham and turned out for local cricket teams. Clough, according to Taylor, was so quick and alert he might have fielded to Test match standard and he dreamed of opening the batting for England. In later years he became a good friend of Yorkshire and England opener Geoffrey Boycott.

'In all the cricket we played together, I never saw Brian look anything better than a reasonable club batsman,' Taylor commented. 'Football, though, was something else. Week after week, I stood in Middlesbrough's goalmouth watching Brian at the other end make my predictions for him come true. You can either score goals or you can't. Blessed with the scorer's knack, he would have stuck goals away in any company. They said he lacked mobility but Brian was mobile where it mattered. He saved his energy for the penalty box; he lurked there always, awake to the faintest chance and applying the clinical finish.'

Taylor kept goal for the Teessiders when Middlesbrough came to Trentside on Saturday 10 November, 1956. He – and I in a crowd of 20,800 – saw the twenty-one-year-old Clough give centre-half Bob McKinlay a torrid time as he hit his first Football League hat-trick. Boro's 4-0 victory put them third in the Second Division, two places above Forest with one point more. Skipper Jack Burkitt, Bill Morley, Peter Small, Doug Lishman and Eddie Baily were all in the home side. In this, his second season, Clough scored thirty-eight League goals in forty-one appearances. He scored twice in three FA Cup games. But Middlesbrough fell away and they finished in sixth place. Forest were promoted as runners-up to Leicester City with Liverpool missing out at third. Jim Barrett was Forest's top scorer with twenty-seven League goals from thirty-two games and three in five FA Cup appearances. Forest reached the sixth round before going out to Birmingham after a replay. Notts County just escaped relegation in twentieth place. Derby County were Third Division North champions – their first title – with Ilkeston-born former coalminer Ray Straw, signed from Ilkeston Town, equalling a club record thirty-seven goals first set by Jack Bowers in 1930/31.

By the end of January, Middlesbrough's high hopes effectively were dashed but Clough's were rising rapidly. He was selected for a 'B' international against Scotland at Birmingham on 6 February, 1957. Clough shone under the St Andrew's floodlights and although he didn't score himself, he played an active role in all of the England goals in a 4-1 victory. 'I don't think I've ever seen him distribute the ball better,' commented Bob Dennison, his club manager. Later the same month, Clough made his debut for the England Under-23 side again against Scotland. This time he disappointed, missing three fine chances created by inside-forward Johnny Haynes, and the game at Ibrox, Glasgow, finished 1-1. He had another trying time playing for Young England against Billy Wright of Old England at Highbury. But he did go close with a couple of good shots and a fine header in a 2-1 defeat. It was enough to secure a place in the Under-23 tour to eastern Europe. He scored with 'a flying header' in a 2-1 defeat to Bulgaria in Sofia, where the England side were down to ten after the sending off of Stan Anderson of Sunderland. Left out against Romania in Bucharest and Czechoslovakia in Bratislava, both England victories, he returned home disappointed.

Scoring one and making two other goals for an FA Representative XI who beat the RAF 5-2 was not enough to win back his Under-23 place. Then he hit five when the FA beat the Army 6-3. He was maturing swiftly and being talked about for the full England side, which had been diminished by the tragic Munich air crash in February 1957 that had taken the lives of Manchester United stars Roger Byrne, Duncan Edwards, David Pegg and centre-forward Tommy Taylor. Clough scored forty goals in forty League games and two more in the FA Cup during 1957/58. He got back into the Under-23 side against Wales and was chosen to travel with the twenty-man England squad to Yugoslavia and Russia but was left out of both matches. England lost 5-0 in Belgrade and drew 1-1 in Moscow. Clough was annoyed and seemingly clashed with both manager Walter Winterbottom and captain Billy Wright. Before the flight home, he was told there was no place for him in the squad to go to the 1958 World Cup finals in Sweden. Derek Kevan of West Brom was preferred. England went out at the group stage after losing to Russia in a play-off. They failed to register a win in four games, scoring only four goals with Kevan getting just one of them.

Feeling even more frustration, he put in another transfer request. Dennison responded by making Clough captain. 'He had almost three years' League experience behind him and I am sure that he has the aptitude for the job,' the manager explained. Age did not matter. 'Brian has that drive on the field that can win matches and as captain I'm certain he can inspire his colleagues.'

It was a controversial appointment not helped by the fact that before long, Clough and Taylor were meeting Dennison in his office on a Friday afternoon to pick the team for the next afternoon. 'I was aware of a certain amount of resentment towards me from some of the other players,' Clough admitted. 'I always said what I thought. I was bloody good at what I did and made no excuses for believing I was the best'. As if to underline this, he started the 1958/59 season by scoring five goals in Middlesbrough's 9-0 drubbing of newly promoted Brighton.

After such a bright start, Boro's form became erratic and in mid-September Dennison agreed a deal with Sunderland manager Alan Brown to buy former England star Don Revie, born even closer to Ayresome Park than Clough. But local loyalties meant nothing as Revie, who had been voted Footballer of the Year in 1956, declined the transfer, dashing any hopes Clough may have entertained of them forging an effective partnership. It wasn't to be the only time the two talented Teessiders would snub each other.

Selection for a Football League XI against the Scottish League at Ibrox on 8 October was a welcome distraction from club discontent for Clough, who scored in a 1-1 draw. Middlesbrough were heading for mid-table obscurity but he made what he described as the best move of his life. Peter Taylor had long told him that what he needed was a girlfriend. He had seemed too devoted to football to show much interest. Then he saw a girl in a local café, introduced himself and bought her a coffee. She lived less than a mile away, just across the park, and her father was a Middlesbrough fan who went on about this young centre-forward who was scoring all the goals. Her name was Barbara Glasgow and, said Brian, 'she had a smile as wide as Stockton high street'. They were married on the morning of Saturday 4 April 1959, choosing the date 'to qualify for a tax rebate'. After a rushed reception, he went off to Ayresome Park to play and score in a 4-2 victory over Leyton Orient.

Middlesbrough finished the 1958 season thirteenth despite Clough scoring forty-three goals in forty-two League games. The England selectors were unimpressed. He was left out of the side taken to the Americas and beaten by Brazil, Peru and Mexico before a final flourish with an 8-1 win over the USA. Boro thrashed Derby County 7-1 at the Baseball Ground in the third game of the 1959/60 but Clough was not on the scoresheet, his twin centre-forward partner Alan Peacock hitting four goals. He was still to open his account when the side went to Plymouth, where he scored four in fourteen minutes in a 6-2 win. He then earned a call-up for the Football League against the Irish League. The match was played in Belfast on Barbara's birthday and he delivered a present of all five goals in a 5-0 victory. 'Here was his answer to those selectors who for so long have rated him no more than a successful goal-getter in the Second Division,' reported the *Daily Mail*. 'Get that England No. 9 jersey ready for Brian Clough,' demanded the *Daily Mirror*.

It was. A fortnight later he got his full international call-up against Wales at Cardiff. At the team hotel he felt nervous and vulnerable. Then he spilt his breakfast of bacon and beans on his lap. His footballing hero Tom Finney came to the rescue, taking him back to the bedroom and then arranging for his only pair of flannels to be cleaned. 'Tom, among the nicest men you could wish to meet, was quite simply one of the finest footballers I have ever seen,' Clough wrote in his autobiography. His problems weren't over. He had forgotten his boots. Bob Dennison rushed them down to Cardiff but, perhaps unsurprisingly, Clough did not distinguish himself. Jimmy Greaves got the England goal in a disappointing 1-1 draw.

Eleven days later World Cup finalists Sweden came to Wembley and Clough kept his England place. Alongside him were Jimmy Greaves and Bobby Charlton. The Swedes won 3-2 and Greaves commented, 'They took us apart.' Clough thought the three of them were too similar in styles and ended up chasing the same ball and making identical runs. 'It didn't work, it couldn't work,' he wrote. Dennison, who had been at Wembley with a party of Boro players, claimed Clough told Winterbottom he would have to drop either Greaves or Charlton. No wonder he didn't get another chance, his club manager said.

Clough wrote,

> I seem to remember that I could have saved the game. One of the Swedish defenders attempted a back-pass. I was always ready for that kind of thing. I saw mistakes before they happened! But this time everything happened very quickly. I was on to it and hit an instant shot. I can still see the ball hitting the bar. If it had gone in, perhaps history would have told a different story. Perhaps they would have given me a third England cap. There were to be no further chances for me. I was cast aside at the age of twenty-four by a manager who, in my opinion, didn't know his job.

Peter Taylor later commented,

> The tragedy of Brian as a footballer, and I'm not thinking of the premature end to his career, was the failure not only of his club but also of his country to capitalise on his extraordinary talent. England capped him only twice because manager Sir Walter Winterbottom and his amateur selectors wanted runners, forwards like Derek Kevan and Ray Pointer, who covered every blade of grass while scoring once in a thousand miles.

When Middlesbrough took the train north to Edinburgh for a friendly match against Hibernian, Clough and Taylor sat apart from the other players, who were playing cards, and discussed the Sweden match. They were analysing Clough's performance and what went wrong for him. This apparent aloofness may have led to a rebellion against his captaincy. Players and coaching staff were called to a meeting with the chairman, directors and manager. 'Players expressed their views and it was a harmonious meeting,' chairman W. S. Gibson said. But Clough handed in a transfer request, saying he wanted to get away and concentrate on football. It wasn't granted. When Fiorentina of the Italian Serie A expressed an interest, however, Middlesbrough admitted they 'might not say no to a big offer for Clough'.

In an unhappy time for the club, with some players even accused in a match-fixing scandal, Clough carried on scoring. On the train back from a game in London, he lambasted some teammates: 'If I can manage to score four next week, you never know we might even win.' He struck forty goals in forty-two games in 1959/60 and thirty-six in forty-two in 1960/61. In six seasons with his home town club, he had scored 204 goals in 222 games.

Peter Taylor signed for Port Vale for £750 – 'my benefit money' – on 12 June 1961. Clough refused to sign a contract for the 1961/62 season and was transfer-listed. Billy Walker was prepared to bid £40,000 to bring him to Trentside but both Arsenal and Sunderland were keen on him. Clough fancied Wolverhampton Wanderers, as he admired their disciplinarian manager Stan Cullis. He needed advice. Taylor was sunning himself in a deckchair on the beach at North Bay, Scarborough, when his friend turned up and together they decided to find the nearest phone box to speak to Wolves. Tayor learned that Cullis was away. 'I had to speak to his chief scout George Noakes who, oddly for his profession, had only one eye and that eye was not focused on Brian Clough,' Taylor wrote.

Not the best sailor in the world, Brian nevertheless decided to treat Barbara to a Mediterranean cruise. 'There was something romantic about life on board,' he said. 'It was a little different from Middlesbrough.' They arrived back in Southampton at 5 a.m. on Monday 10 July, and to their surprise saw Sunderland's manager Alan Brown waiting for them on the other side of the barriers as they disembarked. He had cut short his own family holiday at Bude, Cornwall, to drive 140 miles through the night to meet the Cloughs off the boat. Brown reached over the fence, shook hands and told him Sunderland had agreed a £45,000 fee with Middlesbrough. Clough was offered £40 a week.

Before the deal was announced in the press, Taylor placed an £18 bet on Sunderland for promotion in the coming season. 'I had been laid a fantastic price of 100-6,' he said. 'I could win £300 for my outlay of just over a week's wages before the odds tumbled to 7-2 against.' Unfortunately, Sunderland missed promotion by a point.

Clough was happier with Sunderland than at Middlesbrough. There was immediate respect. He wrote,

It was Alan Brown who taught me about discipline: the value of decent behaviour which, years later, was to become a hallmark of Clough teams and the reason why we the favourites among referees. We made their job so much easier. He ran Sunderland from top to bottom. He was the boss. What he said mattered and people responded. Alan Brown was not simply my manager, he was my mentor. He wasn't to know it at the time, of course, but he was teaching me the right way to go about a task that was to present itself far quicker than anyone imagined.

Clough's arrival unleashed a new wave of enthusiasm on Wearside. Season ticket sales doubled. He was just as prolific a goalscorer as he had been at Middlesbrough and made watching Sunderland exciting. In sixty-one League matches in a Sunderland shirt he scored fifty-four goals. Nearly 1 million fans went through the Roker Park turnstiles, an increase of more than 250,000 on the previous season, and the club made a profit of nearly £17,000. But their promotion push was in vain. Thousands of supporters travelled in overnight trains to Wales for the last game of the season. Clough seized on a loose ball and evaded two challenges to open the scoring but Swansea equalised midway through the second half so great expectations came to nothing.

He was enjoying what he described as 'the happiest time of my life in football' when misfortune struck and he became one of the first casualties of a ferocious winter. It caused chaos for two months. The FA Cup Final was put back by three weeks, hundreds of matches were postponed and the pools panel was created to guess the results of unplayed games. Boxing Day 1962 was a biting, forbidding day with a torrential hailstorm worsening conditions as Sunderland faced Bury at Roker Park. Clough wrote in his autobiography, 'It was the kind of day when seagulls fly backwards to stop their eyes watering.'

Half an hour had passed. No score but a penalty missed by Sunderland. Then came an overhit through-ball and Clough gave chase. He recalled,

I sprinted across the muddy surface towards the ball, my eye on it the whole time. I was never to be distracted in circumstances like that. I sensed an opportunity to score another goal. Suddenly, it was as if someone had just turned out the light. The Bury goalkeeper, Chris Harker, had gone down for the ball and his shoulder crunched into my right knee. I was slightly off balance with my head down. I didn't see him. My head hit the ground and for a second or two I didn't know a thing. Only blackness. It must have been a fleeting moment, though, because I spotted that the ball had run loose again. My instinct told me to get after it. I tried to lever myself off the ground but couldn't. I started crawling. Something kept urging me: Get up, get up.

He tried but couldn't. Bob Stokoe, the Bury centre-half, shouted, 'He's only coddin', ref.' But the referee, Kevin Howley, himself a Middlesbrough man, replied, 'He doesn't cod, not this lad.'

Unable to stand, Clough was carried from the field and then from Roker Park to Sunderland General Hospital. Both the medial and cruciate ligaments were completely torn. Sunderland went on to lose 1-0. In the 1962/63 season Clough had scored twenty-four goals in twenty-four Second Division appearances with four more in the League Cup. It took eighteen months of harsh physical work – running up and down the Spion Kop at Roker Park and along the beach – and mental torment before he could attempt a comeback.

Sunderland finally won promotion in 1964 and by the start of the 1964/65 season he was back in training with the squad. He returned to the side as a second-half substitute in a mid-August friendly against Huddersfield, then scored for the reserves in a 2-2 draw at Grimsby before hitting a hat-trick for them in a 7-1 win over Halifax at Roker Park. Alan Brown had resigned as manager in July to join Sheffield Wednesday. Former Sunderland and England full-back and captain George Hardwick was now in charge and he restored Clough to the first team to play at West Bromwich Albion, but they drew 2-2. He scored with a header in 3-3 draw at home to Leeds. A week later, he played in another drawn game against Aston Villa. He was dropped for the visit to Arsenal and never played again. 'I hadn't a clue that I was insured for £40,000; peanuts now but a princely sum then,' he wrote. The club banked the money 'settling with me for little more than £1,000'.

Clough had been happy at Sunderland, where his sons Simon and Nigel were born, but now he was desolate. He railed against the directors but later said, 'George Hardwick offered me something that was to be far more significant than cash. He gave me the chance to work with youth players. I found, instantly, that I could teach.' According to Hardwick, 'Brian was a revelation. He loved working with the kids and they loved working with him. Instead of condemning, he was encouraging.' Hardwick made him youth team manager. 'I was always interested in management,' said Clough. 'I used to talk a lot about football and you'd be amazed how many footballers didn't.'

He was persuaded by Hardwick to go on an FA coaching course at Durham. It was run by Charles Hughes, later to become technical director of the FA. 'Hughes preached a primitive "long-ball" game based on percentages – one that I regard as absolute bloody garbage,' Clough wrote. 'He reached the same shortlist as me, years later, when I was interviewed for the job of England manager. That says everything about the way football is run in this country. I've worked with a few coaches and managers in my time but never with anyone who had less idea about football than Charlie Hughes.' Despite the friction, Clough was one of the youngest in the game to earn his full FA coaching badge. At Sunderland he scrapped the 'dreadful, monotonous laps' from the training routine. 'I put a ball down and we played football, five- and six-a-side games,' he wrote. John O'Hare, who later played for Derby, Leeds and Forest, was a member of his youth team.

Hardwick was asked by the directors why he had promoted Clough and was told to get rid of him. He refused and later was sacked himself. 'I was fired because I stood by Brian and refused to climb down,' he claimed. Clough asked the new manager, Ian McColl, to confirm that he could continue working with the youngsters. He couldn't, saying, 'I don't think the directors will be too pleased if you stay here.' Clough was out of work but collected £10,000 in proceeds from a testimonial match attended by 31,898 supporters.

Meanwhile, Peter Taylor had moved out of League football to join Burton Albion of the Southern League and was appointed manager in 1963. On the night of his testimonial Clough was offered the chance to become the youngest manager in the Football League, at thirty years old. That same night he rang Taylor with the question, 'Do you fancy joining me?' The remarkable Clough-Taylor managerial partnership was just about to begin.

6

Sweet and Sour

Leaving Aston Villa was a wrench but quitting the game altogether was unthinkable to Billy Walker. He had prepared himself for management with the help of the Villa office staff and had mugged up on the Football Association and the League rules and regulations. He recalled,

> It did not take me long at my studies to realise that the players' and the managers' points of view are two entirely different things. I was in need of a complete reorientation but now I was equipped with the necessary fundamentals – the three Rs of management - and more than twenty years' experience as a pro and amateur player.

Sheffield Wednesday were struggling near the foot of the First Division when the board accepted the resignation of Bob Brown as secretary-manager. They had won only two of their last eleven games and, having conceded six goals at Wolverhampton and four at Sunderland, were desperately in need of inspiration. Walker was under no illusion about the size of task ahead of him when just before Christmas 1933, two months after his thirty-sixth birthday, he took the managerial chair at Hillsborough. 'Wednesday were in a pretty bad way when I got there,' he said. 'They were second from bottom and morale was about as low as their position. However, I was always one to accept a challenge. I set about the task of transferring as much as I could of the Villa spirit to my new club. It worked like a charm.'

With his arrival, the team went on an unbeaten run of sixteen matches, including four FA Cup ties, and they finished the 1933/34 season mid-table. The sequence ended in late February at Maine Road, where Manchester City won a fifth-round replay 2-0 on their way to winning at Wembley. The rot had been stopped by 'a combination of restored confidence and luck', Walker claimed modestly. 'In the rebuilding of the Wednesday, I had pursued the policy that has always been mine – I insisted on good football.'

Two important decisions facilitated his successful start in management. The first was to contact his old friend Jimmy Hogan and Hugo Meisl, architects of the 'Wunderteam', and invite them to Sheffield to talk about the tactics and coaching methods that had greatly impressed him as captain of England in 1932. Despite the limitations of some of the players he had inherited, he wanted to copy the smooth and speedy passing game he had so admired. FK Austria Wien, champions of Central Europe after winning the 1933 Mitropa Cup, toured England during the 1933/34 season playing against Liverpool, Fulham and Birmingham City as well as at Hillsborough. Much to Walker's delight, the Wednesday beat the Viennese, who included Mathias Sindelar, Austria's greatest-ever player, 3-0. 'The Austrians gave us a banner and we gave them a magnificent cup, which impressed them no end, and presented all their players with Sheffield-made knives,' Walker said. Hogan, who had been Vienna's first manager in 1911, interpreted.

Walker's second significant step was to restore Ronnie Starling, who under the previous management had lost form and been dropped, to the side. Not only that, Starling was given the captaincy and the attack was built around him. Starling had joined Wednesday from Newcastle United and thrived on the faith that Walker placed in him. He was 'a strange genius', his manager said, 'a bit of an odd man out when I started my remoulding task'. It was just the morale boost Starling needed and he became a model of consistency, leading the team to an FA Cup Final triumph and making almost 200 appearances before moving to Aston Villa for £7,000 in 1937. An England international with two caps, he played twelve games for Walker's Forest in wartime football.

So many players were shipped out that only four of those who started in the manager's first Wednesday team that beat Liverpool 3-1 at Anfield on 9 December 1933, remained to take part in the Cup Final at Wembley on 27 April 1935. Those who departed included fan favourites like Jack Ball, who had scored thirty-five goals in 1932/33 and veteran England full-back and former captain Ernest Blenkinsop. Ball went to Manchester United as part of a deal to bring in Walker's first big signing, Scottish international centre-forward Neil Dewar from Manchester United – he scored fifty goals in ninety-five games for Wednesday. Blenkinsop was replaced by Joe Nibloe, another Scottish international and known to Walker from his Villa days.

Two young players who were on the Walker wanted list would develop into legendary stars. They were Stanley Matthews and Tommy Lawton.

He was never likely to pick up Matthews, who had signed amateur forms for Stoke City a few years earlier. Lawton, who had recently left school, was impressed by Walker, whose offer included lodgings, ten shillings a week as pocket money and a job outside football until he was old enough to turn professional. 'Mr Walker was very nice to me,' the young prospect recalled, 'but my mother thought I was too young to go so far away on my own.' Instead, he joined his local League team, Burnley.

Walker's second season was an outstanding success for the tyro manager. Wednesday finished third in the First Division behind champions Arsenal and Sunderland and a point better than Manchester City, whom they succeeded as FA Cup holders. On the way to Wembley, Wednesday beat Oldham Athletic at home and Wolves away before, in the fifth round, being drawn away to mid-table Second Division side Norwich City, whose tight little ground in Rosary Road, known as the Nest, was shorter and narrower than any they were used to. The Canaries 'flew' to Carrow Road the following season.

To prepare his players, Walker had the expansive Hillsborough turf marked out to the exact dimensions of the Norwich playing area. On the Tuesday morning before the game, he invited supporters along to watch a full-scale practice match and several thousand turned up to stand around the touchlines. 'After about twenty minutes our players had got used to confined space and were controlling the flight of the ball as if they had been playing on small grounds all their lives,' the manager said. 'They went on for nearly two hours, not only to hammer the lessons home but also to give our co-operative supporters a run for their money.' Walker's planning paid dividends as City were beaten 1-0. League leaders Arsenal were beaten 2-1 at Hillsborough in the sixth round and Walker took his side to Villa Park for a semi-final against Burnley, who like Norwich were in Division Two. True to form, the Owls were 3-0 winners.

Another idea of his was to watch practice matches from the vantage point of the broadcasting box in Hillsborough's main stand. He used loudspeakers to give instructions as the players tried out tactical moves he had devised. These were usually held behind locked doors but, occasionally, training sessions were conducted in public. He also installed Turkish baths, laid on table tennis, supervised the preparation of special meals and organised entertainment for the players and their families. Not all Wednesday supporters appreciated his approach. To some diehards, his innovations were 'stunts'. Undeniably though, at this stage it was results that counted.

Wednesday won only two of the seven League games before the final and on the Monday before the big day drew 1-1 in a 'rehearsal' against the other finalists West Bromwich Albion at the Hawthorns.

Albion were unbeaten in their seven matches after the semi-final but 'rested' players for the league game. Starling was one of the Owls' players left out. His place was taken by a Walker discovery, Jackie Robinson, spotted playing in a junior match in his native Tyneside. The young debutant went on to become one of Wednesday's finest and an England international. He scored twice in the 6-3 defeat of Germany in Berlin in 1938, remembered for the reluctant but notorious Nazi salute the players had to give before the kick-off to avoid an international incident. The war interrupted Robinson's career, which ended when he broke a leg playing for Lincoln City.

Starling returned for the final, for which West Brom were overwhelming favourites. But Walker calmed nerves. 'All along I have taken the view that it is to be our Cup this season, and this is my opinion still,' he said. 'We shall not vary our tactics in the slightest.' His confidence was justified. Left-winger Ellis Rimmer scored twice in the last five minutes to give Wednesday a 4-2 victory. Leading national sports journalist Henry Rose wrote, 'Starling, as befits captain, was the inspiration of his fellows in a hectic second-half when Wednesday took the lead, lost it, and gained it again. He took over a big portion of that half and wrote his name all over it. He pirouetted hither and thither, changed position with the magic of a trapdoor acrobat in a pantomime, rallied his mates and made himself a nuisance to his foes.' Starling himself commented, 'The boss believed in me from the start. I should be travelling in a circus now if it were not for him.'

At inside-right in the cup-winners' side was Jack Surtees, a Geordie who had been released by Northampton Town in November 1934. On the recommendation of his brother Albert, a Villa teammate of Walker's, Surtees was given a month's trial at Hillsborough. His fine form was such an eye-opener that after being given a first-team chance on Christmas Day, he kept his place for the rest of the season and played in six FA Cup ties. Surtees lost his place to Jackie Robinson and was transferred to Nottingham Forest in October 1936. He scored twenty-three goals in ninety-three Second Division games for the Reds up to the outbreak of war and also played for Walker in a few wartime games.

Wednesday's form slumped alarmingly in 1935/36 and they were embroiled in a relegation battle. West Brom, Liverpool and the Owls finished on thirty-eight points and down went Aston Villa with thirty-five and Blackburn Rovers with thirty-three. It was a fate deferred. They were given the wooden spoon at the end of the following season and were accompanied into Division Two by Manchester United. They fared little better in the lower division and were next to bottom of the table when Walker handed in his resignation on Sunday 7 November 1937.

Tuesday morning's newspapers reported that:

> A summons has been taken out by Mr Darrell H. Foxon, of Sheffield, against Mr William H. Walker, secretary-manager of the Sheffield Wednesday Football Club, alleging assault and damage. It is answerable at Barnsley on Thursday 18th November. Barnsley and Sheffield Wednesday played at Barnsley last Saturday and Mr Foxon, who is a member of Sheffield City Council, was a spectator.

The next day the club's chairman, Mr W. G. Turner, issued this statement after a three-hour board meeting: 'Mr W. H. Walker handed in his resignation as secretary-manager. This has been accepted and his engagement with the club has been terminated on terms mutually agreed upon. There is nothing further to be said.' It was very different from the fulsome welcome he had received from Mr Turner and the board on his appointment in December 1933, when a welcoming banquet had been held for him. 'Mr Walker will be club manager from top to bottom,' Mr Turner had told the gathering. 'With his great experience and ability, he is qualified to go on the field and give our players the benefit of his advice and, in fact, his position is one of full power and full responsibility.'

Walker said his authority was gradually seeped away and he fully believed that, given time, he would have got the team out of trouble. The club was in profit, its bank overdraft had been reduced from £10,788 to £3,534 and £10,000 profit had been made on transfers. He described being 'made a scapegoat' with interference in his handling of the players and team selection. 'There were powerful interests at work' against the manager. 'However, that's football and I have always accepted whatever fortune the game has brought me, good or ill.'

On Friday 19 November, the headline in the *Daily Independent* announced 'SUMMONSES AGAINST BILLY WALKER FAIL', reporting,

> Barnsley magistrates yesterday dismissed summonses brought against Mr W. H. Walker, formerly manager of Sheffield Wednesday Football Club, by Councillor Darell H. Foxon for assault and fifteen shillings damages to his spectacles. They unanimously thought that the payment of court costs by Walker – amounting to four shillings in each case – would meet the position.

Mr W. E. Wise, prosecuting, told the court that Mr Foxon had been a Sheffield Wednesday supporter for many years. At the Barnsley match on 6 November he stood next to a wall dividing the players' entrance from the terraces. Wednesday were being heavily beaten and there was a lot of shouting by the spectators. 'Mr Foxon heard someone walking rather sharply down the gangway and, turning round, he saw Walker who said something to him. He failed to catch what it was. He then received two fairly violent blows to the face, one on the bridge of his nose and the other on the left side of the eye. These blows were delivered by Walker,' it was alleged. The paper reported that Mr Wise went on: 'This affair happened at a football match to which people had paid to go to be entertained. It is a place where criticism is given vent to by the spectators. Defendant is a man with the utmost experience of the game both as a player and as a manager. He has many times earned the plaudits of the crowd when his team has done well, and he has had to accept criticism when it has done badly. The manager of a football club must be able to take the good with the bad without losing control of himself.'

In reply to Mr R. J. Craig, representing Walker, Mr Foxon agreed that in his opinion 'the management do not seem to have the faintest notion of running a football club'. He had written to the press to express that view and told the directors they should appoint a new manager. And he had shouted that the players should take no notice of Walker's instructions. Foxon admitted he had never been involved in football management. 'What would be your attitude if Walker circularised your clients saying what a rotten chartered accountant you were?' asked Mr Craig. 'That is not the same thing,' Mr Foxon replied. 'Would you consider it fair comment and fair criticism?' 'If right, yes.' 'You would not consider it a personal attack?' 'No.' Mr Foxon said he had seen Wednesday eight times in the previous season and once in the current season. 'I put it to you that this incident at Barnsley was the culmination of two and a half years' campaign by you of vicious and vindictive persecution,' Mr Craig said. This Mr Foxon denied.

According to the *Independent*, Mr Craig asked the Bench to take into consideration the circumstances that had been mounting up for a very long time. Walker acted in self-defence, believing that he was about to be assaulted, and that he was justified in this belief because of the personal nature of the attacks that Mr Foxon had made upon him for over two and a half years. 'So seriously did the directors of the Wednesday club regard the complainant's behaviour that they were seeking powers to have him debarred from their ground,' Mr Craig said. 'Twelve steady, prominent citizens, who were also sportsmen, would not go to such a length as that unless they had been given reasonable grounds for so doing. During the game at Oakwell, Mr W. Foster, a director of the Barnsley club, was so disgusted with Foxon's conduct that he called him to shut up and watch the match. Whether Walker was convicted or acquitted the case would do him serious harm in the football world which was his livelihood.'

Dealing with the incident at Oakwell, Walker said in evidence that near the end of the game he saw Foxon coming towards him. 'I was under the impression that he was coming to strike me. I have never seen a man look so ferocious,' he told the magistrates. 'I knocked his hat off with my left hand and knocked his glasses off but I certainly did not strike him with my fist. They were open-handed blows.' Cross-examining, Mr Wise asked Walker, 'Are you a bad-tempered man?' The reply was, 'No.' 'Have you had an argument with a referee and were you cautioned by the Football Association?' Walker admitted he had been warned not to interfere.

In the witness box, the Barnsley director Mr Foster said that during the game Foxon kept up a continual barrage against Walker and near the end of the match used an offensive word. Walker then struck him. 'I should have done what Walker did,' Mr Foster added. Wednesday trainer Sam Powell said Foxon shouted to the players to 'take no notice of Billy Walker'. Councillor William Fearnehough, a Sheffield Wednesday director, said Foxon shouted to him in the street to 'Sack Billy Walker'. Another director of the club, Councillor Donald Craig, said that Foxon rang him up at midnight to tell him to sack Walker.

Chairman of the Bench, Mr B. F. Canter, said they were very sorry that the case had come to court. The *Daily Independent* reported Walker saying after the dismissal:

> I want to forget the matter as soon as possible. I have had many congratulations by all kinds of people on the result of the case. They are from friends in Sheffield as well as outside and have come by telegram and over the phone. A lot of them I know but there are many I don't know at all. I don't know what my plans will be yet but I am going to have a holiday.

On 24 January 1938, Billy Walker was appointed secretary-manager of Chelmsford City FC, an amateur club with ambitions to become professional and join the Southern League. 'I jumped at the opportunity to help them become a limited liability company,' he said. 'Probably it was the best thing I could have done. I got a valuable insight into company law and business administration. We went to the public with an offer of five-shilling shares and raised £3,500 within a few months.' He put together a new team, retaining only the amateur goalkeeper, and his signings included former England left-half Eric Keen from Derby; Jackie Coulter, the Irish international and Everton outside-left; and Jack Palethorpe, his centre-forward from Sheffield Wednesday. With a team and supporter base, the next stage was ground improvements, with new terracing and an extended main stand.

Having been accepted by the Southern League, Walker's City embarked on an FA Cup run beyond the dreams of Chelmsford supporters. Progressing through the qualifying rounds, they beat Kidderminster Harriers 4-0 in the first round proper on 26 November 1938, Darlington 3-1 in the second round on 10 December, Southampton 4-1 on 7 January in the third round, at which stage Derby, Forest and Arsenal were among the teams knocked out. In the fourth round on 21 January, the run ended at Birmingham with a 6-0 defeat, but the little Essex side had gone as far as Notts County, Leicester City and Tottenham Hotspur, who were all also beaten.

This success merely reignited the manager's desire to find a Football League club. 'So ended this brief but exciting period of Cup stimulation, and with it went my interest in non-League football,' he wrote. 'I had a go while it lasted but could not escape the feeling that there was something better for me than this,' he said. His disillusion was exacerbated by a failed attempt to sign a player from Plymouth Argyle on a free transfer only to find a £500 fee was demanded. 'I had a most unpleasant time with my directors at Chelmsford for that money was going to take a lot of finding,' Walker wrote. 'I decided it was not for me and bowed out.'

Walker went back to live in Walsall. 'I just sat tight and waited,' he said. 'Then Nottingham Forest approached me and that was that.'

7

Derby Fallout

Brian Clough leapt at the chance to manage Hartlepools United (as the club was then known) when owner and chairman Ernie Ord offered him the post. It meant the youngest manager in the Football League began at the bottom. Hartlepools were regularly having to apply for re-election (this was before automatic expulsion to the Conference) and they had again finished last of all. He needed Peter Taylor's help but Ord would not countenance a managerial partnership. Clough told Taylor his role would be that of assistant manager but to pacify the owner his job title would be trainer.

I knew Peter was desperate to get into League football even though he'd have to take a cut in money to join me. I gave him a two hundred quid to help him decide to help me make something out of a ramshackle, failing, totally skint football club called Hartlepools United. Pete was the bucket and sponge man on matchdays and there was nothing funnier than that. He knew nothing about joints, ligaments and tendons. If it couldn't be cured by sploshing a cold sponge on it and telling the injured player to 'gerrup and gerron wi' it', he had no cure at all, and I certainly didn't.

But we learned at Hartlepools. We learned how to ship out the deadwood and bring in better players. We learned how to lift a team from bottom in October to the safety of eighteenth place by the end of the season. We learned where to place buckets to catch the rain that leaked through the holes in the boardroom and office roof. We learned how to sign a youngster from grammar school whose headmaster wanted him to go to university rather than to Hartlepools United, which wasn't an unreasonable point of view. I persisted, arguing that surely the lad should have the choice, already knowing the boy wanted to sign for me. So John McGovern became a professional footballer instead of a university student. He, Taylor and I were to have good reason to be thankful for the day he put pen to paper at the scruffy little club that gave us all a start. John McGovern of Nottingham Forest was to hold aloft the European Cup on all our behalves, not just once but in two consecutive seasons. Not many players, captains, have done that.

Clough's impact at the Victoria Ground had been immediate and the television cameras were there for his first home game, a 4-1 victory against Crewe Alexandra. To end the season eighteenth in the old Fourth Division doesn't sound great but it was better than they were used to at Hartlepools. To stiffen the defence, Clough, coincidentally, signed full-back Brian Grant from Nottingham Forest for £2,000 and paid £4,000 to Mansfield Town for centre-half John Gill, a former Forest youth player. Gill, said Peter Taylor, was 'terrifyingly tough'.

Financially, the club was in such dire straits that its manager offered to give up his £2,000-a-year salary and work for free until the crisis passed. A public appeal for funds was launched and Clough toured the town speaking in pubs, clubs, at dinners and at meetings. He was at loggerheads with the chairman, Ernie Ord, and complained about interference. 'He didn't seem to appreciate what Taylor and I were doing for Hartlepools,' Clough wrote in his first autobiography. 'I knew how the media worked and never missed a chance to get them there with their cameras and their notebooks. I helped give the ground a fresh lick of paint, I helped the lorry driver unload steel plates for the rebuilding of the stand roof, and I made sure the Press were there to see it all. Hartlepools had never known so many column inches.' Clough taking the limelight added to the chairman's annoyance, foreshadowing what was to follow at Derby County. He announced that his son would in future handle all publicity at the club. 'I said "Piss off" and carried on with whatever I was writing at the time,' Clough commented.

Next, Ord was determined to get rid of Taylor, whom he saw as surplus to requirements. Clough made it clear that if Taylor went he would go too. A boardroom revolt saw the chairman replaced instead. Ironically, Clough and Taylor were about to quit anyway. First, Hartlepools finished the season in eighth place – their highest for a decade – and Clough gained his first trophy as a manager, the Durham Senior Cup, after an aggregate win over Gateshead in the final.

According to Brian Clough, the first to become restless was Peter Taylor. A new chairman had been installed at Hartlepools but 'Pete insisted we were worthy and capable of bigger things'. Former Sunderland and

England star Len Shackleton had become an influential football writer in the north-east working for the *Sunday People* and Taylor was constantly in touch with him. 'Shack' had contacts and Taylor knew that if anybody could find them a better club it would be him. Derby County had a managerial vacancy. They had just sacked Tim Ward, a former England international and stylish right-half who had played more than 230 games for them and had been their manager for five years.

The famous 'silver and gold' inside-forward partnership of Raich Carter and Peter Doherty had helped the Rams win the first post-war FA Cup in 1946 after appearing as wartime 'guest' players. Both had fallen out with the directors soon afterwards and the club twice broke the British transfer record to replace them with Billy Steel and Johnny Morris. But after finishing fourth in the First Division in 1948 and third a year later, Derby went into decline, falling into Division Three by 1955. Taylor's mentor Harry Storer got them back into the Second Division in 1957. Ward, Storer's successor, complained that lack of investment had held him back. 'The trouble with this club is that you can't put a threepenny stamp on a letter without consulting the board,' he said. 'I was told money was available but I could never get an answer when I asked how much.'

Cheltenham-born Ward was perhaps too decent a man and when he did make a stand, insisting on signing twenty-year-old Kevin Hector from Bradford Park Avenue for £20,000, it led to his departure. The young inside-forward was an outstanding recruit but the chairman, Sam Longson, claimed the credit for the deal. Inconsistent, Derby finished the season seventeenth and Ward's contract was not renewed. Chief scout Sammy Crooks, a great Derby and England right-winger, also left. 'There is potential here for a great team but under the present set-up I see no chance of an improvement,' the departing manager said. After the final match, fans chanted, 'Sack the board, bring back Ward.' Hector's goals would help Clough's side become champions of the Football League.

Shackleton set up a meeting for Clough with Longson, who had made a fortune in the road haulage business, at a hotel at Scotch Corner. 'Longson had the kind of voice that could shake stone from quarry walls,' Clough said. 'It took Shackleton and me hardly any time at all to convince him I was his man. The job was mine before the main course arrived.'

Taylor was in his element. He had watched Carter, Doherty, Crooks and Jackie Stamps in the Baseball Ground's brief golden age but he said, 'Derby meant nothing to Brian. His ambitions were set in the North East managing Sunderland or Newcastle United.' Once he had overcome the difficulty of the directors reacting badly to his demand for Taylor as his assistant, Clough took down the photographs of Steve Bloomer,

Carter, Doherty and the other Derby greats that lined the corridors at the Baseball Ground. The focus was to be on the future rather than past glories. Other managers, like Dougie Freedman at Forest and Clough's former player Roy Keane at Sunderland, wanted players to be reminded of a club's traditions. Just as Billy Walker had at the City Ground, Clough drew up a rulebook, which he called the 'Players' Ticket'. His emphasis, however, was on restrictions and prohibitions – no smoking at the ground during training, no riding motorcycles, no going to dances later in the week than Tuesdays and no going to 'licensed premises'.

Longson pledged a transfer pot of £70,000. Clough made a big bid for former Notts County striker Tony Hateley, who was unsettled at Chelsea, but it was Liverpool who signed him for £100,000. A week before the start of the season, the first newcomer arrived at the Baseball Ground. Clough had spent £21,000 on a nineteen-year-old reserve forward from Sunderland named John O'Hare, not a great goalscorer and neither particularly tall nor quick, but a player he'd worked with in the youth side on Wearside. 'I have to confess that he was one of my favourites who, like John McGovern, I was to take with me to Leeds and to Nottingham Forest,' Clough wrote. 'O'Hare was the gentlest of men but also, on the field, one of the bravest, because he always received the ball with his back to the defender. People used to say he had weaknesses in his game. Absolute balls! O'Hare could receive and control a ball on his thigh, his chest, his head, his ankles or his knees. And he had a heart as big as a bucket.'

McGovern, later to play an even more significant role at Forest, was another key arrival, Clough said.

> He couldn't run and often looked ungainly on the field. But he would always stand up straight, he would always strive to get and to pass the ball, and he would do that whether the team was losing three-nil on a filthy night at Walsall or winning four-nil on a sunny afternoon at Wembley. He was the absolute genuine article – one who made the upmost and more of the talent at his disposal, rather like O'Hare. My kind of footballer.

On Taylor's recommendation, Clough doorstepped a terraced house on Merseyside to snatch 'an uncut diamond' in Tranmere's nineteen-year-old central defender Roy McFarland from beneath the noses of Liverpool and Everton. And they shopped at the City Ground to buy outside-left Alan Hinton, who had pace, a powerful shot and could cross a ball with accuracy. Clough thought Hinton was unappreciated by Forest and its fans. In fact, supporters were never convinced that manager Johnny

Carey got the best of the deal when he swapped 'Flip' Le Flem for Hinton, then of Wolves, in January 1964.

For Clough and Taylor, wheeling and dealing was all part of the fun. 'Taylor and I were always at our best and fired with the greatest enthusiasm when we were dismantling teams and rebuilding them,' Clough said. Even so, Derby finished their first season in eighteenth place, one place lower than Tim Ward had managed before being sacked. There were directors with an anti-Clough agenda, 'a hostile atmosphere backstage' and even hate letters arriving from disgruntled fans. 'If there was a single moment of inspiration that transformed Derby from a humdrum, dilapidated, down-in-the-dumps club, it was when Taylor took me on one side and said, "We must get some experience in this side. Go and sign Mackay." To me, like most people throughout the country, Dave Mackay was the famous Tottenham Hotspur wing-half, a very big name, someone we used to read about in the newspapers.' Clough told Taylor, 'You must be bloody joking.' But he turned up unannounced at White Hart Lane, blurted out to Spurs' revered manager Bill Nicholson that he had come to talk to Dave Mackay. He was told Mackay was off to Edinburgh to become assistant manager of Hearts. But they met, haggled over a signing-on fee and eventually a deal was done.

At Derby, Mackay was to be a 'sweeper' alongside young McFarland and the thirty-three-year-old veteran, who had suffered two broken legs, recognised the role as a way of prolonging his career. Derby paid Spurs a £5,000 transfer fee and gave Mackay £14,000 for signing. Taylor thought McFarland was the best signing he ever made. Clough counted Mackay his best-ever capture. 'Not only did he have everything as a player, he was the ideal skipper; a supreme example to everybody else at the football club,' Clough declared. 'And not only that, he even taught us how to play cards.'

Mackay led the Rams straight into the First Division, seven points clear of runners-up Crystal Palace, and he was elected by the Football Writers' Association as Footballer of the Year 1968/69 (jointly with Tony Book, the Manchester City right-back). 'We had so much confidence it was coming out of our ears,' Clough said. 'We felt unbeatable and it all stemmed from Dave. He brought a swagger to the team, to the whole club.' Mackay also spent hours practising with Clough's two sons, Simon and Nigel, kicking ball after ball into a wooden shooting box beneath the main stand at the Baseball Ground.

Derby finished fourth in their first season in the First Division (Forest were fifteenth) and ninth in 1970/71. Arsenal were 'double' winners. A year later Brian Clough, then thirty-seven, was manager of the League champions. Manchester City were five points clear at the beginning of

March, a lead they squandered but then beat Derby in their penultimate match. Clough's side overcame Liverpool to go a point ahead of City and Don Revie's Leeds, who had a game in hand and a much superior goal average. Clough took a family holiday in the Isles of Scilly while Taylor flew with the Derby players for a break in Cala Milor, Majorca. Only a couple of days after beating Arsenal to win the FA Cup, Revie's side went to Molineux needing only to draw with mid-table Wolves to claim the 'double'.

There were five bookings and two claims for Leeds's penalties, and Geoffrey Green, the doyen of football writers, reported in *The Times* that they were 'justifiable' with one a blatant handball. But the home side, in front of a 53,000 crowd, were 2-0 ahead with half an hour left to play. Billy Bremner clawed a goal back for Leeds but Wolves defended doggedly and when Leeds lost, the title was Derby's. 'Leeds died like heroes,' wrote Green, calling theirs 'a brilliant failure'. The news filtered through to the island of Tresco and Clough ordered champagne for every guest in the dining room of his hotel.

Clough and Taylor had paid their first six-figure fee to Forest for classy Welsh international Terry Hennessey. 'We saw him as an eventual replacement for Mackay because although a fine midfielder he was unflappable as a sweeper,' said Taylor. Their undeniable bargain buy was Archie Gemmill from Preston for £64,000. Gemmill was 'a tiger on the pitch and a lamb off it' but a perfectionist always striving for a flawless performance. He won forty-three caps and captained Scotland twenty-two times. Centre-back Colin Todd arrived from Sunderland for a then British record fee of £175,000 just before Mackay left to become player-manager of Swindon Town. The Todd signing was made without the knowledge of Longson and the chairman got a shock when he learned the size of the fee. Longson had called Clough his 'adopted son' but the relationship was cooling and would soon become icy.

Having already acquired Hennessey, Clough knew Nottingham Forest was selling its best players to balance the books. Ian Storey-Moore remained at the City Ground until all hope of First Division survival had gone. His parting gift to the Forest fans was a goal that he ranked as the best of his career. There were 42,750 on Trentside for the visit of Arsenal on 27 December 1971. They saw Storey-Moore receive the ball from a throw by goalkeeper Jim Barron and begin a run that took him more than 70 yards into the Arsenal 18-yard box, chased most of the way by Alan Ball, recently signed by the Gunners for a British record £220,000 from Everton. What stuck in Storey-Moore's mind was not Ball's ginger hair nor his yellow away shirt but a pair of white boots thudding on the turf behind him and trying to catch up.

There were still half a dozen defenders confronting him but he twisted and turned to find an opening and then beat goalkeeper Bob Wilson with a shot inside his near post.

Although he was to score twice more for Forest, in defeats by Leicester City at home and Southampton away, that goal was the golden memory he left behind. His last game in Garibaldi red was at the Baseball Ground on 19 February 1972, when Derby put Forest to the sword 4-0. Storey-Moore had come to the club as an apprentice eleven years earlier. He made his First Division debut as an eighteen-year-old in a 2-1 victory against Ipswich, the team from the town where he had been born. Top scorer in the four seasons leading up to his controversial transfer, he scored 118 goals in 271 Forest appearances. Capped only once at senior level by England – against Holland in 1970 – he played in two Under-23 internationals and twice represented the Football League.

Gillies accepted a bid for him of £200,000 from Manchester United manager Frank O'Farrell and so began a 'Tug-o'-Moore', perhaps one of the most unedifying of all transfer sagas. Clough pounced when it seemed the player could not agree personal terms. He matched the United bid and got Storey-Moore's signature. The Forest player was paraded at the Baseball Ground as a new signing and watched the Rams beat Wolves. But no transfer forms had been signed by Forest officials and they refused to confirm the transaction. Storey-Moore went home to Bingham and there he was visited by O'Farrell and Matt Busby, then a United director. A deal was done.

In his Clough biography *Nobody Ever Says Thank You*, Jonathan Wilson writes that, 'furious' at the turn of events, Clough sent off a four-page telegram to the Football League in protest but he was not supported by his chairman, Sam Longson, who apologised on Derby's behalf. It did not prevent his club being fined £5,000 and Clough receiving a warning about his conduct of transfer business. Storey-Moore made his debut for United against Huddersfield at Old Trafford on 11 March. At the City Ground just 9,872 disgruntled supporters – the lowest crowd for seventeen years – turned up to see Forest beaten 2-0 by Ipswich Town and sent on their way to twenty-first in the table and relegation. Their mood was not improved when an announcer gave out the information that United had taken the lead at Old Trafford 'and the scorer is Ian Storey-Moore'.

There was an amicable ending to the sorry saga. Clough, during his eighteen great years at the City Ground, would become a lasting friend of Forest secretary Ken Smales, the man he said had 'whipped Ian Storey-Moore's transfer forms back from me at Derby'. Clough also said,

'The secretary's position is a difficult one. It's never easy for a manager to have the club secretary as a friend because he has to serve his board of directors.' At Derby he had been warned by Taylor and by a director not to trust the immaculately suited secretary Stuart Webb. 'No matter how good you are, or how powerful you think you are, all chairmen listen to their club secretaries,' he was told. 'Further down the line, I learned to appreciate working with Ken Smales at Nottingham Forest, the most trustworthy secretary I ever knew,' Clough said.

The relationship he had with Longson had already begun to deteriorate and the Storey-Moore incident did more damage as the chairman worried about his own standing within the game as his manager seemed to delight in flouting authority. To make matters worse, the Clough-Taylor partnership was becoming seriously strained. Both were beginning to feel insecure. 'Even as the corks popped, we sensed that our honeymoon with Derby County might be ending,' Taylor wrote. He had become increasingly upset by the perks Clough was receiving and the pair had a furious row when Webb told him his efforts were being belittled by his partner in board meetings. Clough went so far as to demand that Longson sack Taylor who, he claimed, had become impossible to work with, but the chairman refused. The dispute was smoothed over with conciliatory interviews in the Press. And even Clough was enraged when he learned a director had demanded that Taylor explain exactly what was his contribution. 'He was degrading a man whose record was unequalled,' Clough said. 'Peter Taylor had nothing to prove to anyone but a complete fool.'

Then Taylor found out only after seeing a contract lying on Webb's desk that Clough had been given a secret £5,000 pay rise when he had received nothing. He had suffered a heart attack helping to build a winning team and this was his thanks. 'Groups of men rarely remain united for long; differences are inevitable and football boards are especially prone to form factions,' he wrote, adding, 'Nor is it always sweetness and harmony between managerial partners.' Longson, he felt, should have apologised for paying the money on the sly and Clough for accepting it while leaving him in the dark. Instead, the chairman wanted to know how he had found out. There had been an agreement from their Hartlepools days that bonuses and outside earnings should be shared equally between them.

After winning the championship, Clough disclosed that he and Taylor had been close to joining Coventry City and there had been negotiations with a Sunderland consortium planning a takeover of the Wearside club. Birmingham City had also made an approach. More surprisingly, there had also been genuine interest from Barcelona and from the Greek FA seeking a national team boss. 'We never discouraged offers; it was good for our standing and self-confidence to be in demand,' Taylor commented.

Liverpool cruised to the championship in 1972/73 with Derby fourteen points behind in seventh place. There was consolation for Clough in Europe. Perhaps recalling Wolves' defeat of Honved on a Molineux mudbath in 1954, he ordered the Baseball Ground pitch to be heavily watered for the visit of Benefica. The Portuguese champions and their star Eusebio were bogged down and Derby took a 3-0 lead to Lisbon. FIFA president Sir Stanley Rous ticked him off for gamesmanship. The second leg was goalless.

Progressing to the semi-final stage and a tie with Juventus, Clough recruited John Charles, venerated in Turin after a six-year career with the Italian club, as their goodwill ambassador. Nothing went right for Derby when they lost the Turin first leg 3-1 in controversial circumstances with allegations of collusion between the home club and the referee. Journalist Brian Glanville, widely respected in Italy as well as the UK and a fluent Italian speaker, translated comments for Clough and later wrote, 'Though strange and suspicious things may have happened, Juventus won it fairly and squarely on the field.' The second leg at the Baseball Ground ended 0-0 with Alan Hinton missing a penalty. In the final Juventus were beaten by Ajax of Amsterdam 1-0.

'Sometimes I wish 1973 had been wiped off the calendar,' Taylor commented. 'It was a year of troubles for us and the shemozzles in Turin were far from the worst of them. The climax, of course, came in the autumn with uproar over our resignations from Derby County.' Clough admitted in his autobiography that he was involved in the meetings where the players plotted and planned their moves that brought mayhem to the Baseball Ground. 'Even I underestimated the impact our resignations would have,' he wrote. 'Bedlam broke loose.' The Bring Back Clough protest movement was organised and the team even considered decamping to Spain rather than fulfilling their next fixture at the Baseball Ground against Leicester City. 'Hey, hang on a second, you can't do that,' Clough claimed to have told them. 'That's pushing it too bloody far.'

Clough was convinced he would beat Longson just as he had Ernest Ord at Hartlepools but Derby determined that a quick managerial appointment was needed to try to diffuse the situation. They got permission from Nottingham Forest to approach Dave Mackay. 'It was ironic that my key signing who launched the great revival of the old club would be brought in to replace me as manager,' wrote Clough. 'To be fair, he did a terrific job. Derby went on to win the League title two seasons later and Mackay deserves the utmost credit for the way he tackled and endured the task he inherited.'

A fortnight after quitting Derby, Clough and Taylor were back in business, surprisingly on the south coast, where property developer Mike Bamber, chairman of Third Division Brighton and Hove Albion, was prepared to hire them even though a charge of bringing the game into disrepute hung over his new manager. Two weeks later an FA disciplinary commission heard the case and Clough was cleared.

8

The Happy Forester

Just as Sheffield Wednesday had been, Forest were in freefall when Billy Walker took over.

The 1938/39 season's opener was a match at the City Ground against Notts County in aid of the Football League's Jubilee Trust Fund. A crowd of 9,505 saw the Reds win 4-1 but hopes of better things in the Second Division were soon dashed. Forest went eight games without a win and then, after beating Bradford Park Avenue, let slip a three-goal lead to allow visiting Sheffield Wednesday to take home a point. That was followed by a 7-1 beating at Chesterfield. After a 1-1 home draw with Fulham before 9,341 fans on 11 March, the decision was taken to part company with team manager Harold Wightman. He was the first to have that role. Wightman, a Nottinghamshire man who had guested for the Reds during the First World War, had successfully managed Luton Town before succeeding secretary Noel Watson and taking the new job title in 1935. Watson remained as secretary, and later also as honorary treasurer, serving the club for thirty years and becoming a life member.

Ten days after Wightman's dismissal, Forest appointed Walker as the first club manager. He could not have had a tougher start, away to Blackburn Rovers who would be crowned champions. Unsurprisingly, the Reds were beaten but it was only by the odd goal in five. Jack Surtees, who had been an FA Cup winner with Walker's Wednesday, celebrated their reunion with one of the Forest goals. He was also on target in each of the three wins gained in the next four games and took over the captaincy from the injured Tommy Graham when, once again, Forest faced a relegation battle away from home on the last day of the season. But this time they knew that, with a superior goal average, they could survive a defeat at Norwich so long as it was by fewer than four goals.

'Boy' Martin had left to join Notts County in November and at centre-forward was twenty-three-year-old Bob McCall, who would later establish himself as wing-half and then full-back before returning to his home town club, Worksop Town, as player-manager in 1952. The home side were restricted to a single goal, scored in the 49th minute. Forest's fine defence had kept them up and the Canaries joined Tranmere in relegation.

The Reds were in eighth place in Division Two when the outbreak of war in September 1939 brought down the curtain on the Football League season. Forest went to war heavily in debt to the bank, with the committee finding money from their own pockets to keep the club going. Mr. H. R. Cobbin, a committee member since 1912 and its chairman until 1948, handed over 'a very large cheque' without a word to his colleagues. In *The Club in Wartime Football*, his 1947 booklet, Walker wrote,

> A crisis meeting was called. And, although things looked very black, the committee decided they owed it to the boys who were going to war, and as a means of keeping up morale, to carry on." Players' contracts were cancelled as they went into the Forces, civil defence work, armament factories or back into the pits.
>
> I decided I had a wonderful opportunity of finding young talent on our own doorstep. In September, 1939, I started our Colts team and I am proud to claim that I was the first manager in wartime to embark on such a venture. During the war years I tried out more than 1,000 young local players. Many are still in the game, with Forest or other clubs, many, I regret to say, were killed in the war. Of those 1,000 'discoveries' only about fifty made good.

Future first team regulars such as Frank Knight, Geoff Thomas, Jack Hutchinson, Bill Morley and 'Tot' Leverton were wartime 'finds'.

Throughout the war years, Forest competed in regional football and made use of the 'guest player' system, although Walker was not an enthusiast for it. The 'guests' included the Derby County wingers Sammy Crooks and Dally Duncan, Ron Burgess of Tottenham and Andy Beattie of Preston, who was to succeed Walker at Forest on his retirement. The manager himself played for the team in the first two full wartime seasons. In 1940/41 he kept goal in a City Ground friendly against the RAF, which was won 4-1, and a Midlands Cup tie at Lincoln, where Forest were beaten 2-1. He was then at outside-left when the Reds lost 4-0 in a regional league match at Stoke. In 1941/42 he was again an emergency goalkeeper for a League Cup qualifier at Chesterfield and conceded the decisive goal.

The Midland Cup was the trophy Forest came closest to collecting during the war when the final was settled by a 'golden' goal. The Reds and West Bromwich Albion shared four goals in the first leg at the Hawthorns on 29 April 1944. A week later, 14,438 saw Forest take a 3-2 lead late in extra time and some supporters, thinking it was all over, invaded the pitch to carry the players shoulder-high for the presentation by the Lord Mayor of Nottingham. But there were still two minutes left, police restored order, and Albion grabbed an equaliser on resumption. The sides were deadlocked at the end of extra time and the match continued until a deciding goal was scored. That 'sudden death' goal was put past Forest's 'guest' goalkeeper Ray Middleton to give Albion an overall 6-5 victory.

During the 1945/46 season, Forest flew to war-battered Germany to play the Rhine Army team in Cologne. The soldiers were 4-1 winners and their left-wing pair impressed. At inside-left was Billy Steel, who became a Scottish international and a Derby County star before emigrating to Canada. He was unaffordable but his partner George Lee, fast with a powerful shot, was brought to the City Ground a week before the 1946/47 season started. Walker paid York City £7,500 for him and commented, 'I fully believe him to be the best left-winger in the country today.' He also signed the army side's right-back Jim Clarke, who hailed from the manager's home town, Wednesbury in Staffordshire, and went to the same school there. So despite the defeat and an alarming return flight – a hurricane buffeting the plane, forcing it to make an unscheduled landing near the south coast – the trip was well worthwhile.

Thirty-four years later, the Reds would revisit Cologne's Müngersdorfer Stadium on 25 April 1979, and record a famous victory. Ian Bowyer scored the vital goal that carried them through to the European Cup Final by a 4-3 aggregate after drawing the first leg against FC Cologne 3-3 in the semi-final first leg at the City Ground.

One of the shrewdest strokes of business pulled off by Forest's astute manager at the end of the Second World War was the signing of England wartime international inside-forward R. A. J. Brown from First Division Charlton Athletic. Robert Albert John Brown, who liked to be called Bert but was forever known in football as 'Sailor', had starred for the Londoners in the 1946 FA Cup Final, which had been won 4-1 by Derby County after extra time. Deep into the second-half, with the scores level at 1-1, 'Sailor' dribbled past five defenders but just failed to find his skipper Don Welsh with a pass that might have produced the winning goal. His ear, as ever, close to the ground, Walker picked up that afterwards there had been a sharp fallout between Brown and his manager, Jimmy Seed. The player was going to be moved on and, naturally, he wanted to stay in the top flight. His preferred destination was Aston Villa but Seed did not want to see his star go to another Division One club and Forest snapped him up for £6,750.

A year later, 'Sailor' was transferred to Villa for a club-record fee of £10,000. Had there been an arrangement? Who knows? But Forest certainly did very well out of it. Brown played forty-five Second Division games for the Reds, scoring seventeen goals. He also featured in four FA Cup ties and a couple of friendlies, including a 2-2 draw against the Combined Services in Hamburg. Ironically, before Walker's time, the club might have signed him for nothing. On 3 May 1934, Forest had played a friendly at Gorleston and won 5-2. Brown was in his home town's side and may have been the reason for Forest's visit because he had been recommended to the club by scout Billy Latham. He was invited to the City Ground for a trial but nothing came of it. Centre-half Tom Graham, who had played against him, suggested he should try again with Forest but by then the youngster was already booked for Charlton.

'Sailor' scored on his debut for Forest at Barnsley on 31 August 1946 but George Robledo got a hat-trick for the home side, who won 3-2. His last game, on 27 September 1947, was also a defeat in Yorkshire. Despite George Lee putting Forest ahead in the first minute at Hillsborough, Sheffield Wednesday were the victors at 2-1. Walker thought highly of him. 'Bert Brown is the captain and schemer of the side with original ideas on tactics,' he wrote in his shilling handbook. 'A vital link in any line in which he plays, Brown can stay the course to the end. Another of Forest's humourists, his forte is dialect stories and verse. Is keen to become a football manager, otherwise is quite rational.'

Unfortunately for Forest, Brown's transfer to Aston Villa coincided with the sensational arrival of England's then centre-forward Tommy Lawton at Third Division Notts County from Chelsea. Walker saw England's inside-right Raich Carter as a perfect City Ground counter-attraction. Silver-haired Carter and blond Irish star Peter Doherty were the 'silver and gold' inside-forward partners who, after being wartime 'guests' at the Baseball Ground, helped Derby win the FA Cup against Brown's Charlton. They were together for the start of the first post-war Football League campaign in 1946/47 but Doherty made only fifteen appearances, scoring seven goals, before moving to Huddersfield. Carter didn't stay at the Baseball Ground much longer. He left in March 1948, having scored thirty-four goals in sixty-three appearances. Both had fallen out with the Derby board.

Carter had played for Forest in wartime League South on 12 September 1945 in a draw with Fulham at the City Ground. At the time, he was in the RAF and stationed at a pilot rehabilitation centre at Loughborough.

So Walker thought he might have a chance of persuading him to come and Derby to sell. He was thwarted by the player's management ambitions. There was an offer from Hull City and Carter reasonably considered his prospects in that direction much brighter on Humberside than on Trentside. And so it proved. Within a couple of weeks Major Frank Buckley quit the Hull job to take over at Leeds and, in his place, Carter was appointed the Tigers' player-manager. He led his charges to the Third Division North championship and, ambitiously, signed England centre-half Neil Franklin and Don Revie. When a second promotion didn't materialise, ever the perfectionist Carter resigned in September 1951. Subsequently, he led Leeds United to the top flight in 1956 but, after ruffling the feathers at Elland Road, was sacked in 1958. He had one more promotion to achieve, taking Mansfield Town out of the Fourth Division in 1963 before finishing his career with three lean years at Middlesbrough.

Forest went into the war having made a loss of £4,877, which doesn't seem much by today's reckoning but was a considerable concern at the time. Profit and loss accounts stayed in the red until 1943, when a profit of £1,571 was made. Profits rose steadily to £2,919 at the end of the 1946/47 season. A comfortable enough sum, but Walker had forked out £4,500 on the recommendation of Bert Brown for winger Freddie Scott from York City, a record fee for the selling club. 'Sailor' had partnered him in wartime football at York and Charlton and knew his worth. A former England Boys outside-right, Scott was then only a month from his thirtieth birthday but he went on to play 323 games for Forest and was only a month from turning forty when he made his last appearance in September 1956.

With the height and weight of a jockey, Scott had the pace and skill to take on the strongest defender. A fine positional player, he could play on either wing and was shrewd enough to make the ball do a lot of the work. Walker said he would do even better if he cut in towards goal a little more 'and had a crack'. In fact, Scott's twenty-eight goals for Forest included one in his last game, which Rotherham won 3-2.

For the 1946/47 season, Billy Walker introduced a palm-sized four-page card of players' instructions containing thirteen training rules and regulations. The day would begin at 10 a.m., they were told, and training would include running, sprinting, skipping, punching the ball, walking, football dribbling and practice games. Any player absenting himself from training would be held to have broken his agreement and his wages would be stopped pro rata. Friends were not allowed in the club rooms and gambling of any description was strictly prohibited. On the back was an admission ticket and players were to carry the pass and show it to the gateman at all home matches. In effect, it was a Forest identity card and, psychologically, it must have given players a sense of belonging.

When Larry Platts died in a Lincolnshire nursing home on 4 September 2006, aged eighty-four, it was said that he 'was a Forest man right up to the end'. He was one of Walker's 'colts' and made his first team debut in goal for a friendly match at Lincoln City on 19 October 1940, just twelve days before his nineteenth birthday – it was won 3-2. Larry was also on the winning side in his last game when the Reds beat Port Vale 2-0 in the Third Division South at the City Ground on 29 April 1950. Wally Ardron and Gordon Kaile scored in a match watched by a crowd of only 5,908. In all, he made seventy-two first team appearances – all but ten of them in wartime football.

But it is Forest's famous FA Cup fourth-round victory over Manchester United on 25 January 1947 that gives him an honoured place in the club's history. Because of war damage to Old Trafford, the game was played at Manchester City's Maine Road ground, where there was a 34,059 attendance. Forest were in the lower half of the Second Division with United lying third in Division One. Goals by Eddie Barks and Colin Lyman made Forest giant-killers but it is remembered as 'Larry Platts' match'. Nottingham journalist Arthur Turner reported, 'Platts kept a fantastic goal – it was the game of his life.' Army call-up made that his last for a couple of years.

The Forest team was Larry Platts, Harry Brigham, Bob McCall, George Pritty, Ted Blagg, Frank Knight, Freddie Scott, 'Sailor' Brown, Eddie Barks, Jack Edwards and Colin Lyman. Johnny Carey, later to become a Forest manager, was in the United line-up along with Johnny Aston, Allenby Chilton, Jimmy Delaney, Johnny Morris, Jack Rowley and Stan Pearson. The quality of the home side was shown in their next match when they beat Arsenal 6-2 in the First Division at Highbury. The young goalkeeper had made his Football League debut at the City Ground only a week earlier when Southampton were despatched 6-0 with goals by Lyman (2), Edwards, Barks, Brown and Brigham. There were 24,591 present.

Eddie Barks was Walker's first signing for Forest in April 1939, coming from Heanor Town. Locally born Barks was 'one of the best club players I have ever had', said Walker. 'He is the real 100 per cent player who never gives up; a real tryer. A real glutton for work, he is ready and willing to play anywhere and his whole-hearted efforts in the unaccustomed position of centre-forward, he is really a wing-half, will not soon be forgotten by Forest supporters.' Barks played seventy times for the Reds between August 1946 and September 1948, scoring six goals, and then joined Mansfield Town, making 225 appearances for the Stags.

With Platts now in uniform, Griff Roberts was in goal for the fifth-round tie against Middlesbrough of the First Division. A crowd of 32,000, paying £3,842, saw England's Wilf Mannion score an own goal in a 2-2 draw. Freddie Scott got the other Forest goal. The replay at Middlesbrough was watched by 27,000. Barks and Edwards scored for Forest but Mannion hit a hat-trick in a 6-2 home win. Lyman became a 'passenger' for the remainder of the match after twisting his knee in the 30th minute.

City Ground supporters had seen Mannion in September playing for an FA XI against a Combined XI in a benefit match organised by Billy Walker for Newark-born England star Willie Hall, who had lost both legs after being struck down by thrombosis. In a memorable international match against Northern Ireland in 1938, Hall, formerly of Notts County but then a Spurs player, had lit up a dull November day with a three-minute hat-trick. He went on to score a record five goals in a row as England won 7-0. The FA X1 included such stars as Frank Swift, George Hardwick, England captain, Stan Cullis and Billy Wright from Wolves, Tom Finney and Raich Carter. In Combined XI were Ray Middleton, Leon Leuty, Len Shackleton, Jack Rowley of Manchester United and Forest players Bill Baxter, Bob McCall and Tom Johnston. Mannion got a goal and the game ended properly as a 2-2 draw.

Floods, fog and snowfalls during the winter of 1946/47 caused such disruption that the football season ran into the middle of June. Forest's match against Manchester City in November had to be played at Notts County's Meadow Lane because the City Ground was deep underwater. A crowd of 32,000 saw the visitors win 1-0. Trent floods returned with a vengeance in March, when the water crept up almost to the height of the crossbars and swans from the river glided majestically the full length of the pitch. Floodwater swamped the club's offices and important records were lost. No home matches were played that month and those fixtures were postponed until the end of May.

The match at Fulham in December was abandoned because of fog with Forest leading by a Barks goal and only fifteen minutes remaining. The match at Millwall in March was finished in a snowstorm.

Forest were not safe from relegation until their last three matches, all at home and all victories. A Johnston goal was enough to see off Chesterfield on 27 May and four days later Plymouth Argyle were thrashed 5-1. Johnston netted another two and Brown, Edwards and Knight also scored. It was raining heavily and only 8,429 turned up when Forest ended the season with a 4-0 victory over Bradford Park Avenue at the City Ground on 14 June. Versatile Tom Johnston, who had been a part-time pro with Peterborough United and joined the Reds during the war, scored a hat-trick, taking his goal tally to twelve and making him the season's second highest scorer after 'Sailor' Brown on sixteen.

A significant newcomer who made his debut in a 1-1 draw at Fulham on 26 May was 'Mr Consistency' himself, George Henry 'Harry' Walker, who had helped Portsmouth win the FA Cup against Wolves at Wembley in May 1939. 'As safe as houses', he was tall and confident in judgment and handling. An ever-present in Forest's Third Division South championship-winning side, he played 304 games for the club before injury forced his retirement aged thirty-nine in May 1955. Walker warded off challengers for his place like Reg Savage, Griff Roberts, Harry Orgill and, of course, Platts.

Walker wanted his team to play a high-speed passing game and, needing a schemer to replace the departing Brown, paid Brentford £7,000 for thirty-year-old George Wilkins, who was described as 'a clever, calculating craftsman'. He scored on his debut in a 4-2 home win over Doncaster Rovers on 27 December 1947, and averaged a goal every four games but, plagued by injuries, his appearances became increasingly spasmodic. The father of Ray Wilkins of Manchester United, Chelsea and England, he managed only twenty-six starts in nearly two years. Another thirty-plus Londoner proved a more enduring signing. Blond centre-half Horace Gager cost a record £8,000 fee to Luton Town but became the pillar of the Forest defence for the next seven years. He retired in 1955 after playing 258 league and nine FA Cup games. He scored the penalty goal that gave Forest a 2-2 draw at Barnsley on 17 April and made them safe from relegation.

It was a temporary respite for, despite a final flourish with six wins and a draw in their last nine games, they were doomed on the closing day of the 1948/49 season to go down in twenty-first place with bottom club Lincoln City. With one game remaining, the Reds were two points behind Leicester but with a superior goal average. Forest were at home to Bury while City had to travel to fourth-placed Cardiff. A 26,754 crowd at the City Ground saw a second-half goal by George Lee give Forest both points. All now depended on the result at Ninian Park, where the game had kicked of a quarter of an hour later. Cardiff were holding a first-half lead but then, two minutes after the City Ground game had finished, Forest fans were crushed as the Foxes' centre-forward Jack Lee grabbed a saving equaliser.

Walker himself was in despair and described that last Saturday of the season as 'the blackest of my whole career'. In his autobiography he wrote,

> From the beginning I was so nervous of the outcome that I went into my office and stayed there. So much depended on every kick of that game that I could not bear to see a single one of them. All I could do was to sit there and listen to the roars of the crowd from time to time and wonder for whom they were roaring! At times like these the position of the manager of a club that has been having a bad time is almost the same as that of the captain of a ship that's in trouble. As I sat there trying to forget the game and its dire potential, I was fortified by one voice out on the terracing. This voice kept up the morale-boosting shout of 'Come on, Forest' that did my heart good.

Chairman Jack Brentnall, a musical-instrument dealer, knocked on the locked door of Walker's office. The manager opened it reluctantly. But Brentnall had a smile on his face. 'Cheer up Billy', he said. 'You told me we'd get back in two years if we went down. Well, we're down and I believe you. Remember I'll back you and I'll be out with you if we don't do it.'

The next day he went to the ground in some trepidation for a meeting with the committee. Their response was in sharp contrast to the reaction at Sheffield to a similar event just over ten years earlier. 'It was hard to believe from the way they behaved that we had just been sent into the Third Division,' he wrote. 'You might have thought we had won promotion! It did not seem possible that seven men could look as happy as these did in these circumstances but I knew my great friend Jack Brentnall had created this atmosphere especially to help me.' His chairman and the committee showed they believed in him. 'I thanked them and went home at lunchtime a very much happier man.'

9

Sea Fret

'People go to Brighton for various reasons: for a holiday, for a day trip, for a place to retire, for a Tory Party conference or for a dirty weekend,' wrote Brian Clough. 'With all due respect to the club and its fans, you don't go there for the football. Brighton is not a big-time club and is never likely to be.' Taylor, who saw the potential, believed he had pushed his mate into accepting the job but Clough's heart wasn't in it. What would they have said had they seen Albion in 2016 attracting crowds in excess of 28,000 and third in the Championship ahead of Derby.

Just as the duo were arriving on the south coast I was leaving for a new editorial appointment in Nottinghamshire. I cursed my luck as the *Evening Argus* welcomed the dynamic partnership with front-page headlines and high hopes. I knew from personal experience that Clough was wrong about East Sussex, just as I had been on moving to the area three years earlier. Based at Eastbourne as sports editor and then chief subeditor of the town's *Herald* and *Gazette* newspapers, I was also a correspondent for the Press Association.

Eastbourne had county and club cricket, archery, bowls and croquet at the Saffrons ground near the Town Hall and pre-Wimbledon professional tennis at Devonshire Park. There were two sailing clubs and Eastbourne Eagles speedway. But football? Actually, yes! It was the most popular sport of them all. Eastbourne Town, the senior club at the Saffrons, and Eastbourne United at Princes Park Oval were both semi-professional teams and Eastbourne and District Football League dwarfed organised cricket and rugby. That was in 1970. Today, Eastbourne has three major football clubs and the biggest is Eastbourne Borough of the Conference, which in my time there had been a junior side called Langney Sports. The Sussex County League is one of the largest and best organised in the country.

My first assignment took me to the Dripping Pan at Lewes, where Eastbourne United were to play. The ground's unusual name comes from it being sited at the spot where monks from Lewes Priory used to dry water from the nearby River Ouse to make salt. Lewes FC was formed in 1885. It was another sixteen years before the county's leading professional club, the Albion, came into being at Brighton. The Pan, as it is often called, has a 3,000 capacity with seating for 600. By 2008 its rivalry was with Eastbourne Borough, not United, as the two clubs battled for the Conference South championship. Lewes became champions and in the same season faced Mansfield Town in the First Round proper of the FA Cup, losing 3-0 at Field Mill. Their fortunes declined after that and faced several winding-up orders before becoming the Lewes Community Football Club in 2010. The club is now owned by members, one of whom is playwright and director Patrick Marber. A few years ago the Pan was voted one of the best away venues in non-league football.

I really enjoyed covering Brighton's games at the traditional Goldstone Ground in Hove in the early 1970s. Walking to the match with the enthusiastic crowd from Hove train station to the Goldstone, Albion's home for ninety-five years before it was demolished to make way for a retail park, gave one the same sense of anticipation as going to northern and Midland grounds. Before Albion moved in, it had been the ground of Hove FC, an amateur club. Taylor, I sense, took on board the history and culture of football in East Sussex and the potential at Brighton but to Clough all this may as well have been lost in a sea fret, the wet mist or haze that comes in from the sea to shroud the towns of the Channel coast.

Albion's manager in the three years I was working in Sussex was the imposing Pat Saward, a former Republic of Ireland international wing-half who had captained Aston Villa to victory against Manchester United in the 1957 FA Cup. In charge of Villa was Billy Walker's old mate Eric Houghton. Saward succeeded former Manchester United defender Freddie Goodwin in July 1970, a few months after I had joined the Eastbourne papers. Born in County Cork like Forest favourite Roy Keane, he gained eighteen international caps before becoming a youth coach and then assistant manager at Coventry City under Jimmy Hill.

Tall, broad-shouldered and darkly handsome, Saward had an extrovert personality and infectious good humour. His commitment to an attacking style of play made him hugely popular with Albion supporters. He got the Seagulls promoted in his second season but they dropped back to the Third Division in 1972/73. His sacking in October 1973 angered supporters just as Clough's departure had done at Derby. Their protests were nowhere near as well organised as those in the Midlands and were no more effective. Ambitious chairman Mike Bamber was to seize the moment.

Saward was a pleasant, thoughtful and approachable man. We met soon after his appointment at pre-season training held at Sussex University's sports complex at Falmer, near Lewes, coincidentally since 2011 also the home of the Albion. He readily agreed to my request for a regular column to be contributed to the *Herald* by one of his players. We discussed who among them might be interested as well as being appealing to Eastbourne readers. There was no long debate. It had to be goalkeeper Brian Powney. Born, bred and still living at Seaford, a 9-mile coastal walk across the South Downs Way from Eastbourne, Powney had played for East Sussex Under-15s before joining Eastbourne United. FA staff coach Jack Mansell was full-time manager at Princes Park Oval and ran the club on professional lines. United were in the Metropolitan League at the time playing against the likes of Arsenal 'A', with whom he also had trials. But at sixteen he joined the Goldstone ground staff, signing pro forms on his seventeenth birthday. His league debut for Albion was against Derby. Powney and I got together regularly and put together a sort of diary of a goalkeeper, which proved popular with *Herald* readers.

Powney played almost 400 games for the Seagulls under five managers. 'I enjoyed playing for Pat Saward most,' he said. 'As a coach he was second to none. His knowledge was immense and he really motivated us by getting us to enjoy the game.' This is his take on his last manager at Brighton, given to Charlie Bamforth for *The Footballer* magazine, on which I was leader writer:

> Brian Clough tried to motivate by fear. I didn't like him at all. I am well aware that there are players at other clubs who would give you a different view but I can only speak as I find. Clough joined us when our morale was at an all-time low. We had no confidence and it just got worse. The media following was mindboggling. But the things that were said, the slagging off of players, shattered our confidence.

He had spoken about Clough to John McGovern when they were both on holiday in Majorca. Asked what the manager was like, he had replied 'hard but fair'. Powney got the impression that if Clough asked him, McGovern 'would have jumped over Beachy Head for him'. In fact, McGovern had a stronger character than that and rejected approaches by Clough and Taylor when they wanted him to go with them to Brighton.

Oddly, the first club to approach Clough as he was hesitantly moving on from the Baseball Ground had been Forest, who needed a replacement for his successor Dave Mackay. Committee member Stuart Dryden met

Clough and Taylor in Nottingham and told them they were wanted to re-energise the club. He asked Clough to call the City Ground the next day and a firm offer would follow. The call wasn't made. Clough met Bamber twice, in London and then Derby, before agreeing, perhaps reluctantly, to join struggling Albion.

A goalless draw at Chesterfield was Brighton's fourth game unbeaten but it was marred by an incident remarkably similar to the Mourinho clash with club doctor Eva Carneiro leading to her departure from Chelsea. Albion physio Bert Parker was banned from attending matches after protesting when inside-right Ken Beamish was forced back onto the field despite having damaged an ankle. He had carried an injury for a week and before the match had had an injection. It wasn't working and he was struggling. It was too painful and he signalled his distress to the bench. 'I was made to carry on,' he said. 'It didn't anger me but I thought it was strange.'

Clough's biographer Jonathan Wilson wrote that Parker, a qualified physiotherapist, was banned from attending matches. 'That broke Parker's heart,' Brian Powney commented, 'He was a very loyal club man and he was such a gentleman. It really upset him and it upset the players because after that we didn't have a good physio.'

Brighton faced non-leaguers Walton and Hersham, with a future Forest manager Dave Bassett in their side, and lost 4-0 to go out of the FA Cup. Hot on the heels of this setback came an 8-2 thrashing by Bristol Rovers – the heaviest defeat in the history of the club. John Vinicombe wrote for the *Evening Argus*:

> The danger at the Goldstone is that the cure prescribed by Dr Clough might kill the patient. That Albion were ailing before Clough took over is beyond doubt. But has the latest emetic proved too much of a purgative? It would appear so. The stomachs are too weak for the Clough medicine. Albion are clearly the sick men of the Third Division – a disturbing state of affairs in a town famous for its health-giving ozone.

Powney thought the manager was depressed because 'he'd lost his bluff game at Derby'. But there were distractions. 'It was a showbiz environment in which you could walk along the prom and bump into people you had seen on television,' wrote Clough. Mike Bamber was a nightclub owner, well-known in the entertainment business and had many theatrical connections. 'If you're on your own and feeling in need of some company, come down to the nightclub whenever you wish,' Bamber told him. Clough and his wife met film, TV and stage comedy actress Dora Bryan at a twenty-first birthday party for Bamber's son. And she told Barbara, 'If you would like somewhere nice to live while you find a place of your own, you can have our house. We have a hotel so we spend our time there. It's yours if you wish.' But Clough continued to live in Derby and to many Brighton fans never committed to his new club. 'I was manager of Brighton for about nine months and I must have spent eight of them on the M1,' he said himself.

Taylor and Clough's first signing for Albion was former Forest goalkeeper Peter Grummitt from Sheffield Wednesday. Grummitt, discovered at Bourne Town, Lincolnshire, had made his debut for the Reds as an eighteen-year-old replacement for Chic Thomson and what a shock he had got when in the first minute of his first game Jim Iley scored an own goal against him. This was in front of nearly 19,000 fans at the City Ground on 12 November, 1960. But Colin Booth spared the blushes of both teammates with two goals to earn a draw with Bolton Wanderers. Grummitt never did have time for introspection. He was one of the most acrobatic goalkeepers of his time, relying on agility and amazing reflexes. Many an opposing forward has held his head in his hands as the England Under-23 international saved a seeming certainty at point-blank range. Unfortunately, he suffered serious injuries, including a broken arm, and after making 313 appearances for Forest was transferred to Wednesday in 1970.

Grummitt's arrival at the Goldstone meant that Powney lost his place until, once again, injury struck the former Forester, who fractured his pelvis in a 1-0 defeat at Shrewsbury. Powney had also suffered, having broken two fingers diving at a forward's feet at York. 'You're going to have to play,' Clough told him and proffered a brandy. He turned down the drink but grabbed the opportunity of a game, strapping the injured fingers together. 'It was a bit difficult to punch the ball, to say the least, and my little finger was dislocated but they put that back,' he recalled. Manager and player were happy with the outcome – a 4-1 victory over Cambridge. Like Grummitt, he was not the tallest of goalkeepers but a reputed shot stopper, quick and brave. Brighton finished nineteenth in 1973/74, two places above the relegation zone, and Powney learned by letter that he had been given a 'free'. He became player-manager of Sussex County League side Southwick, taking them to a title and a FA Cup game against Bournemouth. At the Goldstone he had seen off competition from former Wolves and Aston Villa goalkeeper Geoff Sidebottom and Tony Burns, ex-Arsenal. But Grummitt went on to make more than 100 League appearances for Albion.

Powney was certain Clough intended only a short stay on the south coast and the news of his decision to return the north to take the Leeds job came as no surprise. 'Cloughie never moved down to Brighton and stayed in a hotel,' he said. 'We players never saw him apart from an hour before kick-off on match days and the odd time in midweek for a practice match. He never coached us or talked tactics. I think it was pretty obvious from the start that Cloughie hated Southerners.' Bamber 'loved rubbing shoulders with famous people', Powney said. He brought stars like Bruce Forsyth and Des O'Connor down to the ground and into the dressing room. Clough and Taylor were big news and that was their appeal to the chairman. 'I wasn't surprised when Clough left Brighton because he didn't want to be there.'

Taylor agreed. While Brighton were engaged in a relegation battle at Cambridge in January, Clough was in New York for the world heavyweight fight between Muhammed Ali and Joe Frazier. On his return, he started planning a cricket trip to the West Indies in February. Then he flew to Tehran in March to discuss an invitation to manage the Iranian national team. He also left the team to canvass in Derby during the 1974 General Election. 'I had fallen for Brighton,' wrote Taylor, who had a seafront apartment and whose daughter worked for the *Argus*. 'I loved the club, the people and the place but Brian never took to the South Coast. We weren't a unit at Brighton. His mind was elsewhere.'

The break came in July when the FA sacked Sir Alf Ramsey, England's 1966 World Cup-winning manager, and appointed Don Revie of Leeds United. Clough, Taylor and Bamber met Manny Cussins, the Leeds chairman, in Hove. 'I could read Brian's ambitious mind,' Taylor wrote. 'He saw himself jumping straight from the Third Division into the management of a European Cup side.' Clough seized the moment but Taylor shocked him by saying, 'Count me out.'

Don Revie had been born in Middlesbrough eight years before Clough. His father was a joiner and his mother a washerwoman, who died of cancer when he was only twelve. He learnt the rudiments of football playing with a ball made of rags in the tiny yard behind their home. This influenced his thinking and, in later life, he reasoned that young players should learn skills by using smaller footballs on compact pitches. He began his professional career at Leicester and joined Hull, then managed by Raich Carter, before becoming the key member of the Manchester City side that introduced the 'Revie Plan', based on the style of the 1953 Hungarians. Revie operated as a deep-lying centre-forward in the manner of Nandor Hidegkuti, who had invented the role. I was at Wembley to see Revie mastermind the 3-1 FA Cup Final victory over Birmingham City in 1956, when Manchester's German goalkeeper Bert Trautmann famously played on despite suffering a broken neck diving at the feet of opposing forward Peter Murphy. Revie's elegance and superior passing talent was impressive and he was named Man of the Match.

England international Revie joined Leeds United in 1958 and they were a struggling Second Division side when he was appointed player-manager in March 1961. He looked upon everyone at Elland Road from cleaning staff to players as his 'family' and took an interest in all of their lives. His superstitions included a belief that birds conveyed bad luck and so he had the owl on the club badge removed and changed the nickname from Peacocks to Whites, based on his choice of team strip. He gave up playing in 1962 to concentrate on management and Leeds were promoted to Division One in 1964.

Surprisingly for one who had been such a cultured player, he encouraged a physical approach and produced lengthy dossiers on opposing teams to exploit weaknesses and nullify threats. Clough hated what he saw as their cynicism, gamesmanship, manipulation, dirtiness, time-wasting and haranguing of referees and, what's more, as soon as he arrived at Elland Road he made no bones about it. In his first team talk, which was made remarkably a week after his arrival, he told the players, 'The first thing you can do for me is throw those medals in the bin because you've never won anything fairly; you've done it by cheating.' He then addressed each player in turn and none emerged unscathed. Midfielder Johnny Giles, Revie's and the team's choice for the manager's job, said later that in those few minutes Clough 'cut his own throat'.

The first competitive match of the season was the now infamous Charity Shield encounter with Bill Shankly's Liverpool at Wembley. It was to be Shankly's farewell before retiring and a week earlier Clough had rung Revie to invite him to lead the side out alongside the Liverpool legend for the last time. The Don declined, and the season opener is now best remembered for the double sending-off of Leeds' captain Billy Bremner and Liverpool's Kevin Keegan. Clough said Keegan had been provoked and he was sorry for him.

Clough's first signing was Forest forward Duncan McKenzie, a City Ground favourite, for £250,000. 'We all agree, Duncan McKenzie is magic, is magic, is magic' Trent Enders would sing and they were dismayed by his departure. Two familiar faces, John McGovern and John O'Hare, followed from Derby County. His manager thought McGovern in particular was being persecuted and passes were being played short or overhit to make him look bad. This was strongly denied. Peter Lorimer described the two ex-Derby men as 'smashing lads but, frankly, not good enough to get into our team'.

McGovern's recollection is very different. He told me they were ostracised. There was hostility in the stands and no favours from Revie's old guard on the pitch. Targeted by the boo-boys, he decided to face them and strode into the supporters' lounge after a match. It was a bit like a Western film as he made his way to the bar and asked for a half of Guinness. The bartender hesitated and looked nervously round the room but then filled his glass. McGovern took his time over the drink and then left in silence. If nothing else, he had shown he would not be intimidated. Clough stayed at Leeds for only forty-four days. 'I had to stick it out for seven months,' McGovern said. 'By the time Brian asked me to join him at Forest, I'd have gladly walked down the M1.'

Leeds lost three of their first five games – only one fewer than in the whole of the previous season – and slumped to next-to-bottom of the table after a 1-1 draw against Luton with the Elland Road crowd booing Clough. A League Cup tie at Third Division Huddersfield Town was to be his last as manager of Leeds. Revie was present in the directors' box watching three Leeds players – Paul Madeley, Norman Hunter and Alan Clarke – in his role as England manager. He was spotted in his sheepskin coat by visiting fans who began to chant his name. Lorimer spared Clough further humiliation with a last-minute goal to earn a replay.

At the chairman's home that night Clough was told he was being dismissed. The next day at Elland Road he agreed a pay-off of somewhere around £100,000 after tax and was allowed to keep his club Mercedes. Compensation for trainer Jimmy Gordon, who had come with him from Derby, was also settled.

Clough then went to the studios of Yorkshire Television to be interviewed by Austin Mitchell and found Revie there, too. It became a dramatic debate with two protagonists, Clough generally being considered the clear winner. But Revie landed two or three late blows. Had Clough met the players on his first day? No. Had he introduced himself to the players, the coaches, the staff? No. Addressing the staff on the first day would seem natural for a manager in any walk of life, Revie insisted. 'Why didn't you get everybody together?' 'Because I didn't think it was necessary,' Clough answered.

Leeds recovered to finish ninth in the table as Dave Mackay's Derby won the title.

On 6 January 1975, Brian Clough was appointed manager of Nottingham Forest. Fourteen months after he had first approached him, Stuart Dryden had got his man.

10

Up the League We Go (Part I)

'The bravest centre-forward who ever drew breath.' That was TV chat show host Michael Parkinson's take on Wally Ardron in his 1968 book *Football Daft*. Well, Wally was certainly manager Billy Walker's most significant signing and one of Forest's all-time greats. He made a promising start in the Garibaldi with a goal at the Goldstone Ground to earn a point from the opening match of the 1949/50 Division Three South season, a 2-2 draw with Brighton and Hove Albion.

Ardron was then a part-timer and worked as a fireman on the railway, but he had scored 230 goals in nine seasons, including wartime, for Rotherham, and his thirty-eight in the first season after the war is still a club record. The deal was done at the Crown Hotel, Bawtry, convenient for both clubs, and chairman Brentnall accompanied the manager. But first, Ardron had a question for them. He wanted to know if they realised how old he was and, according to the player in his autobiography *Goals Galore*, Walker's reply was, 'Yes, you are thirty-two and you will do me for five seasons.' Ardron comments, 'This I, in fact, did and scored nearly 130 goals for him. Rotherham were happy, too – the money they received, £10,000, enabled them to buy their Millmoor ground from British Railways.' Wally's age on signing may have been slightly exaggerated. According to former club secretary Ken Smales's records, he was born on 19 September 1919. Another source makes his year of birth 1918.

Not particularly tall but stocky and powerfully built, as befits a champion shot-putter and useful pugilist, Ardron could handle himself all right. Bruce Woodcock was the first post-war British heavyweight champion and held both British and Empire titles from 1945 to 1950. Wally was his mate and sparring partner. My dad, the boxing fan, got me out of bed in the early hours of 18 May 1946 to listen with him to the BBC broadcast of

Woodcock's fight with Tami Mauriello of the Bronx at Madison Square Garden, New York. At stake was a shot at the world heavyweight title held by the legendary Joe Louis. Mauriello won with a fifth-round knockout and the American press unkindly dubbed the Englishman 'the horizontal heavyweight'. The title fight took place that September at Yankee Stadium in the Bronx but that didn't do Mauriello much good as he was dispatched by the Brown Bomber before the end of round one.

Manager Walker insisted that his new centre-forward give up his railway job and the player responded magnificently to becoming a full-time pro. He scored twenty-five goals in his first season and became so influential that Walker acted on his advice to buy left-wing pair Tommy Capel and Colin Collindridge. Twenty-six and an ex-Royal Marine, Capel came from Birmingham City in exchange for a £14,000 cheque, the largest Walker had signed, and made his debut on 5 November 1949, when 18,471 turned up at the City Ground for a 2-0 victory against Crystal Palace, John Love scoring both goals. Capel had a powerful left foot and made his presence felt with nine goals in twenty-four league games in his first season.

Tommy Lawton-led Notts County were still, of course, the big boys in town. On 26 November, when 15,567 were at the City Ground to see Forest beat Bristol City 1-0 in the first round of the FA Cup, there were 28,584 at Meadow Lane for the Magpies' cup tie against non-league Tilbury. Forest played the Essex port town's team in a City Ground friendly at the end of the season to raise funds for Hyson Green children.

The first-ever Third Division matches between the Nottingham clubs and the first in the League for nearly fifteen years resulted in home and away defeats for Forest in front of huge crowds. Notts were top of the table with Forest hard on their heels when the two sides met at the City Ground on 3 December before a crowd of 38,903. In the 28th minute the Magpies took the lead with a goal headlined in the *Daily Express* as 'Lawton's Leap'. Here is how reporter Crawford White described it:

From a corner Broome placed a high dropping centre rather farther from goal than usual. No greyhound ever left a trap quicker as he darted in to take his chance. He made a spectacular leap, timed the flight of the ball uncannily and nodded his head. The next thing the crowd saw was the ball hurtling past the Forest goalkeeper. Even dyed in the wool Forest fans had to applaud this piece of soccer sorcery.

Former Aston Villa and Derby winger Frank Broome made it 2-0 after the interval and, with only three minutes remaining, Tommy Capel pulled one back for the Reds.

The return match on 22 April attracted an all-ticket crowd of 46,000, breaking the Meadow Lane attendance record. Jackie Sewell headed Notts in front after fifty-eight minutes and two minutes later Lawton got another – with a header, of course. The 2-0 victory gave the home side their first-ever double over Forest. It also assured promotion. Lawton was the division's top scorer with thirty-one goals. Wally Ardron was second highest, six behind the Magpies' captain. Forest finished fourth with forty-nine points, nine fewer than the champions Notts.

Forest supporters had lots to celebrate in 1951. After two seasons in Division Three South, the club had been promoted as champions, six points clear of runners-up Norwich, scoring a League record 110 goals while conceding only forty. Walker had fulfilled his promise. What's more, the reserves had won the Midland League nine points clear of second-placed Rotherham United after scoring 103 goals against forty-five. Forest were the highest scorers in all four divisions (including Third Division North) of the Football League and had conceded fewer than any other League club.

Forest signed Collindridge just in time for the start of the promotion season. Earlier, they could have had him for no more than a £10 signing-on fee but his transfer from Sheffield United was secured for £12,000. They were not alone in missing his talent. Rotherham had released him shortly after his seventeenth birthday. Wolverhampton Wanderers also let him go and he declined Forest's offer of only part-time terms. After serving in the RAF, he helped Sheffield United win the League North title in the transitional 1945/46 season, scoring sixteen goals in nineteen games. He was also the Blades' top scorer in each of the three post-war seasons. When Walker heard that Collindridge was keen on a move to Preston, he stepped in with an offer, knowing that the player had married a Nottingham girl during his RAF service and hoping that he might like to live in the city. The approach was successful and a week after signing he scored on his debut in a season-opener at Newport. Johnson got the other goal in 2-0 win. A cheery character and an excellent club man, the winger was a huge favourite with Forest fans who admired his speed, skill, direct play and powerful left-foot shot.

Collindridge struck up an immediate rapport with his inside partner Capel and the goals began to flow from all along the forward line. Forest scored seven without reply against Aldershot at the City Ground at the end of September. Ardron hit a hat-trick and Scott got two with one each from the left-wing pair. In the middle of November a crowd of 20,639 on Trentside saw Capel hit four, a hat-trick from Ardron and Johnson score two in a 9-2 trouncing of Gillingham. A week later, it was Johnson's turn to register a hat-trick as Torquay United were beaten 6-1 in the first round of the FA Cup. When Crystal Palace were beaten 6-1 in south London in January, every Forest forward scored. Johnson got another hat-trick in a 5-0 win at Exeter and the Reds finished the season with four successive victories – two at home and two away.

Wally Ardron had revelled in having Scott and Johnson to his right with Capel and Collindridge on his left flank. He scored a still-standing club record thirty-six goals. Capel hit twenty-three, Collindridge sixteen, Johnson fifteen and Scott nine goals. 'Tot' Leverton, who deputised chiefly for the injury-prone Johnson, contributed six goals in twenty-two appearances. It wasn't all down to the attack, of course. Forest had an outstanding half-back line with captain Horace Gager at centre-half and two home-grown wing-halves, Bill Morley and Jack Burkitt. In front of the reliable goalkeeper Walker were full-backs Bill Whare and Geoff Thomas, who went on to establish a sound, long-lived partnership. Jack Hutchinson at full-back, former Manchester United wing-half John Anderson, and inside-forward John Love made up the promotion-winning squad.

On 1 May, 1951, Billy Walker received a letter from chairman Jack Brentnall that he said was 'as much a treasured possession as my own Villa cup medal'. The chairman wrote:

Dear Billy,
I felt that I would like to write to express my gratification and sincere appreciation of your untiring efforts to bring about the Championship that we have just obtained.

I am fully aware of the anxiety and numerous difficulties throughout the season that have caused you to be so uneasy and restless. Along with you I have, as you know, at times been very concerned, but your personality and confidence on these adverse occasions, which you have always been so ready to pass along to me, have been reassuring. We, together, have seen dark days, but at the moment I feel the times are going to be much better, and with your valuable help and experience, which as you know I have always appreciated, gives me confidence to say that the set-back we had two years ago has been overcome and the future, without a doubt, is going to be much brighter. No committee man and chairman could have had a better guide than yourself. We both may have been doubted by some of our colleagues and supporters on many occasions but my confidence was never shaken.

I am so pleased that we have been able to stick together to retrieve our position and I sincerely trust we shall be together many more years to further same. Whatever happens, and in football as you know it is

very difficult to foresee the future, I hope we shall be the staunch and
true friends that we have been in the past.

Very many thanks, Billy

(signed) Jack Brentnall, Chairman

Walker wished 'that all club executives could think and talk so sweet'. He
recalled that twenty-five years earlier as an Aston Villa player he scored a
goal that sent Forest down into the Second Division.

> That far-back game was a particularly mixed day for me because, by
> that time, my old colleague Sam Hardy, the greatest goalkeeper of
> them all, was playing for Forest, and it was my goal that beat him and
> Forest. Now, with the First Division well in our sights, was a time of
> tremendous exhilaration, and that summer flew past on wings. But, in
> spite of the fact that I had put Forest back into the Second Division
> with the help of my committee and my players, the nigglers were still
> at it. They wondered if we should go straight forward, or if we should
> go back. They wondered if we had a good enough team, if we'd a good
> enough ground (although it is, in my opinion, the best ground and the
> best piece of turf in the country). And so it went on, harassingly, from
> the kind of people who are never satisfied. Well, it did not take very
> long for us to show them.

Walker was confident that his promotion-winners would do well in the
higher division and added only wing-half Alan Orr from Third Lanark
and Dubliner Noel Kelly, an inside-forward from Crystal Palace, to his
squad. The Reds did so well that they led the division for six weeks until
defeated by West Ham on 22 March 1951. They might have had back-to-
back promotions but for bad luck with injuries to key players including
skipper Gager and, even more damagingly, Collindridge, who broke a
leg in December and did not return to the side until Good Friday to play
only the last five games of the season. Winger Alan Moore was signed
from Hull City and made his debut in a 3-2 win over Notts County at the
City Ground on 19 January. There was a crowd of 40,000, 4,000 fewer
than there had been at Meadow Lane in September, when the Magpies
had scored twice in the last five minutes to force a draw. Forest finished
their first season back in Division Two a creditable fourth.

Tommy Lawton came to the City Ground in September 1952, this
time leading the Brentford attack, but his side were without success as
the home side were comfortable 3-0 winners. Jack French, a wing-half
signed from Southend United for £10,000, and inside-forward Tommy

Martin, a record £15,000 buy from Doncaster Rovers, made their debuts against Rotherham United at Millmoor at the beginning of November in an attempt to end a run of five defeats in seven games. It succeeded but Forest dropped to a seventh-place finish.

Now in his mid-thirties and becoming more prone to injury, Wally Ardron made just fourteen appearances in 1953/54 but still managed to score ten goals. Alan Moore was top scorer with nineteen and Tommy Capel got eighteen. When Forest beat Notts 5-0 at the City Ground on 10 October the visitors fielded five former Reds – Aubrey Southwell, Bill Baxter, Jack Edwards, Tommy Johnston and 'Tot' Leverton. The 4-2 defeat of Derby on 7 November was the Reds' ninth successive home win. Forest had regained fourth place when the season ended but Tommy Capel and Colin Collindridge had played their last games for the club, the left-wing pair being transferred to Coventry City during the summer.

Ardron played his last match for the Reds across the river at Meadow Lane on 12 February 1955, but did not score and Notts were the victors at 4-1. He and Tommy Lawton were rival but very different centre-forwards though both were accomplished headers of the ball. Who had the biggest impact? Lawton drew the crowds to the Lane and inspired promotion to Division Two but County slumped after his departure. Ardron's goals and grit drove Forest forward and they were able to build on his achievements. He is remembered reverently still in the stands at the City Ground, where his ashes were spread on the pitch after his death in 1978.

'Billy Walker told me he wanted First Division soccer and the FA Cup,' Ardron wrote in his book. 'Both were achieved but, unfortunately for me, after my enforced retirement through injury.' Although Forest were fifteenth in 1954/55 they reached the fifth round of the FA Cup and took eventual winners Newcastle United to a second replay. The match at the City Ground on 18 February attracted 25,252 and ended 1-1. New outside-left Peter Small from Leicester City, who had been injured and taken to hospital for an X-ray, returned to the field to put Forest ahead with just five minutes left. Two minutes later Jack Milburn equalised. Across the river on the same afternoon, Notts County's Cup clash with Chelsea attracted nearly 42,000. At St James' Park, the Reds were two down at half-time but came back with goals by Jim Barrett and Fred Scott. A coin was tossed to decide which club would stage the second replay and it fell for Newcastle. Tommy Wilson shot Forest ahead in the 22nd minute but the home side equalised and got the winner in extra time.

Judging by comments in his 'The Manager's Review' in a Forest programme in March 1953, Billy Walker stored what he had seen in his memory for future action. Here's what he wrote after an eight-match unbeaten run had been ended at Upton Park:

In the West Ham side last week I saw for the first time their young inside-forward, Barrett, who is the son of old Jimmy Barrett, the former West Ham centre-half, who had some twenty years' service with the club. While old Jimmy stood about 6ft and weighed something like 15 stone, young Jimmy is 5ft.8in and only about 11 stone. He is unlike his father in build but, on last Saturday's display, he is a grand player, very constructive, and always having a crack at goal.

Walker signed Jim Barrett for £7,500 from West Ham in December 1954. He was Forest's top scorer for three successive seasons. In their 1956/57 promotion-winning season, young Jim hit thirty league and cup goals.

In time Walker came to appreciate that Ardron's natural successor was the local boy Tommy Wilson, signed in 1951 from Cinderhill Colliery, but before claiming the No. 9 shirt as his own he had to see off lively competition from Peter Higham, brought in from Preston North End. It was immediately obvious, however, that Bobby McKinlay was the player to take over from Horace Gager, who played only five times in 1954/55 before retiring. Gager had made 268 appearances in a seven-year career at the City Ground. Outside-left Stewart Imlach was a new recruit in the summer. The Scot, who had built up his fitness and speed-running on the beach at Lossiemouth, was unhappy and unsettled at Derby. He found the Wembley-sized pitch at the City Ground much more to his liking than the cramped Baseball Ground. A prelude to promotion, Forest climbed back to seventh place in 1955/56. With Doug Lishman having been signed from Arsenal on transfer deadline day in March and Eddie Baily to join him in the Garibaldi early in the new season, the key to the First Division door was in Forest's hands.

Forest began with away victories at Leyton Orient by 4-1 and at Bristol City 5-1. In a new season's message for the first home match on 25 August 1956, when Fulham came to the City Ground, chairman G. S. Oscroft wrote,

As you know, we are a club with limited resources. However, with a 100 per cent effort by our players and, more important still, your whole-hearted support, we may all feel confident and hopeful that the arduous campaign ahead will bring us to our ambition - First Division football for Nottingham.

The Fulham side that day included Roy Dwight at centre-forward and Tony Barton, who joined Forest in December 1959, on the right wing. Eddie Lowe, who later managed Notts County, was at inside-left. The winning start continued with Jim Barrett hitting a hat-trick, taking his goal tally to seven in three games.

Forest then led the division on goal average from Sheffield United and Swansea. Bristol City went away with a 2-2 draw at the City Ground at the end of August but the Reds began September in spectacular style, outplaying Swansea at the Vetch Field to triumph 4-1. It was their biggest win at Swansea for twenty-eight years. The national press raved about the quality of their football: the passing and movement, players supporting each other, keeping the ball, keeping it down, on the ground – 'the Walker Way'.

Doug Lishman scored two of Forest's goals against Swansea and went on to hit the target in four successive games. He had been a Football League championship winner with Arsenal in 1953 and a prolific scorer for the Gunners with 137 goals in 244 games. An astute signing by Walker for £8,000, the England B international had scored on his debut against Middlesbrough at the City Ground in March 1956.

A crowd of 18,699 watched the Reds beat Port Vale 4-2 at the City Ground on 22 September. They witnessed a match of greater significance than the result, important though that was. It had been highlighted in the newspapers as a clash between two former North London idols: Lishman against Eddie Baily, an England international inside-forward signed by Vale from Tottenham Hotspur nine months earlier. Billy Walker saw enough to know that if he could pair these two, Forest would have a goalscoring force of true promotion potential. His bid of £7,000 was accepted and Baily, wearing borrowed boots because of the speed of the transaction, made his debut at Huddersfield on 6 October. The Reds lost 1-0 but at home to Bury the following week nearly 22,000 saw the Cockney 'cheeky chappie' Baily score twice with ex-Commando Lishman also on the scoresheet in a 5-1 win.

Lishman and Baily again got the goals when Forest beat Notts County 2-1 before a 31,585 crowd at Meadow Lane a week later. The two linked up well together and with strike partners Barrett and Tommy Wilson. The immaculate passing of the former push-and-run Spurs star also brought the best out of speedy left-winger Imlach.

An eleven-match unbeaten run in the league from the end of December was broken on 30 March by a 2-1 home defeat to Leicester City, who were now home and dry in the promotion race. Forest were left to battle for second place with Blackburn Rovers and Liverpool. Forest had beaten Liverpool at the City Ground in December with a goal by Baily, but at Anfield on 20 April, 47,621 saw them gain revenge 3-1.

So to the dramatic finale. Sheffield United came to the City Ground on 22 April hoping to get back into the hunt, but they were seen off 2-1,

Peter Higham and Wilson scoring goals to delight 29,000 fans. Many Forest supporters (including me) were at Bramall Lane five days later for the return match, which we needed to win to ensure promotion. There were 28,000 fans occupying three sides of the ground – in those days one length of the pitch was open to the cricket field.

Even the most optimistic of us could not have imagined such a masterly performance as Forest blunted a Blades' team that included goalkeeper Alan Hodgkinson, centre-half Joe Shaw, wing-half Jim Iley (who was later to join Forest from Spurs) and England international inside-forward Jimmy Hagan.

Dynamic and deadly, Lishman crowned a brilliant performance with a never-to-be-forgotten hat-trick with Wilson the other scorer in a 4-0 triumph. It was Lishman's swansong. He retired aged thirty-four at the season's end to manage the family furniture business.

A crowd of 32,000 went to the City Ground on the first of May to celebrate promotion at the final Division Two match of the season and saw Imlach and Wilson score Forest's goals. But Notts County scored four. Typical Forest. Defeat did not stop the celebrations as thousands of fans swarmed onto the pitch to cheer as the players appeared in front of them waving from the committee/directors' box. Most thought Notts would follow the Reds to Division One. Instead, County went into decline and descended first into the Third Division and then Division Four.

Barrett scored twenty-seven Second Division goals and three in the FA Cup. Lishman delivered sixteen and Wilson posted just as many, including two in the cup. In his debut season, Imlach scored twelve. Forest's ninety-four goals was a club record for the Second Division and Barrett's total of thirty was the best by an inside-right.

Billy Walker asked, 'What do records matter at a time like this? Forest were back in the First Division again – back to the heady highlands of the game after thirty-two years in the scrubby foothills.'

Up the League We Go
(Part II)

T-shirts on sale in the club shop have a Clough quote across the chest: 'Rome wasn't built in a day but, then, I wasn't on that particular job.' Rebuilding Nottingham Forest was to be no quick fix either. But the manager knew the people he needed and immediately set about bringing them to the City Ground. He recruited trainer Jimmy Gordon, who had been with him at Derby and Leeds, and tried but initially failed to persuade Peter Taylor to leave Brighton. The key signing, however, was John McGovern. He and centre-forward John O'Hare had been with Clough at Derby and were taken by him to Leeds for a combined fee of £150,000. After the manager's sudden departure, both were in limbo at Elland Road and were relieved when Forest paid a total of £60,000 to reunite them with him at the City Ground.

Scotsman O'Hare was born in the Dunbartonshire village of Renton, whose football club he is keen to point out, won football's first world championship. Renton, Dumbarton and the Vale of Leven, all from the football hotbed of Dunbartonshire, were early winners of the Scottish Cup. Renton beat Cambuslang 6-1 in the 1888 final and then won a challenge match against the English Cup-winners West Bromwich Albion 4-1 to determine the 'Champions of the United Kingdom and the World'. The world-championship trophy, made of pewter and around a foot high, is displayed in the Scottish Football Museum at Hampden Park.

Clough had won his first game in charge of Forest, the FA Cup third-round replay against Spurs at White Hart Lane on 8 January, thanks to a goal by inside-right Neil Martin. The team stayed in London and trained at Bisham Abbey in preparation for the Second Division game against Fulham at Craven Cottage three days later. Martin's strike partner Barry Butlin scored the only goal. Fulham were also Forest's fourth-round opponents and the tie went to three replays before the Londoners triumphed 2-1 in front of a 23,240 crowd at the City Ground on 10 February. McGovern and O'Hare made their debuts at the end of the month and found themselves in a relegation fight. After the league win over Fulham, the Reds went sixteen games before getting another at home to bottom club Sheffield Wednesday thanks to a penalty by George Lyall. Only 14,000 were present. Fewer than 12,000 saw Butlin score twice in the 2-1 defeat of sixth-placed West Bromwich Albion that ended the league season with Forest sixteenth, five points clear of relegation.

On that last day Newcastle United captain Frank Clark was stunned to learn from his manager Joe Harvey that he was finished at St James' Park after thirteen years and more than 400 games with the club he had joined from Crook Town. He was nearly thirty-two and available on a free transfer. Clark, an Inter-Cities Fairs Cup winner in 1969 with a wealth of top-flight experience, was already in talks with Doncaster Rovers when, thanks to a tip-off from journalist Doug Weatherall, he came on Clough's radar and was persuaded to swap the Tyne Bridge for Trent Bridge. The summer also saw Ian Bowyer, John Robertson and Martin O'Neill sign new contracts and a recognisable Brian Clough team was taking shape. Viv Anderson and Tony Woodcock took part in a successful tour in West Germany and Bowyer, wearing the number eleven shirt, scored successive hat-tricks against Ballymena and Coleraine in Northern Ireland.

Season ticket prices had gone up from £15 main stand and £7 terraces in 1973/74 to £22 main stand and £10 terraces when Forest opened the 1975/76 campaign with a 2-0 victory over Plymouth Argyle at the City Ground on 16 August. The attendance was just over 13,000. The team lined up: John Middleton, Viv Anderson, Frank Clark, Sammy Chapman, Liam O'Kane, John McGovern, George Lyall, Paul Richardson, John O'Hare, John Robertson and Ian Bowyer. Terry Curran, a twenty-year-old winger signed from Doncaster Rovers for £60,000, made his debut in the next home league match at the end of the month but a last-minute Les Bradd goal gave Notts County the points.

A serious injury to O'Kane led Clough to approach Manchester City for reserve full-back Colin Barrett, who at first declined a loan move. But Clough wasn't about to give up the chase and spoke to the twenty-year-old over the phone. 'You're playing in the reserves and I've got a place in my first team for you,' he said. They met outside Leek Town's ground and agreed a loan deal to the end of the season. Barrett played at right-back in the remaining ten league games and his appearances coincided with the season's best run of results. His impressive form encouraged Clough to pay City £30,000 to make the loan permanent. Barrett was to be an important asset over the next two seasons. Martin O'Neill and

John Robertson had gained regular places and Forest finished eighth on forty-six points, three fewer than fifth-placed Notts County.

Word got around during the summer that Jimmy Armfield, Clough's successor at Leeds, was considering letting Duncan McKenzie go to finance a move for Sheffield United midfield playmaker Tony Currie. When Stuart Dryden got a call from Clough inviting him for a drink at Widmerpool Cricket Club, where the manager and McKenzie had both been playing in a testimonial match, the committee man assumed a transfer deal was in the offing. It turned out that Clough's target was not the player but Peter Taylor. 'I'm off to Cala Millor to fetch him,' he informed Dryden. He had heard from scout Maurice Edwards, who had turned down an invitation to be assistant manager at Brighton, that failing to gain promotion for the south coast club had been unsettling and Taylor would not be averse to them linking up again, but was not willing to make the first approach.

Armfield accepted a £200,000 bid from RSC Anderlecht and McKenzie went off to Belgium. After his debut against the Bayern Munich of Franz Beckenbauer, Gerd Muller and Sepp Maier, one Belgian newspaper reported, 'We thought we'd signed an Englishman but we have ourselves a Brazilian.'

McGovern and O'Hare had noticed a difference in Brian Clough during the past season. 'I know what it is,' McGovern told his teammate as they travelled from Derby to Nottingham for training. 'I think he's kind of going through the motions.' It was a niggling feeling they shared until Taylor's arrival when, McGovern judged, 'Brian Clough would always be top man yet his change of mood was clearly visible.' Taylor himself commented, 'We both knew we were banging our heads against a brick wall on our own. Together we could do any job. There was no point delaying.'

Taylor, born in the Meadows, had come home. McGovern recalled,

With Peter Taylor now on board I knew things would be different. 'It's just a matter of when,' I told the rest of the players. 'When what?' one or two asked. 'When we get promoted,' I declared. 'Don't you mean if we get promoted?' they said. 'Not if, just when,' I confidently replied.

The bookies agreed and ranked Forest among the favourites for promotion along with Wolves and Bolton.

Forest returned from a successful pre-season tour in West Germany to play their first competitive games in the Anglo-Scottish Cup. Unbeaten in their qualifying group, which included Notts County, West Bromwich Albion and Bristol City, they went through to the knockout phase of the tournament. Kilmarnock came to the City Ground in the first round and were beaten 2-1. The away leg was drawn 2-2. Ayr United were next up and Forest won the home leg 2-1 with goals by new signings Larry Lloyd, who had joined from Coventry on loan, and Peter Withe, a £44,000 striker from Birmingham City. Gedling schoolboy Stephen Burke, just sixteen years and twenty-one days old, came on as substitute to replace Martin O'Neill and became the youngest-ever Red. An England Youth international, it was his only game for Forest but in an eleven-year career he made a total of 156 League appearances and scored fifteen goals, including five in sixty-seven matches for Queen's Park Rangers and eight in fifty-seven outings with Doncaster Rovers.

The second leg at Ayr took place in a torrential downpour with only 3,000 prepared to be drenched. Recalled from a month on loan at Doncaster, twenty-year-old striker Tony Woodcock and Withe were paired for the first time and both scored in a 2-0 win. It was a taste of triumphs to come. Leyton Orient were the opposition in the two-leg final played in the middle of December. A Robertson penalty enabled Forest to draw the London match and a 4-0 home win made the aggregate 5-1. Full-back Colin Barrett, pushed forward to inside-right, scored two goals and McGovern lifted his first piece of silverware as captain of the club.

Having made his senior debut for Forest as an eighteen-year-old at Villa Park in April 1974, Eastwood-born Woodcock only really established himself in the promotion season. He loved to run at defenders with the ball at his feet, often collecting it from a deep position and darting down one of the flanks. Yet he hated it when Brian Clough played him on the left wing. He plucked up the courage to tackle Clough about it and asked to be played up front. The manager wanted to know why he should make the change. 'Because I'll score goals for you,' the player replied. 'Good answer, young man,' his manager replied.

With his pace and control, Woodcock was difficult to contain and provided a perfect foil for big striker Peter Withe. After the latter's departure for Aston Villa, he linked up equally effectively with Garry Birtles. Ron Greenwood reunited Tony and Peter as an England striking partnership for the 1982 World Cup in Spain. Woodcock was awarded the first of his forty-two England caps against Northern Ireland on 16 May, 1978. He scored sixteen goals in full internationals and five in his two England Under-21 appearances. In the promotion season, Withe scored sixteen goals in thirty-three Second Division appearances and Woodcock eleven in thirty. They also scored four and six respectively in Cup games.

Lloyd returned to Coventry when his loan period expired at the end of October, resisting Clough's efforts to persuade him to sign permanently.

Signed from his home town club Bristol Rovers by Bill Shankly as successor at Liverpool to veteran captain and centre-half Ron Yeats, he had won three international caps while at Anfield and played in all fifty-four matches in 1973 when they won the league championship and UEFA Cup. After Shankly's retirement in the summer of 1974, Lloyd left for Coventry, who paid a club record transfer fee of £240,000. Handicapped by a back injury, he did not have a happy time at Highfield Road and his playing career was at its lowest ebb when the Sky Blues tried to sell him to Third Division Walsall for £40,000. The player refused to consider the deal and wasn't keen on dropping a division for a loan move to Forest. The Clough psychology worked, however, when he said, 'Come and see if you like it at Forest. It's not about us having a look at you, it's about you having a look at us.' Back at Coventry, he was still undecided but manager Gordon Milne made it clear he wanted more mobile centre-backs. Forest bid £60,000 and Milne was so keen he was prepared to lose almost £200,000 on the transfer. Clough – and in particular, Taylor – had got the big centre-half they wanted at the heart of their defence. Lloyd was a heavyweight 6 feet 2 inches tall and, perhaps, Taylor recalled Shankly frightening visiting centre-forwards at Anfield by offering to take them on 'a tour around our centre-half' when Ron Yeats was at the height of his powers.

Forest's league progress was interrupted by a third-round FA Cup tie with Bristol Rovers that went to a second replay before they went through 6-0 at Villa Park with two goals from Woodcock and one each for Withe, Bowyer, O'Hare and Anderson. A run of fourteen games without defeat had been ended by Charlton Athletic at the Valley four days earlier. The biggest crowd of the season, home or way, 38,284 saw the fourth-round clash with Southampton finish 3-3 at the City Ground. There were 29,401 at the Dell for the replay, which the Saints won 2-1. Successive 2-1 defeats at Wolverhampton and at home to Luton were deflating before Southampton came again to the City Ground, this time in the league, on 16 February. It was looking bleak for Forest when Nick Holmes put the visitors ahead before half-time. Luckily for the Reds, during the interval thick fog billowed in from the Trent and two minutes into the second half referee Roy Capey abandoned the game. The Reds won the rearranged match 2-1.

Further bad weather caused more cancellations and blank weekends so the team headed off to Torremolinos in Spain for five days. Then came the announcement that George Hardy, who had replaced Sam Longson as chairman of Derby County, had sacked manager Dave Mackay and wanted Clough and Taylor to return to the Baseball Ground. Forest chairman Brian Appleby gave permission for a formal approach and negotiations appeared to go well. A celebratory bottle of champagne was opened. Appleby was said to have arrived at the City Ground on the morning of 21 February and enquired, 'Has he gone yet?' But overnight Clough, much to Taylor's dismay, had changed his mind. Clough told the *Evening Post* at Nottingham that the reason he had remained at the City Ground was loyalty to Stuart Dryden who came in for him after he had been sacked by Leeds. Perhaps also he thought the Forest committee would be more malleable than Derby's board of directors, especially as he had wanted Longson and Stuart Webb dismissed. So there was dejection at Derby but relief in Nottingham, though there would be more times when Forest fans felt their emotions had been put through the wringer by Clough's restless opportunism.

A serious knee injury in October had put right-winger Terry Curran out of the side for four months, forcing a tactical change that would prove critical to Forest's success. Robertson had been seen as almost a midfielder really, with Curran an orthodox flanker. Now Robertson advanced further forward on the left and O'Neill adopted the slightly withdrawn role on the right. It was still a lopsided 4-4-2, only with the opposite winger pushed high. Robertson lacked pace except when he had the ball at his feet, when he could outwit and leave straggling more than one defender before crossing accurately. Curran got back into the side briefly and scored the only goal in the victory at Hereford on 2 March. He then made one appearance at centre-forward and three as a substitute.

The match against Hull City, watched by a 15,000 crowd at the City Ground on 12 March, was notable not just for goals by Withe and Woodcock in a 2-0 win but for the debut of twenty-year-old local lad Garry Birtles, who would go on to become the scorer of Forest's first-ever goal in the European Cup.

A 2-1 defeat by Notts County, watched by 31,000 at the City Ground, preceded the Hull game, which was followed by a 2-0 loss away to Sheffield United on 19 March, putting Forest in seventh place, three points behind their neighbours but with a game in hand. Then came the home game with Southampton, rearranged after the earlier abandonment. Only 12,393 turned up but the Reds, with goals by Woodcock and O'Neill, began a five-match winning run that included a crucial 3-1 defeat of Bolton Wanderers at the City Ground.

A drawn game at Meadow Lane did neither Notts nor Forest any favours and it was followed by defeat for the Reds at leaders Chelsea and then to lowly Cardiff City by the only goal after failing to score at home in the league for the first and only time. Frustrated Clough was furious and demanded better. His team responded, beating Oldham 3-0 at the City Ground, picking up an away point against Bristol Rovers and remaining in the West Country to defeat Plymouth Argyle two days later. This left Forest in the third promotion spot behind Wolves and Chelsea with fifty points from forty-one games, two points ahead of Notts, three more than Bolton and with a vastly superior goal difference. But Notts had a game in hand and Bolton three. 'It's better to have the points,' Clough commented.

The pressure was on the chasing pack but Forest needed to beat Millwall at the City Ground in their final league match of the season on 7 May as defeat could allow Notts, Bolton and Blackpool to leapfrog them. The gate was a surprisingly low 23,529 and the game was as tense as expected. The Reds attacked in waves but the visitors held on until a Robertson cross was headed into his own goal by Jon Moore. Bolton drew and needed five points from their remaining three games to deny Forest the final promotion place. Notts failed to get even a point from their last two fixtures and finished eighth.

Clough's message as he and his squad flew off to Mallorca for a post-season holiday was 'Let Bolton worry.' Their flight left East Midlands Airport at 3 p.m. just as Bolton were kicking off against Wolves, who were already champions. Kenny Hibbert scored and then had to go in goal after the Wolves' goalkeeper was injured, but his effort proved enough. With a phone call to Nottingham from Palma airport, the Foresters learned they were as good as up because Bolton, thirteen goals behind on goal difference, needed to win by a cricket score to stop them. They drew and finished a point behind.

Colin Barrett recalled, 'It was a week of mayhem in Mallorca. Celebrations, headaches but it was all good fun, and Ian Bowyer pointed out, 'It wasn't about Bolton. We played forty-two games to get there.' Back in Nottingham fans gathered in the Old Market Square to celebrate.

12

Storming Start

When the reigning champions – the famous Busby Babes of Manchester United – came to the City Ground on Saturday 12 October 1957, they faced a newly promoted Forest side that had taken the First Division by storm, winning eight of the first eleven games played. The victories had included a 7-0 drubbing at the City Ground of star-studded Burnley, full of internationals including centre-forward Ray Pointer and winger John Connelly of England, Scottish goalkeeper Adam Blacklaw and Northern Ireland inside-forward Jimmy McIlroy, led by wing-half Jimmy Adamson. All five Forest forwards scored with two each for Wilson and Imlach.

A then-record crowd of 47,804 were there to welcome United, some of them sitting on bench seats in the new East Stand in use for the first time. Others were allowed to sit on the pitchside of the concrete wall in front of the terraces. No health and safety fears then – and no football hooligans. Don Davies of the *Manchester Guardian*, who wrote under the nom de plume 'The Old International', reported that, 'This was the perfect occasion, a case where the flawless manners of players, officials and spectators alike gave to a routine league match the flavour almost of an idyll.' With United in an all-white strip, Forest in their blood-red shirts and the sun shining, there was the tingling sense of a great event. Forest fell behind within four minutes of the kick-off. Winger David Pegg, deep in his own half, was picked out with a throw by goalkeeper Ray Woods and he raced 70 yards down the touchline before delivering an accurate cross for Billy Whelan to volley into the net. But, as Davies admitted, if they had not 'squandered scoring chances as freely as they made them', Forest should have been ahead at half-time.

A minute after the restart, Stewart Imlach 'crept up behind Blanchflower unawares and gave that Irish international the shock of his life by

95

suddenly thrusting a grinning face over his shoulder while he nodded a long, high centre from Quigley unerringly home'. Imlach's equaliser was answered twelve minutes later when Dennis Viollet restored United's lead. After that, reported Davies, there seemed 'almost a continuous bombardment of the United goal with only the broad bulk of Duncan Edwards and the safe hands of Ray Wood intervening to save their side from disaster'.

He concluded:

> Forest supporters will take some convincing that Foulkes, Blanchflower, Byrne and Edwards were enjoying the shots that bruised their ribs. But what will be acknowledged without dispute is that this was a great exhibition of football, in which skill was the final, the only, arbiter, and where the splendour of the performance was enriched by the grace of sportsmanlike behaviour.

Stapleford-born Peter Watson made a rare appearance in place of Bobby McKinlay, a victim of influenza, and with great style subdued England centre-forward Tommy Taylor. The Forest XI consisted of Thomson, Whare, Thomas, Morley, Watson, Burkitt (captain), Gray, Quigley, Wilson, Baily and Imlach. England captain Roger Byrne led the United side of Wood, Foulkes, Byrne, Colman, Jack Blanchflower, Edwards, Berry, Whelan, Taylor, Viollet and Pegg. The match ball signed by both teams and their famous managers Billy Walker and Matt Busby is a prize item still displayed by Forest. It is made all the more significant as four months after that classic encounter came the disaster at Munich airport on 6 February 1958, an air crash that shocked the world and tragically ended the lives of twenty-three people, including eight of the Busby Babes.

Fate dictated that Forest would be Manchester United's first league opponents after Munich. United had only two survivors from the pre-disaster squad, goalkeeper Harry Gregg, who had been signed a few weeks before the crash and was hailed a hero for his rescue efforts at Munich, and full-back Bill Foulkes. They had recruited inside-forward Ernie Taylor from Blackpool and half-back Stan Crowther from Aston Villa and had won an FA Cup tie against Sheffield Wednesday. There were 66,346 people at Old Trafford for the match against Forest on 22 February 1958, the biggest crowd since the war. Before the kick-off and at half-time collection boxes were passed along the terracing and through the stands. In a snowstorm that conjured up memories of television pictures from Munich, the Dean of Manchester conducted a short memorial service for the dead and then a welter of noise and tumult was unleashed as the game began.

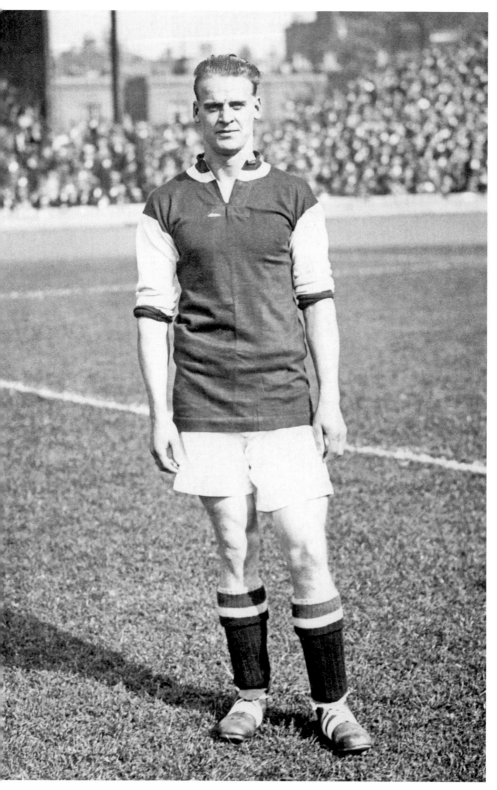

Billy Walker with Aston Villa in 1923. (PA Archive)

The Aston Villa FA Cup-winning team, April 1920, with Billy Walker third from right in the middle row and goalkeeper Sam Hardy, just returned from 'guesting' with Forest, standing fourth from right. (PA Archive)

Billy Walker with England. He is seated second from left in the team that played Wales in 1925. (PA Archive)

Bert 'Sailor' Brown of Charlton Athletic challenging Derby County centre-half Leon Leuty in the 1946 FA Cup Final at Wembley. Soon afterwards he was signed by Billy Walker for the Reds. (PA Archive)

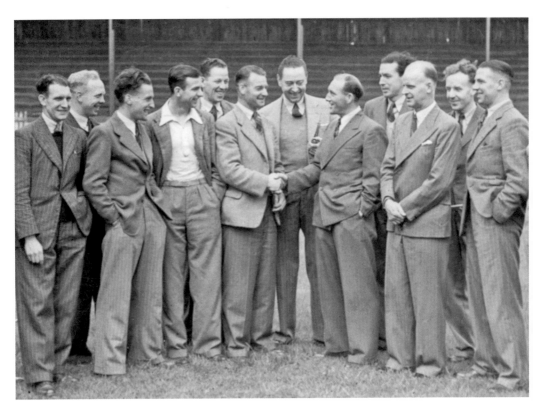

Bob McCall welcoming 'Sailor' Brown to the City Ground in July 1946. Committee member (later chairman) Jack Brentnall stands between them with Billy Walker and, far right, Bob Davies. (*Nottingham Post* Archive)

Wally Ardron in action for the Reds against Fulham at Craven Cottage, December 1954. (PA Archive)

Wally Ardron at Forest, 1954. (PA Archive)

'Sailor' Brown with Forest, 1946/47. (PA Archive)

Jack Burkitt leading out the Reds, followed by goalkeeper Chic Thomson. (PA Archive)

Above: Billy Walker and the team take to the field with Luton at Wembley, 2 May 1959. (PA Archive)

Below: Centre-half Bobby McKinlay heading away from the Luton attack at Wembley. (PA Archive)

Above: Roy Dwight, arms alofts, celebrating his FA Cup Final goal. (PA Archive)

Below: Dwight is stretchered off after breaking his leg in the first half-hour of the final. (PA Archive)

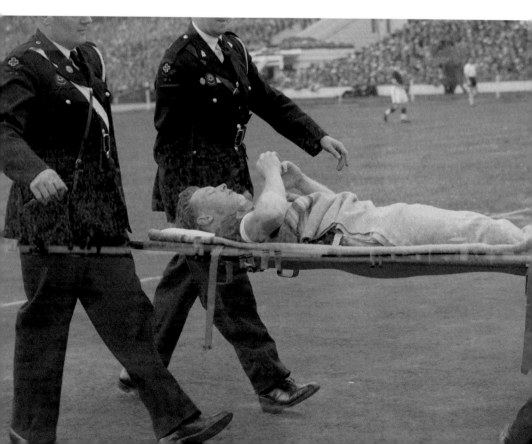

His teammates carry Jack Burkitt shoulder high as he holds the FA Cup aloft. (PA Archive)

The Forest players are congratulated by fans after collecting the FA Cup and their winners' medals. (PA Archive)

David Coleman interviews Jack Burkitt for the BBC after the final. (PA Archive)

Chic Thomson, Johnny Quigley, Joe McDonald, Bill Whare and Roy Dwight share a bath. (PA Archive)

Billy Walker, seated left, and trainer Tommy Graham, right, with their FA Cup winners. (PA Archive).

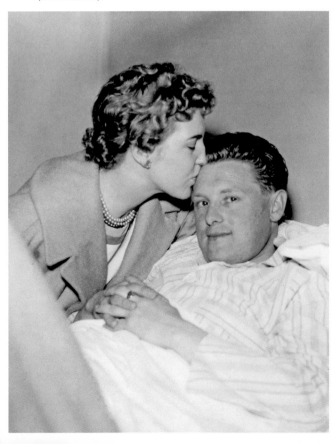

A kiss of congratulation and commiseration for Roy Dwight from his wife, Connie, Wembley General Hospital. (PA Archive).

Forest fans on their Wembley special bus. (PA Archive)

Jack Burkitt has his arm in a sling from a Wembley injury but that doesn't stop him taking the air at Hove, Sussex, with his wife and son, Roger. With them are Billy and Mrs Gray, 3 May 1959. (PA Archive)

Still holding the FA Cup, Jack Burkitt gets a kiss from his wife at the Savoy Hotel, London. (PA Archive)

Right: Stewart Imlach, a Forest Wembley star. (PA Archive)

Below: Five days after the FA Cup was won, Billy Walker took the trophy to Thieves Wood Special School near Mansfield. Here he is with the children and Malcolm Bird holding the Cup. (*Nottingham Post* Archive)

Opposite: Brian Clough has a quiet word with fellow striker Jimmy Greaves during an England training session at Highbury in October 1959. (PA Archive)

Below: A shot on goal by Brian Clough for Middlesbrough against Leyton Orient in London on 15 November 1958. (PA Archive)

Brian Clough with bride Barbara Glasgow leaving St Barnabas' Church, Middlesbrough, after their wedding on 4 April 1959. (PA Archive)

Brian Clough with Peter Taylor after their testimonial match at the City Ground on 1 May 1978. (PA Archive)

Skipper John McGovern, holding the League Championship trophy, leading teammates with other trophies won during the 1977/78 season on a lap of honour at the City Ground. (PA Archive)

Brian Clough with his son Nigel at the National Park, Tokyo, before the world club championship game between Forest and Nacional of Montevideo, Uruguay, 9 February 1981. (PA Archive)

Brian Clough and Peter Taylor celebrating the European Cup Final victory over Swedish champions Malmo in the Olympic Stadium, Munich, at the end of May 1979. (PA Archive)

Making their way back to the City Ground from the muddy training pitch by the Trent, Brian Clough with Des Walker and Darren Wassall, February 1988. (PA Archive)

Brian Clough taking part in a protest march on behalf of redundant Nottinghamshire miners, November 1992. (PA Archive)

The two managers, Brian Clough and Terry Venables, holding hands as they walk out for the 1991 FA Cup Final at Wembley. (PA Archive)

Opposite: Brian Clough receives his Master of Arts degree at the University of Nottingham, 13 July 1990. (PA Archive)

Above: Brian Clough with wife Barbara at Nottingham Council House during his Freedom of the City ceremony, 23 March 1993. (PA Archive)

Right: Two rebels. Brian Clough at the Robin Hood statue beneath the castle wall, March 1993. (PA Archive)

A farewell to Forest fans from Brian Clough after his last match at the City Ground against Sheffield United, 1 May 1993. (PA Archive)

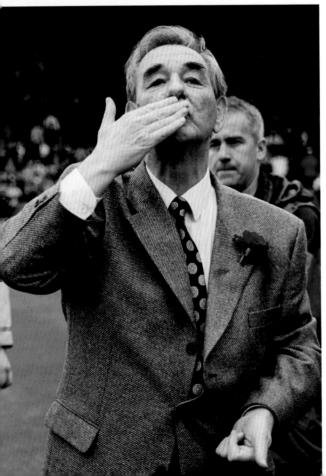

Brian Clough thanks fans at the City Ground after the naming of the Brian Clough Stand, 19 September 1999. (PA Archive)

Forest display the trophies won under Brian Clough, 2004. (PA Archive)

'Walkies time' for Brian Clough on retiring in April 1993. With him is two-year-old granddaughter Susannah and Labrador 'Del'. (PA Archive)

Above: Brian Clough relaxing at home after retirement. (PA Archive)

Below: Frank Clark, Forest manager at the time, presents his former boss Brian Clough with an Edinburgh Crystal punch bowl on behalf of Barclays Bank to commemorate Clough's record number of awards in football management, 1994. (PA Archive)

Above: The Duke of Edinburgh posing with the bust of Brian Clough during a visit to the City Ground in December 1999, as part of the royal visit with the queen to Nottingham. (PA Archive)

Below: Brian Clough with members of his two European Cup winning sides at the City Ground, 2 May 2000. (PA Archive)

Above: Tributes laid at the City Ground in memory of Brian Clough, 20 September 2004. (PA Archive)

Below: Forest fans congregate in the Old Market Square to show their respects to Brian Clough before the match with West Ham United, 26 September 2004. (PA Archive)

Overleaf: Forest fans cheering in front of a big screen image of Brian Clough at the game against Derby County at the City Ground on 12 September 2014. (PA Archive)

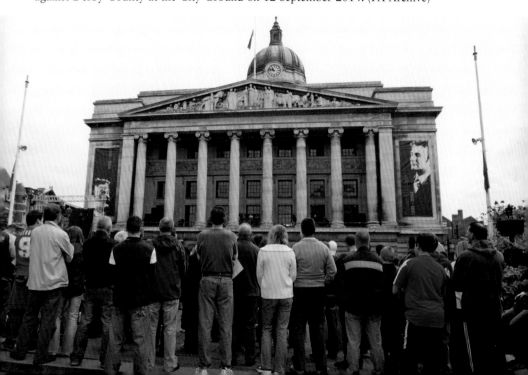

Above: Nottingham Forest's riverside City Ground, showing the Brian Clough and Trent End stands and the neighbouring boathouses.

Below: The Brian Clough statue unveiled at Speakers Corner by his widow, Barbara, 6 November 2008. (PA Archive)

The Forest players answered the understandably fanatical fervour they faced with cultured football and commendable restraint. After half an hour, Tommy Wilson chased a poor United clearance out to the right and cut the ball back to the edge of the penalty area. Imlach instinctively drifted in from the left and from 20 yards drove the ball past Gregg into the net. It was the first goal against the stricken club and was met with silence. In an emotional second-half, United, surging forward to a continuous roar of support, got the equaliser they deserved when Alex Dawson forced in a corner before the final whistle. The fighting furies of United were Gregg, Foulkes, Greaves, Goodwin, Cope, Crowther, Webster, Taylor, Dawson, Pearson and Brennan. Forest's eleven were Thomson, Whare, Thomas, Morley, McKinlay, Burkitt, Gray, Quigley, Wilson, Chris Joyce (Barrett was absent with flu) and Imlach.

Billy Walker made just two signings during the close season in preparation for Forest's new start in Division One and they proved bargain buys. Billy Gray came from Burnley initially to fill the right wing position mainly occupied by Higham or Small in the promotion side and Charlie ('Chic') Thomson arrived from Chelsea to replace Harry Nicholson in goal. The total outlay was about £10,000. Gray, on the small side but quick and strong, had won the Northumberland schools boxing title for four years in succession before 'kicking a tin around' and turning to football. He was a first team regular at Chelsea and then joined Burnley, becoming their top scorer in his first four seasons. But he went on to make 223 appearances for Forest, more than for any previous club. Thomson, whose father had been a Scottish League goalkeeper, joined Chelsea from Clyde in 1952 and had four seasons at Stamford Bridge, keeping goal for the last sixteen games of their 1954/55 championship season to qualify for a medal.

Their pace-setting start made Forest early leaders. Barrett scored in seven consecutive games. Then, on 7 December 1957, the player and the club suffered a severe blow when Barrett, their main marksman, tore ligaments in his right knee just twenty-six minutes into a home game with Sunderland. Wilson scored twice to give the Reds a 2-0 victory but Barrett's season had ended. Again he had been in brilliant form and scored twelve goals in seventeen games. Forest were tenth in the table at the end of the season and went off on tour to West German, Belgium and Holland, during which they played Flamengo in Liege and drew 2-2 with the Brazilians.

In March the Reds took an Italian break when they went to Florence, where they had the support of a contingent of sailors from Royal Navy ships anchored at Livorno, but could only achieve a scoreless draw with Fiorentina. Making his debut at centre-forward was Northern Ireland international Fay Coyle, signed from Coleraine. He made his First Division start in another goalless draw at Chelsea on 4 April and then played two more league games at Sunderland and Arsenal before going off with the Northern Ireland squad to the World Cup finals and winning his fourth cap against Argentina. He returned homesick to Coleraine that summer without playing a single game at the City Ground and in 1964 captained Derry City, his hometown club, to an Irish Cup final victory over Glentoran and, consequently, into European competition for the first time in their history.

It was a busy summer for Billy Walker, who made three key signings in July. In order of arrival, they were full-back Joe McDonald from Sunderland, winger Roy Dwight from Fulham and wing-half Jeff Whitefoot, a former Busby Babe, from Grimsby Town. As every pub quiz contestant knows, Dwight was the uncle of music star Elton John (real name Reg Dwight). He was also the costliest recruit at £14,000. The fee paid for Whitefoot was £10,000 and Sunderland accepted just under their asking price of £5,000 for McDonald, a Scottish international who had played for Great Britain against the Rest of Europe in an Irish FA anniversary match at Windsor Park, Belfast, in 1955. Dwight had been Fulham's top scorer in each of the past two seasons. Walker had wanted to sign Whitefoot from Manchester United eight months earlier and a transfer had been agreed by all parties but the player wanted a guarantee of first team football and went to Grimsby for £8,000. His family could not settle there and so, having liked Nottingham and the house offered to them, Whitefoot welcomed Walker's second approach. It proved a happy move.

A former schoolboy international, Whitefoot was one of the original Busby Babes and had learned how to control a ball playing with his father outside their home in a cobbled cul de sac in Cheadle. He became the youngest to play in the League for United when he made his debut against Portsmouth in April 1950, aged sixteen years and 105 days. A member of the Championship-winning side of 1955/56, he gained an England Under-23 cap against Italy in Bologna and made nearly 100 League and Cup appearances for his club. With Forest, Whitefoot played 285 League and Cup games before retiring after a stay of ten seasons. McDonald made 124 League and Cup appearances in three seasons and fully repaid Walker's faith in him while Dwight, despite the sickening blow that was to come at Wembley, scored twenty-seven goals in fifty-three games for the Reds.

After an opening-day shock 5-1 defeat by Wolves at Molineux despite a debut goal from Dwight, and a 3-0 drubbing by Manchester United in front of a 44,971 crowd at the City Ground, Forest found their shooting boots to beat Portsmouth 5-0 and West Ham 4-0, both at home. Dwight, Wilson and Quigley shared the goals. Then Quigley hit a hat-trick as Manchester City were beaten 4-0, also at the City Ground. After a second-half hat-trick by Dwight on a foggy November afternoon had given the Reds their first win at Leicester for fifty years, they stayed in a challenging position in the league table as the FA Cup campaign loomed large.

It began on 10 January on a deeply rutted pitch that was icy and covered with snow at the small Sandy Lane ground of amateurs Tooting and Mitcham United, who had already knocked out two League sides, Bournemouth and Northampton. This was their first-ever appearance in the third round and the ground was packed with a record attendance of 14,300. The home side mastered the conditions early on and were two up by half-time. After the break they were forced on the defensive and wing-half Murphy, who had scored Tooting's second goal in the thirty-fifth minute, put one into his own goal seventeen minutes later. Tooting's misfortune continued when a defender handled the ball in the penalty area and Billy Gray sent the spot kick high to the right of the goalkeeper's outstretched hand to equalise with fifteen minutes remaining.

The kick-off for the replay a week later was at 2 p.m. to allow for possible extra time and even more respect for the amateurs was shown by a City Ground attendance of 42,320. This time the result was never in doubt with Dwight, Wilson and Imlach taking Forest through. They were in the fourth round and met Grimsby Town of Division Two at the City Ground only four days later. The tie was virtually decided by half-time. Whitefoot scored after three minutes and Gray got two in six minutes, including a penalty a minute before the break. Wilson made it four on the hour before winger Scott got a consolation goal for the visitors in the 76th minute.

Whitefoot, Dwight and Wilson gave Forest a comfortable home win against Bolton Wanderers in the league on 7 February to set them up for a fifth-round visit a week later to St Andrews, where 55,000 saw Birmingham City a minute away from victory, but a spectacular Wilson header dramatically saved the day. The replay drew a crowd of 39,431 to the City Ground on 18 February. It was goalless at full-time. Then John Gordon put Birmingham ahead in the 15th minute of extra time. With five minutes to go, Roy Dwight lobbed the 'keeper to force a second replay. This took place on the afternoon of Monday 23 February at Leicester's Filbert Street before 34,458 spectators.

Here's how Jeff Whitefoot saw it:

We were a good footballing side ourselves but so too were Birmingham. They had some fine players at the time and we knew it would be a tough tie to get through. In all honesty, I think we felt as though we were going out in the first two games but there was a great spirit in the Forest side and we managed to keep going and get vital equalisers to see us through. We expected it being just the same at Filbert Street but it was just one of those days when everything went well for us. I remember Roy Dwight scored an early goal, which helped very much, and after that we kept playing our football. And the goals came. Roy ended up with a hat-trick and Billy Gray scored the other two, including a penalty. A nap-hand. Fantastic.

After three matches and 300 minutes' play, Forest had eclipsed the Blues with a dazzling display. Billy Walker commented, 'This was easily our best performance in the Cup and on that day we would have beaten anybody. It was a team triumph with no one player better than another and everyone pulling together for the team. That's as I like it.' The irony was that, just over two weeks later, the Reds met Birmingham at home in the First Division and lost 7-1. Whitefoot recalled,

It certainly brought us down to earth. I remember us having a goalkeeper called Willie Fraser, who came in for Chic Thomson for that game and another match against Luton that we lost 5-1 just before we met them at Wembley. I don't think he played another game for us and, after those two experiences, you wouldn't have been surprised to have heard that he had a nervous breakdown. But, as everyone knows, it all turned out well and gave us some very special memories.

Reigning cup-holders Bolton Wanderers came to the City Ground for the quarter-final tie. It was an all-ticket game and 44,414 fans saw Tommy Wilson score for the Reds after only three minutes and add another goal just two minutes after half-time. Bolton were limited to a 62nd minute reply through winger Brian Birch. Bill Ridding, their manager, was generous in his post-match comments, anticipating continuing success: 'We could not wish to hand the Cup over to a better bunch of footballers and sportsmen. This was their day and I hope it's the same at Wembley.' Walker agreed that this was 'one of the most sporting games I have seen for many a long day'. Bolton, he added, 'were most chivalrous in defeat and made the match as near a classic as could well be'. He had special praise for full-backs Bill Whare and Joe McDonald for restricting crosses from the wings and for centre-half Bob McKinlay for keeping quiet the man the manager had identified as the main threat, England centre-forward Nat Lofthouse.

Nearly 66,000 paid £16,484 to watch the semi-final with Aston Villa at Hillsborough on 14 March. It was a special day for the Forest manager. In 1920 he had won the Cup with Aston Villa, his only Football League club as a player, and fifteen years later he had won it again as a manager with Wednesday. Now he was one step away from another final and, possibly, another Cup triumph. Walker had noted that this Villa side played a deep, defensive game. Forest would have to be patient. They were. And in the 65th minute were rewarded. Walker described it thus:

> Tommy Wilson crossed over to the left to take Jimmy Dugdale away from the middle, so letting in Johnny Quigley to take up a position around the centre. While Dugdale waited, Wilson slipped the ball across to Johnny, who quickly brought it down from his chest to his feet and, all in the same movement, hit it wide of Nigel Sim's right hand. It was a perfect goal taken by a lad who showed that he at least did not suffer from Cup nerves – and that after only eighteen months out of junior football.

There was overdue recognition in the press that 'Billy Walker has built a team of talented ball-players'. Earlier they had been referred to as 'Billy Walker's misfits, a team of reach-me-downs'. Walker admitted,

> I did not want any ready-made stars. You have only to look at the performances with Forest of the players I brought to Nottingham and against the background of what they had achieved in their previous clubs to realise that all they needed was proper organization in which they could find their true level. This we sought to find for them and in this, as the record shows, we succeeded. We know precisely what we want and even if we have to wait we will get it. We have so far – and I can see no reason for the supply of Forest type material ever to dry up. With this supply of experienced but unappreciated players from other clubs, and with the youngsters whom we are constantly finding and developing around our own doorstep – well, there'll always be a Forest!

First Division form dipped and Forest finished thirteenth, four places above Luton Town, who would be their Cup Final opponents. They had played an unchanged eleven throughout the Cup competition. In the league, however, Walker had been ready to give opportunities to other squad members. Three weeks before the final the Reds crashed 5-1 at Luton and the home side's Scottish international inside-forward Allan Brown scored four of them. He later managed both Luton and Forest.

The 'rehearsal' defeat might have been seen as a good omen. Before beating Derby County to win the Cup in 1898, Forest had lost 5-0 in a league game at the Baseball Ground. During Cup Final week Forest set up training headquarters at Hendon. Walker announced a line-up unchanged from the previous rounds: Thomson, Whare, McDonald, Whitefoot, McKinlay, Burkitt, Dwight, Quigley, Wilson, Gray and Imlach. Luton were also able to name a first-choice team: Baynham, McNally, Hawkes, Groves, Owen, Pacey, Bingham, Brown, Morton, Cummins and Gregory. Syd Owen, Burkitt's opposite number as captain, was chosen as Footballer of the Year by the Football Writers' Association.

Bryon Butler, who went on to become BBC Radio's football correspondent for twenty-three years and write the official histories of the Football League and the Football Association, was then covering Forest for the *Nottingham Evening News*. He interviewed Billy Walker for a souvenir supplement published in the paper a few days before the final. This is what the Forest manager told him:

> My football is the short ball game where an attack can stem from the goalkeeper and progress right through all departments by means of accurately placed passes. I like to see all players in possession moving forward and others moving into position. And I don't like to see the ball stopped before it is in the net. The greatest defences in the world are powerless to stop a team moving with this purpose.

There you have it, on record, fifty years before Pep Guardiola at Barcelona, Billy Walker was expounding the tiki-taka ethos on Trentside.

And so to Wembley.

13

Clough's Champions

Forest had scraped into the First Division in 1977 and were not expected to stay there for more than a season. Pundits had learned little from the exploits of Sir Alf Ramsey's equally unfancied Ipswich side who, in 1962, had become the first in Football League history to win the championship in their initial season in Division One. Ramsey's side began to be taken more seriously after they had thrashed likely title challengers Burnley 6-2 at Portman Road. This was reminiscent of Billy Walker's Reds 7-0 mauling of another highly rated Burnley side in September 1957, soon after their promotion – especially as both Ipswich and Forest had been beaten at Turf Moor shortly before their victories.

Ramsey did not go on a spending spree to prepare for the First Division but bought only one player – inside-forward Dougie Moran for £12,000 from Falkirk. Clough had complained about a lack of support from the Nottingham public but Ipswich had attendances below 15,000. Forest's summer signing was a surprise – £150,000 for Scottish striker Kenny Burns, who came with a fiery reputation from Birmingham. He had just scored twenty goals playing alongside Trevor Francis so eyebrows were raised even higher when it was learned Taylor wanted him as a centre-back. In the first practice match, Clough said to his latest recruit, 'Go and play with the big lad at the back.' And that is how the fearsome, formidable Lloyd–Burns partnership was formed. Taylor saw Burns developing into a Scottish Bobby Moore, just as commanding and more ruthless. Like Colin Todd had been with Roy McFarland at Derby, he proved to be a first-rate defender who was composed and capable with the ball.

Clough and Taylor signed three-year extensions to their original four-year contracts and took the squad off for a pre-season tour in

Switzerland, Austria and West Germany, winning all five games with a combined score of 18-4. Not every game proved friendly. In the second match Austrian champions Wacker Innsbruck, fired up by a boisterous 7,000 crowd, made some rough-house challenges and from one of them Peter Withe got an elbow in the face that broke his nose. To add insult to injury, he was sent off for retaliation. Then he was packed off home for treatment and played no further part in the tour. Even so, Forest won 2-0 with goals by Woodcock and Robertson against a side who went on to reach the quarter-finals of the European Cup. The Austrians knocked out FC Basel and Glasgow Celtic before losing on away goals to Borussia Mönchengladbach.

Coincidences abound in football and, fittingly, Forest's first match back in Division One was at Goodison Park, where on 3 September 1892, they played for the first time in the Football League and helped Everton open their new ground with a 2-2 draw. It was also where the Reds had played their last top-flight game before relegation at the end of the 1971/72 campaign – another draw, this time 1-1. There were 38,000 at Goodison on 20 August 1977, when the team, nervously awaiting a new season in elevated company, was captained by John McGovern, Cloughie's field marshal now restored to his favoured midfield position, and included goalkeeper John Middleton, full-backs Viv Anderson and Frank Clark, centre-backs Larry Lloyd and Kenny Burns, Ian Bowyer in midfield, Martin O'Neill and John Robertson on flanks with strikers Peter Withe and Tony Woodcock. Peter Taylor was telling jokes and anecdotes to relax the players when there was a knock on the dressing room door and former Liverpool manager Bill Shankly made his entrance. Clough welcomed him with the request, 'You give the team talk.' McGovern recalls Shankly telling them to think of the season as 'a marathon, not a sprint'. The bell rang and the team ran out into the August sunshine boosted by the words of Clough, Taylor and the great Shanks.

In the match programme, Everton captain Mike Lyons made a percipient observation regarding prospective title challengers. 'The promoted teams are worth keeping an eye on this time. We will be seeing Nottingham Forest today so there will be first-hand evidence for my hunch that they could be the surprise team of the season.' And the home supporters were shocked when Withe, still recovering from his broken nose, scored with a close-range header from a corner and then Robertson drove in a second off the inside of the post. Centre-forward Jim Pearson pulled one back shortly before half-time, perhaps against the run of play but, with thirteen minutes left, O'Neill hammered home a close-range effort to complete the victory. Duncan McKenzie, then Everton's number 10, said he couldn't believe how composed Forest were that afternoon. Clough, however, kept their feet on the ground, even criticising his captain for trying a couple of shots. 'Give it to someone who can shoot or you're out of the side,' McGovern was told.

However, the national press gave the Reds effusive praise. The *Sunday People* made McGovern man of the match with a nine-points-out-of-ten performance. The *Sun* chose John Robertson while the *News of the World* considered Tony Woodcock as the outstanding performer. The *People's* Stan Liversedge wrote that 'Forest marked their return to Division One by playing it coolly, simply brushing the ball from one red-shirted man to another'. The *Daily Mail* said Clough's players spoke volumes for him on the pitch. The *Daily Mirror* warned that Everton were Woodcock's first victims and he and Forest were going places. Mike Ellis of the *Sun* summed it up: 'It's good to have them back.'

Forest's first home league match was against Bristol City on the 23 August, when the attendance of 21,743 disappointed but may have been due in part to an increase in season ticket prices that some supporters thought excessive. They were £42 for main stand seats and £30 for the East Stand. A young lady from Gedling wrote to the club to say she and her fiancé hoped to marry soon and would not be able to afford £60 to watch football. A Hucknall man also complained that the higher prices might actually reduce revenue for the club. With just eight minutes to go, Peter Withe rose to head home the only goal from a Robertson cross.

Four days later Derby County visited the City Ground for the first time since 1971. Nearly 29,000 fans and ATV's Soccer Special cameras came, too. John Robertson caused panic in the visitors' defence right from the kick-off but the opening goal came from the other flank. Viv Anderson won the ball and sent Martin O'Neill away to force a corner. Tony Woodcock whipped it in with his left foot and when the ball came off Larry Lloyd there was Withe to volley into the top corner despite the close attention of Roy McFarland. Robertson continued to run things in the second half and his long pass enabled Woodcock to race past two Derby defenders and lay off the ball for Withe to score his second. Then, with twelve minutes left, Robertson crowned a virtuoso performance with Forest's third. Television commentator Hugh Johns enthused, 'That was some of the most electrifying football I've seen in a long time.' With just three games gone, Forest were the only team in the division with a 100 per cent record.

Withe scored in his fourth successive game as Forest crushed West Ham United 5-0 in a League Cup tie at the City Ground but the winning run came to an abrupt end at Highbury, where Arsenal won 3-0 and Frank Clark suffered a hamstring injury that kept him out of the side for six months. On the other hand, it allowed Colin Barrett to return to the first team as a converted left-back and he soon made himself at home. What annoyed Clough more than the defeat, however, was indiscipline in the defence where both Lloyd and Burns were involved in off-the-ball incidents that were missed by the referee but they were punished by club fines. The next game at Molineux was the first Clark had missed for two years but goals by Withe, Bowyer and Woodcock got Forest back on course with a 3-2 defeat of Wolves.

Clough was still not satisfied and in the space of a fortnight signed England goalkeeper Peter Shilton from relegated Stoke for £270,000 and Scotland midfielder thirty-year-old Archie Gemmill, an old favourite, from Derby for £20,000 plus John Middleton. Now he and Taylor had got the squad they wanted. And they started to attract better crowds to the City Ground. There were 31,000 for Shilton's debut on 17 September, when Aston Villa were beaten 2-0, and nearly 27,000 saw the Reds go two points clear at the top, never to be dislodged, with a 4-0 drubbing of Ipswich, Withe scoring them all and so becoming the first Forest player to hit four goals in a game since Knocker West in 1907.

The television cameras returned to the City Ground for the visit of second-placed Manchester City on 15 October when 35,572 were also drawn to the banks of the Trent as well as the BBC's *Match of the Day* programme. Neither the Nottingham nor the nationwide audience were disappointed as the game ebbed and flowed. Brian Kidd struck home a loose ball from a corner kick to give the visitors the lead after twenty-one minutes. Then Robertson twisted and turned past three defenders to set up Woodcock to side-foot the equaliser twelve minutes later. Withe placed the ball under goalkeeper Joe Corrigan for a late winner.

There were still observers yet to be convinced by Clough's side. Just a week later after Forest's 2-0 defeat of Queen's Park Rangers in London, former Arsenal goalkeeper Bob Wilson, reporting for *Grandstand* on the BBC, boldly declared, 'Nottingham Forest were lucky to get all the points and although they are now favourites to win the title, I think their bubble will burst.' Clough's response was, 'He's put himself up there to be shot at – and I'm doing the shooting.'

Then the FA upset the applecart. Don Revie had resigned as England manager during the summer and Ron Greenwood had assumed temporary charge. On 5 November Forest were beaten 1-0 by Chelsea at Stamford Bridge but the downer for supporters was the announcement by club chairman Brian Appleby that he had given permission for the FA to approach Brian Clough. The fans pleaded with him to stay. Earlier in the season, Clough had campaigned against foul-mouthed chanting with a poster requesting, 'Gentlemen no swearing please! – Brian.' Now the supporters' response was, 'Brian no leaving please! – The Gentlemen.' Not to be outdone, Clough promptly replied that if they wanted him to stay they should back him. The club sold £3,000 of additional season tickets the following week.

In December candidates to take the England job permanently were interviewed and they included Jack Charlton and Dave Sexton as well as Greenwood and Clough. FA secretary Ted Croker, a former Charlton player, wrote, 'Diplomacy is a quality that is required (of an England manager) and that has not figured too highly with Brian Clough.' Greenwood, then general manager of West Ham and seen as the safe option, got the post. Clough reluctantly accepted the role of youth team manager but never took it seriously. Taylor said the highlight of that job was a free day on the beach at Las Palmas after an international youth tournament.

With the manager settled again, Forest lost Larry Lloyd to a broken toe in the game at home to his former club, Coventry, and learned that he would be out of action for ten weeks. Former Notts County centre-half David Needham was signed from Queen's Park Rangers for £150,000 as a replacement. He made his debut at Old Trafford on 17 December in what many people saw as the defining performance of Forest's season, the 4-0 drubbing of Manchester United in front of a crowd of 54,374. In their yellow away strip, Forest captured the imagination with flowing, one-touch football that swept a full-strength United away and, as *Match of the Day* commentator Barry Davies remarked, made them 'look pedestrian'. Woodcock's shot was deflected in off the post and the body of defender Brian Greenhoff for an own goal to put Forest in front and he thumped home another in front of the Stretford End before half-time. After the break, Archie Gemmill's non-stop running opened up the United defence for first Robertson and then Woodcock to finish off the game with the home seats emptying. 'They don't play with eleven men,' said the bewildered United manager Dave Sexton. 'When they attack, about seven of them come at you and when they are defending, there are about nine of them.'

Paul Fitzpatrick of the *Guardian* wrote, 'There has been a widely held feeling that Forest's success so far has been slightly phoney, based on doubtful virtues that would eventually be exposed. But there was nothing false about Forest.' In *The Times*, Tom German enthused, 'Robertson and O'Neill gave Manchester a roasting on the flanks while Woodcock and Withe were so shrewdly mobile they fooled the central defenders in so many directions that, by the end, they were as bemused as the man in the middle of some particularly impish game of blind man's bluff.' Forest's quality was emphasised just over a week later when, on Boxing Day, Manchester United beat second-placed Everton 6-2.

The big games were coming thick and fast and on 21 January Arsenal, victors at Highbury at the beginning of September, found themselves on a City Ground pitch that was inches deep in mud. Needham headed in a Woodcock corner after half an hour and relentless pressing had the visitors reeling. Midway through the second half, the crowd of 35,743 saw one of the goals of the season. Archie Gemmill intercepted a Liam Brady pass just outside the Forest penalty area and played the ball wide to Withe, who took the ball forward as a diagonal run by Woodcock drew central defender Sammy Nelson out of position. Gemmill had not stopped running, ploughing through the mud to slide Withe's cross past goalkeeper Pat Jennings. It was almost but not quite as good as Archie's famous World Cup goal for Scotland against the Netherlands in Argentina, which was celebrated in the Ewan McGregor film *Trainspotting*. The 'wee man' took the ball into the Dutch penalty area, avoided a lunge by Wim Jansen, went outside Ruud Krol, pushed it between Jan Poortvliet's legs and lobbed it over goalkeeper Jan Jongbloed as he came out. McGregor's character in the movie has just made love and gasps, 'Christ, I haven't felt that good since Archie Gemmill scored against Holland in 1978!' Gemmill's comment on seeing the film was, 'To be fair, I was a bit embarrassed by it.'

Three days later, Forest beat Manchester City 2-1 in front of 38,509 at the City Ground to reach the fifth round of the FA Cup. Then Queen's Park Rangers were knocked out after a second replay. In the League Cup, Forest had beaten West Ham United 5-0, Notts County 4-0, Aston Villa 4-2 and Bury 3-0 to reach a two-leg semi-final with Leeds United. Some 10,000 Reds fans travelled to Elland Road and saw Peter Withe score twice with John O'Hare rifling a third in a comfortable 3-1 win. The second leg, played in front of another 38,000 crowd at the City Ground, was equally easy; Withe, Bowyer, O'Neill and Woodcock scored in a 4-2 victory. The biggest problem for Chris Woods, who had made his debut against Notts as a seventeen-year-old standing in for the cup-tied Shilton, was keeping his concentration during long periods when he saw little of the ball. Now the media, much of which had written off Forest's challenge before Christmas, began to discuss prospects of a treble. But the twenty-two-match unbeaten run came to an end with a 2-0 FA Cup quarter-final defeat by West Brom at the Hawthorns.

A week later, on 18 March, Forest made their first Wembley appearance since the 1959 FA Cup Final triumph and the club invited those players to be guests of honour for the League Cup Final against Liverpool. Barrett was out with a stress fracture of the leg and with McGovern struggling with a groin problem and having to be replaced by O'Hare midway through the second half, Forest were under the cosh. Woods, now aged eighteen years and 124 days but still the youngest goalkeeper ever to play in a Wembley final, showed no nerves and kept the scoreline goalless even after extra time. 'Chris may have been only a kid but he kept us in the game,' John Robertson commented. Clough and Taylor took the squad to Scarborough for a break before the replay at Old Trafford four days later.

Missing McGovern, Forest brought O'Hare into the starting line-up and Kenny Burns was made captain. They were in their yellow away kit instead of the red they wore at Wembley. Once again Woods was magnificent and was beaten only when Alan Kennedy got the ball in the net but had used his hand. Then Phil Thompson cynically tripped O'Hare, who would have been clean through with only goalkeeper Ray Clemence to beat. Under today's laws it would have been a red-card offence. Referee Pat Partridge awarded a penalty that Robertson coolly converted. The Liverpool players were furious and television pictures seemed to back up their claim that contact had been made just outside the box. Thompson, however, acknowledged that it had been 'a professional foul'. It was enough to give Forest their first major trophy of the season.

A goalless draw at Coventry secured the First Division championship with four games still to play. A City Ground crowd of 37,625 saw the championship trophy presented after another scoreless match, this time against Birmingham. And the season ended at Anfield with neither the Liverpool nor the Forest defence conceding. In the end of season awards, Kenny Burns was voted Footballer of the Year by the Football Writers' Association; the PFA chose Peter Shilton as their Player of the Year and Tony Woodcock was named Young Player of the Year. Brian Clough, of course, was Manager of the Year. Forest had won twenty-five and lost only three of their forty-two league games. They had scored sixty-nine goals against twenty-four and finished seven points clear of second-placed Liverpool, who had won the European Cup at Wembley. 'Forest will be our biggest threat to retaining it next season,' Bob Paisley, their manager, predicted.

14

Final Flourish

In their dressing room before the Cup Final, the Forest players were going through the usual rituals – Billy Gray taking a cold shower, Joe McDonald having a smoke in the washroom, Stewart Imlach cracking an egg into a glass of sherry before downing it – when in walked a suited committee man. Unassuming as Frank Chambers was, he was not really welcomed half an hour before kick-off even though he had brought a gift for each player – a pair of frilly knickers for their other halves. Frank, who normally kept in the background being shy of personal publicity, was a lingerie manufacturer and the knickers had been specially made at his factory in Forest colours and with lace rosettes on the sides. 'It was madness but it broke the tension,' said Chic Thomson. 'I've never seen players so relaxed before a big game.'

Ten minutes had not passed when Forest, playing flowing, accurate, passing football, took the lead with five-man move. Left-back Joe McDonald headed a long kick by the Luton goalkeeper infield to wing-half Jeff Whitefoot who played the ball on the bounce for inside-left Billy Gray to glance it on with a flick of his head into the path of left-winger Stewart Imlach. Five defenders tracked back but Imlach cut them all out with a cross pulled back for Roy Dwight, racing in to strike the ball first time with his left foot and send it crashing into the roof of the net. Five minutes later, skipper Jack Burkitt stroked the ball to Imlach who found Gray on the flank. Gray dummied inside, stepped back, and lofted the ball for Tommy Wilson, whose bulging neck muscles showed the power of his header into the net – a header to equal the fabled 'Lawton's Leap'.

It was all Forest until the 32nd minute when the dreaded Wembley injury hoodoo, which to a lesser degree had affected Arsenal full-back Wally Barnes, Bolton wing-half Eric Bell, Leicester defender Len Chalmers, Manchester City's full-back Jimmy Meadows and goalkeepers Bert Trautmann of City and Ray Wood of Manchester United, removed Roy Dwight from the fray and into hospital. Astonished patients had gathered in their dressing gowns on chairs in front of a television set had seen him carried off the field on a stretcher. Now they saw him brought into their ward unbooted but otherwise still in his full kit, lifted into a bed with a cage to keep the blankets off his right leg and settling down to watch the second half with them. With Jack Burkitt struggling with a dislocated shoulder but still inspirational, the exhausted, depleted Reds conceded a 62nd-minute goal. Flagging but still fighting, they found the energy to hang on for a Wembley triumph never equalled, first for grace and elegance and then for determination and endeavour.

It was estimated that 200,000 people saw the Cup come home to Nottingham after sixty-one years. A bedecked open-top coach took the players and committee from the Midland Station on a route encircling the city centre past Chapel Bar and into Angel Row to the Old Market Square. There the players disembarked and led by Jack Burkitt, carrying the FA Cup, walked slowly down the Processional Way to the steps of the imposing Council House. Roy Dwight was with them in a wheelchair, having gained his release from hospital to join in the celebrations. In appreciation an iced cake in the shape of Wembley Stadium was sent by the club to the nurses who had looked after him.

The Cup-winning team was never to play again. Dwight took nearly a year to recover from his injury and, although he scored on his return to the side in a 1-1 draw with Preston at the City Ground at the end of March 1960, he played just two more games for the club. Stewart Imlach made his last appearance at the same time in early April and Tommy Wilson bade his farewell to the City Ground against Newcastle United in September 1960, after manager Walker had moved 'upstairs'. Jim Barrett, put out of Cup reckoning by injury, returned for the end-of-season tour of Portugal and Spain. He scored his last Forest goals at Valencia in front of a crowd of 75,000 and Atletico Madrid, taking him to a total of sixty-nine in 117 appearances during five seasons in the Garibaldi.

Johnny Quigley was determined, industrious and a typical wee Scottish ba' player. He stood just 5 feet 8 inches tall and weighed 11 stone but with the ball at his feet he could withstand the challenges of the heftiest of opponents and surprise them in turn with the ferocity of his tackling. He had the toughness that seemingly comes from being born in the working-class district of Govan, a couple of miles west of Glasgow's city centre on the south bank of the Clyde, once the centre of the Clydeside shipbuilding industry. Other Govanites include Sir Alex Ferguson and Kenny Dalglish.

Johnny was spotted by Billy Walker, who was on a scouting mission north of the border in mid-August 1957. Quigley had begun his career as a 'provisional' signing by Glasgow Celtic, who farmed him out to local Scottish junior club St Anthony's. Celtic didn't retain their interest in him so he joined non-league Ashfield. Walker watched Ashfield against Linlithgow and was so impressed he immediately signed the twenty-two-year-old. The Scot's impact at the City Ground was similar to that of Irishman Roy Keane, who was signed by Brian Clough in the close season of 1990 and given his debut against Liverpool at the end of August. Quigley scored two goals for the Reds' first team against an All Stars XI in a testimonial match for trainer Tommy Graham at the City Ground on 23 September and made his First Division debut at White Hart Lane at the beginning of October, scoring again in a 4-1 victory. A week later he played in the classic match against Manchester United's Busby Babes.

Quigley went on to make twenty-one Division One appearances in his first season, with three goals, and played three FA Cup games, scoring once. He was a key player in the 1958/59 FA Cup-winning season, scoring twelve goals in thirty-nine First Division appearances and appearing in all nine FA Cup games, including the replays. He scored just once in the Cup but what a crucial goal it was, coming in the semi-final and taking Forest through to Wembley. In the same season, he had become the first Forest player to score a post-war hat-trick with goals in the 57th, 74th and 81st minutes in the 4-0 defeat of Manchester City. After six years as a first-team regular, he lost his place to John Barnwell, newly arrived from Arsenal, and in February 1965 he was transferred to Huddersfield Town. From there he joined Bristol City in October 1966, and later became captain of the Ashton Gate club. Johnny also skippered Mansfield Town, whom he joined for £3,000 in 1968. He converted from inside-forward to wing-half, though in truth it wasn't much of a change since in modern terms he had always been an attacking midfielder.

In 1969, Quigley was in the Mansfield team that beat a West Ham United side, including several of England's World Cup winners, 3-0 to progress to the quarter-finals of the FA Cup before losing to Leicester City. He made over 470 Football League appearances for his four clubs, including 236 games with fifty-one goals for Forest. After being assistant manager at Mansfield, he had a spell coaching Doncaster Rovers before going to the Middle East to coach in Kuwait and Saudi

Arabia for five years. Johnny died in Nottingham on 30 November 2004, aged sixty-nine.

Quigley was a typical Walker player, but how did the team view their manager? He was 'a likeable rogue', the Govan man told Gary Imlach, Stewart's son, in an interview for the award-winning book *My Father and Other Working-Class Football Heroes*. Quigley added, 'He wouldna gi' you too much, man.' The quote comes in a chapter about the Forest players' pool, set up before the final to make a little extra cash from their appearance at Wembley, as all teams did. They posed in their kit with the dray horses of the local brewery, Shipstones, opened fetes and held a pre-final dance. Billy Walker had offered to act as the players' agent and seek commercial opportunities. The players turned him down. 'Nobody now can remember how much money the players' pool generated,' wrote Gary Imlach. 'Whatever the sum, Billy Walker had been denied his agent's commission.'

Did the manager want his cut of whatever was going? Possibly, he was careful with money. This is his autobiographical reflection:

> Football is more than a game to me. It is more than a profession. It is a way of life. I played football because I had an inner compulsion to do so. Nothing else mattered. Fame, fortune – I never considered these. It was the game that mattered. Anything I have now has not been derived directly from football. When I was starting out, my grandfather said to me: 'Will, when you get a bit of money put it into bricks and mortar.' I did what he told me.

And that was advice he passed on to his players. Perhaps the pool would have been larger with agent Walker.

A journalist and TV sports presenter, Gary Imlach was rightly praised for a heartfelt and hard-hitting account. But there are two sides to every story. Here's Walker's version:

> I've never been one to see the odd bawbee go by but I have never allowed the business of securing the future of myself and my family to interfere with my obligations both to my team and to myself. Now Nottingham is a comparatively compact city. Everywhere our players moved in the Cup-mad town they were pleaded with, cajoled and pestered. Our form began to suffer. Our old smooth rhythm went and defeat followed defeat.

After being beaten by 'an ordinary Chelsea side', Walker told his players that the 'perks' had got to stop. 'I told them this without bluster, for that is not my way, but as man-to-man. Soccer was no longer to be a side interest.'

Gary Imlach felt his father had been badly treated when he was transferred to Luton, especially as the *Evening Post* seemed to have been told about the deal before the player. He is understandably critical of Forest's manager but the record shows that his father was at his peak in Nottingham with the freedom to express himself that Walker gave him. And he was at his happiest, as Gary Imlach acknowledges. Stewart, a Derby discard, won two promotions, a Cup-winners' medal and four international caps during his five years at the City Ground. He scored forty-three goals in 147 games for Forest, including five in eighteen cup ties; he was jeered by Rams supporters but cheered by the Trent-enders. His career dipped at Luton, Coventry, Crystal Palace and non-league Dover and Chelmsford but he later coached Notts County, when Billy Gray was manager there, as well as Everton, Blackpool and Bury.

With Billy Walker's health failing, 1959/60 was a season of decline. His heaviest defeat was 8-0 at Burnley, yet a week later Leeds United were beaten 4-1 at the City Ground. The Reds reached the fourth round of the Cup but were then beaten 3-0 by Sheffield United at Bramall Lane. Tommy Wilson then scored in six successive games, which brought two wins, two draws and two defeats, but they were still battling against relegation until the penultimate Saturday, when Newcastle United were beaten 3-0 at the City Ground. The last match at Leeds on 30 April was Walker's final league match as manager. His team was Thomson, Patrick, McDonald, Whitefoot, McKinlay, Burkitt, Barton, Quigley, Iley, Younger and Gray. Roy Patrick, signed from Derby in August, was the only change from the Cup Final defence – replacing Bill Whare – with Quigley and Gray still in the forward line. Forest lost the game 1-0 but it was Leeds who were relegated along with Luton Town.

Relegation having been narrowly avoided, Billy Walker retired after twenty-one years as manager and accepted an invitation to join the committee. Forest, on Walker's recommendation, appointed former Scotland and Preston North End full-back Andy Beattie as his successor. Beattie had guested for the Reds during the war and had been manager of Stockport when they knocked Forest out of the FA Cup in the second-round match at the City Ground in December 1949. The Walker era ended with his death on 28 November 1964, four years after his resignation as a manager and elevation to the committee. Fittingly, it coincided with a victory, Forest winning by two goals to nil at Blackpool.

A captain of Aston Villa and England, Walker consulted European coaches as a manager and kept up to date with their techniques. A professorial leader long before Arsène Wenger at Arsenal, he saw it as his responsibility to encourage and develop young players and, along with stability, two promotions and an FA Cup triumph. This was his legacy to Forest and his successors. He was a teacher who let his players express themselves and he was a listener, willing to take on board the advice of senior professionals. All of this made his Reds one of the most attractive teams in the country.

15

Conquering Europe

League champions Forest went to Wembley on 12 August 1978, for the traditional season's curtain-raiser against the FA Cup winners for the Charity Shield. Bobby Robson's Ipswich team had beaten Arsenal 1-0 in the Cup Final but they proved no match for the Reds, who swept them aside 5-0. John Robertson had tormented the Ipswich defence all afternoon and deservedly completed the scoring in the last minute. Martin O'Neill scored twice, Larry Lloyd volleyed another and Peter Withe headed what was to prove his last goal for Forest.

The team had the distraction of a four-team tournament in Spain in the week before the opening match of the First Division season and lost Lloyd to a leg injury that kept him out of four league and two League Cup games. Visitors Tottenham Hotspur were welcomed by a 41,223 opening-day crowd at the City Ground and included their two new Argentinian signings, Ossie Ardiles and Ricardo Villa. Forest took a first-half lead through Martin O'Neill and Withe hit the bar but Ricky Villa equalised and they had to be content with a point. Steel fences had been erected to prevent fans invading the pitch but, sadly, did not prevent fighting after the game. There had always been a sense that such incidents were not part of the Nottingham football scene.

After the match, news broke of a transfer request by Peter Withe, who had not been able to agree a new contract. Newcastle United manager Bill McGarry, who had worked with the player at Wolves in the mid-1970s, made a £250,000 bid that was accepted. The break-up of a prolific Withe-Woodcock partnership was hailed by Clough as 'good business'. The club had made a profit of more than £200,000 with the deal, he pointed out. The problem was that he had only the untried Steve Elliott and Garry Birtles as replacements. Elliott played seven games without scoring before Birtles got his chance. He came into the side in a 2-1 home win over Arsenal on 9 September, when Gary Mills, on as a substitute, became Forest's youngest-ever player in the Football League at sixteen years 302 days. Clough told Birtles he would play against Liverpool in the European Cup the following Wednesday. He hadn't scored but had held the ball up, taken the tackles, felt the pain and shown no fear. That was enough to impress his manager.

Before the draw for the first round, players had hoped for a European adventure with a trip to Spain or Italy and a game against Real Madrid or Juventus. The pairing with Liverpool was a bit of a downer. They'd travelled up the M1 on to the M62 and seen enough of Anfield in the past season, and knew they were loathed by the Scousers. Liverpool had been in terrific early form, trouncing Spurs 7-0 on Merseyside, and were seeking a third successive European Cup triumph. Once again Forest's chances were written off by the national press. But the first leg was at the City Ground.

'That September night will remain with me as one of the most amazing of my career,' Birtles recalled. It was a sultry, sunny evening and over 38,000 excited, noisy fans were crammed into the City Ground. And 'here I was in my third professional game contesting the giant trophy coveted from Milan to Madrid and Benifica to Barcelona.' It was about to get even better. The pace of the Forest attacks exposed weaknesses in a Liverpool defence famed for its tactical awareness and organization. Midway through the first-half, Kenny Burns brought the ball out of defence and chipped it over head of Graham Souness to Ian Bowyer whose flick-on found Tony Woodcock making a penetrating run and forcing goalkeeper Ray Clemence to come out to meet him. As Clemence closed in on him, he squared the ball for Birtles to tap it home in front of the Trent End with Phil Thompson on his heels. 'One goal won't be enough,' Thompson snarled at the elated Birtles.

With time ticking down, it looked as though this would have to do. Then came Colin Barrett's goal. The full-back charged down an attempted pass by Jimmy Case on the halfway line. The ball fell to Phil Neal and his clearance was blocked by the onrushing Barrett. Rebounding into the Liverpool half, the loose ball was collected by Birtles who evaded Case, skipped past Thompson and crossed to the far post where Woodcock nodded it back across the box to Barrett, who had kept running all the way from the Forest half, and he shrugged off the attentions of Emlyn Hughes to volley home an unstoppable drive. After a split-second' of stunned silence, the ground erupted for a second time that night. It was arguably the most important goal in Forest's history, enabling the side to go to Anfield with a two-goal cushion without which their European odyssey may never have begun.

'I'd surely have been fined if I hadn't scored,' reflected Barrett. 'I'm told Peter Taylor was going mad in the dugout, wanting to know what I was doing up there and yelling at me to get back. I think it's likely a fine was on its way.' His full-back partner Viv Anderson commented, 'If you analyse it, it was a phenomenal goal from start to finish. Colin broke up an attack on the halfway line and went on a run that ended with him putting the ball in the net from inside the box. Fantastic.' John Robertson, in his autobiography *Super Tramp*, said, 'It was such a massive goal in our history and without it I often wondered if we would have gone on to achieve the success we did.' Unlucky Barrett suffered a serious knee injury in a home draw with Middlesbrough four days before the second leg that would very soon cut short his playing career. 'It was a tragedy for him and us because there was no doubt he would have been an integral part of our side for years to come,' said Robertson. 'He was playing out of his skin at the time and the gaffer loved him.'

Overtaking Phil Thompson on the way back to the centre circle, Garry Birtles had shouted to him, 'Will two-nil be enough then?' It was. Even though before the second leg, in a poll of the twenty First Division managers only three – John Neal of Middlesbrough, Bristol City's Alan Dicks and Chelsea's Ken Shellito – believed Forest would hold on at Anfield. Clough, who scoffed at talking tactics, nevertheless tweaked things a little. Archie Gemmill was employed on the right flank with responsibility for helping Anderson deal with the forward runs of Liverpool left-back Alan Kennedy and John McGovern was posted in front of Lloyd and Burns as cover for the back four. It worked. Liverpool were stymied. The game was goalless and Forest had a 2-0 winning aggregate. David Lacey in the *Guardian* wrote that Forest played 'precisely the type of tight, containing game with which the European Cup winners of the past two years had frustrated so many opponents away from home'.

Forest were now engaged on four fronts: defending their championship title, retaining the League Cup, and contesting the FA Cup and the European Cup. Peter Taylor made no bones about his priority: victory in Europe. In the League Cup, the Reds had been held to a goalless draw at Oldham but won the replay 4-2. Then, a week after progressing in Europe, Birtles, McGovern, O'Neill, Robertson and Anderson scored as they reached round four with a 5-0 defeat of Oxford United that was watched by only 14,287 at the City Ground. Birtles got a brace and O'Neill scored again as Wolves were beaten 3-1 in the First Division and the crowds returned to Trentside with more than 29,000 fans present. Forest had set a new league record with thirty-five games unbeaten.

Bristol City were overcome by the same scoreline at Ashton Gate before the European journey was resumed in Greece.

Forest were paired with AEK Athens with whom they had drawn 1-1 during a pre-season tour. AEK were managed by Ferenc Puskas, the Hungarian international with a legendary left foot who had starred in the European Cup alongside Alfredo Di Stefano in the great Real Madrid side. A hostile Athenian crowd greeted Forest at the first leg on 18 October but they were subdued by a John McGovern goal, scrambled in with only eleven minutes gone after a quick free-kick from Frank Clark to Robertson led to a cross flicked on by Birtles at the near post. Clark was involved again just before half-time, when his well-timed run from deep in the Forest half beat the offside trap, freeing him to take Robertson's pass and put Birtles through to finish off the move. AEK played the last seventy minutes with ten men after Uruguayan Milton Viera was sent off for rashly planting a left hook on Burns' jaw. They pulled a goal back from the penalty spot after a foul by Burns, who had been booked and was suspended for the second leg.

Puskas was given a warm welcome from a 38,000 crowd at the City Ground as he took his seat in the directors' box for the second leg on 1 November. Needham came into the Forest side for Burns and John O'Hare replaced the injured McGovern. Lloyd, who had survived a row with Clough after refusing to wear a club blazer in Athens, was made captain and young Mills got a taste of European football when he came on as substitute for the injured Clark. Needham opened the scoring with a diving header from Gemmill's cross after thirteen minutes and it was then all Forest. More good work by Gemmill led to Woodcock heading in a perfect cross from Robertson in the 37th minute and Viv Anderson struck a 25-yarder right-footed into the top corner of the net only two minutes later. Two goals by Birtles in the space of six minutes underlined the Reds' superiority and they ran out 5-1 winners on the night and 7-2 on aggregate. 'I cannot think of any team capable of stopping them,' Puskas commented. 'Are you crying, Liverpool?' sang the Trent End.

Victory at Bolton on 25 November took Forest's unbeaten run in the First Division to a league record forty-two games and Robertson, who scored the only goal, had played in every one of them. Goalkeeper Peter Shilton was the only other player to achieve that. The run was made up of an equal number of wins and draws and the fact that Forest scored just fifty-eight goals in those forty-two matches confirms that Shilton and his defensive colleagues were supreme. It was at Anfield on 9 December that the run came to an end with a 2-0 defeat, Terry McDermott scoring both goals – one of them a penalty. Burns had torn his cartilage in a 3-2 League Cup victory over Everton at Goodison, McGovern was still injured, O'Neill was ruled out and Woodcock missed the game after returning from international duty with a badly gashed ankle. It was a huge win for Liverpool, who had not beaten Forest in the six matches they had played since Clough's side gained promotion – two in the First Division, two in the final of the League Cup and two in the first round of the European Cup.

The unbeaten record was previously held by Leeds, who had gone thirty-four games without loss, and Arsène Wenger's 'Invincibles' later surpassed Forest's achievement with Arsenal going forty-nine Premier League games undefeated.

During the international break, Viv Anderson had become the first black player to represent England. He was in the side against Czechoslovakia along with Woodcock and Shilton.

Forest bounced back with a 3-1 League Cup fifth-round victory over Brighton at the City Ground and then beat Aston Villa 2-0 in the third round of the FA Cup at Villa Park. January was a good month in cup competitions with the defeat of York City to reach the FA Cup fifth round and a 3-1 aggregate win over Third Division Watford in the two-leg League Cup semi-final. Graham Taylor's emerging side had beaten Newcastle and Manchester United along the way.

There was managerial uncertainty once again when Clough was linked with the Sunderland job after the departure of Jimmy Adamson for Leeds. But instead of moving to the north-east, he made transfer history and signed Trevor Francis from Birmingham City – Britain's first £1 million player. The previous record fee had been £516,000, paid by West Bromwich Albion to Middlesbrough for David Mills. If Clough was unhappy about having to pay a million, he was equally upset by Francis's obligation to play for American side Detroit Express for a summer season and he stuck the England international in the third team in a Saturday morning game for his Forest debut. It was afterwards found that the player's registration had not been completed and the club had to pay a £250 fine to the Football Association. Francis was ineligible for the FA and League Cup competitions and could only play in the European Cup if the Reds reached the final.

Arsenal were proving a 'bogey' side for Forest and, with Francis on the sidelines, they went out of the FA Cup to a Frank Stapleton goal at the City Ground on 26 February. He'd scored four goals in five games against Forest since their promotion and Arsenal had won three of them. Francis finally made his first-team debut in a 1-1 draw at Ipswich on 3 March, when Birtles scored. Four days later, Forest were again in European Cup action at the City Ground against Grasshoppers, the Swiss champions, who had put out Real Madrid on away goals in the previous round.

Twenty-three-year-old Claudio Sulser, who had scored nine goals in the previous four European games, was the danger man and he made his presence felt after just ten minutes, holding off two challenges to clip the ball past Shilton. McGovern had an effort cleared off the line before Woodcock found Birtles inside the box for the equaliser. In the second-half a handball by a defender stopped Birtles running on to another Woodcock flick and Robertson converted the penalty. Two goals in the closing minutes made the scoreline 4-1. First Gemmill stabbed home a cross from the right and then, from a third successive corner, Lloyd met Robertson's centre to score with a header at the near post.

Colin Barrett marked his comeback from injury with a great goal to earn a point at Everton. He lifted the ball over a defender's head, ran past him and crashed a fierce shot into the net. With Viv Anderson injured, Barrett deservedly kept his place at right-back for the League Cup Final against Southampton at Wembley on 17 March and then switched to left-back, replacing Frank Clark, for the second leg of the European Cup-tie with Grasshoppers in Zurich four days later. On the eve of the final, Clough and Taylor gathered the players together after dinner at their London hotel for a short team talk in the lounge, which became a late-night champagne party.

The League had previously refused Forest permission for both Clough and Taylor to lead the team out at Wembley, so without any discussion with officials it was Taylor, resplendent in his blue club blazer, who emerged from the tunnel at the head of the procession. There had been snowstorms during the week and although the pitch had been cleared and looked fine on the surface, it slowly deteriorated into cloying mud as the game progressed, a situation not helped by the fact that it was still recovering from a recent Horse of the Year show.

Perhaps it was a collective hangover from the night before, but Forest were, in John Robertson's words, 'terrible in the first half'. Southampton's Alan Ball dictated play and David Peach gave them a 16th-minute lead. Going in a goal down at half-time, Robertson said Clough greeted them with the warning, 'Right, you lot, don't go blaming this on last night.' And, according to McGovern, he added, 'How dare you underperform with your wives, girlfriends, relations and supporters in the stands.' The manager's instructions for the second half, Woodcock recalled, were simply, 'Get the ball and just pass it to another red shirt.' It was a Jekyll and Hyde performance. 'Without even thinking about it, we found our rhythm and played our natural game.'

Now the Reds were rampant. Birtles robbed centre-half Chris Nichol and shot high into the roof of the net for the equaliser. He found the net twice more but each time was denied by controversial offside decisions.

Then Barrett won the ball and passed to Woodcock, who found Birtles. The irrepressible striker tore through the Southampton defence to put Forest in front. Gemmill's pass put Woodcock in for the third goal. Nick Holmes scored a late consolation goal for Southampton but Forest won 3-2, beoming the first club to retain the League Cup. Clough had another dig at protocol by insisting that he and the Southampton manager Lawrie McMenemy should climb the thirty-nine steps to receive their medals with the players. Not even Alf Ramsey had done that as England World Cup-winning manager.

There was no time for celebrations. Brian Clough took the League Cup home with him and stuck it on the top of the television set while he watched and ate fish and chips. Confidence was sky-high as the Reds flew out to Switzerland for the European Cup third-round second leg. Grasshoppers needed to win 3-0, or better. After just four minutes, Sulser gave them the lead from the penalty spot after Viv Anderson had been harshly judged to have committed a foul as he challenged for a header. Forest secured the tie before half-time when, from close range, O'Neill bundled the ball in from a cross by Birtles. The game ended 1-1 and the Reds qualified with a 5-2 aggregate for the semi-final against Bundesliga champions Cologne, favourites after Liverpool's exit to win the trophy.

Meantime, in the league, Forest had the luxury of a five-star attack featuring O'Neill, Francis, Birtles, Woodcock and Robertson. They beat Coventry 3-0 and Chelsea 6-0 (O'Neill hitting a hat-trick) at the City Ground before Francis scored his first Forest goal in the last minute at Bolton to save a point. Aston Villa were beaten 4-0 at home and the 'double' was completed over Chelsea with a 3-1 win at Stamford Bridge (Francis scoring in both games) to give the Reds nine out of a possible ten points, scoring seventeen goals and conceding just two, in the three weeks between European engagements.

The first leg of the semi-final was at the City Ground on 11 April, but four days earlier, John Robertson suffered a terrible blow with the news that his brother, Hughie, had been killed in a car accident. Sensitively, Brian Clough told him to take all the time he needed and left the decision about playing entirely up to the player. The rest of his family convinced Robertson that he should play. 'I went into the match with all kinds of different emotions,' Robertson wrote in his book. 'Because of that I had a strange carefree attitude to it all. It was as if football wasn't all that important anymore and it took all the pressure of the occasion away from me.'

Cologne had been involved in European competition throughout the 1970s and made good use of their experience. They surprised Forest and the 40,804 crowd by taking the game to them and led 2-0 after only nineteen minutes with goals by Belgian international winger Roger Van Gool and German star Dieter Muller. Forest fought back and, after Bowyer had struck the bar with a looping shot from 18 yards, Needham knocked a Robertson cross back across the box for Birtles to head past goalkeeper Harald Schumacher into the top corner of the net. Just before half-time, Gemmill ruptured his groin and Clark came on to replace him, taking up the left-back position and allowing Bowyer to move forward into midfield. 'Bomber' had a happy knack of scoring important goals and when a Robertson chip was nodded down by Birtles, Bowyer was there to drive home the equaliser with a right-foot shot from 16 yards. Then Robertson stunned the Germans, the crowd and even himself with a diving header into the net. Forest were ahead until speedy Japanese winger Yasuhiko Okudera came off the bench to squeeze a shot under Shilton for 3-3. 'Forest sunk by Jap sub' screamed a national newspaper headline the next morning.

Once again, Forest's chances were being written off. Even Cologne, with three away goals, were so sure that they would reach the final that they printed a club European Cup Final brochure and booked tickets and buses in anticipation of going to Munich. 'This lot are in for the shock of their lives,' said Brian Clough. The first leg had been frantic, end-to-end football. In contrast, the second game, watched by 50,000 fans in the Müngersdorfer Stadium, had the tactical charge of a chess match. Barrett's knee had let him down again and he was in hospital when the team came out in an all-red strip bowl on a damp, cold and misty night. Anderson and Burns returned to bolster the defence and Clark was at left-back with Bowyer staying in midfield. With keeping a clean sheet imperative, Forest were content to allow the Germans to push forward and then counter-attack them. It was goalless on the hour and then, in the 65th minute, Birtles flicked on Robertson's corner at the near post and Bomber, the master goal poacher, stooped to conquer, heading the ball into the roof of the German net. It was all they needed.

Forest lost only one of their remaining seven First Division games, going down 1-0 to Wolves at Molineux. Three days after returning from Cologne, they had surrendered the championship title after a goalless draw with new champions Liverpool in front of a 41,898 crowd at the City Ground. Forest finished as runners-up, having lost only three times in the league for the second consecutive season.

Seven days before the European Cup Final, Lloyd, Francis and Robertson scored as the Reds beat Mansfield Town 3-1 to win the County Cup. Only 9,000 fans were at the City Ground to see it. However, there were 57,500 in the Olympic Stadium, Munich, on 30 May. Malmo, formed in 1910 and the first Swedish club to turn professional, were managed by their second English coach, Bobby Houghton, who later had a spell as number two to Dave Bassett at the City Ground. The first had been Roy Hodgson, the eventual England manager. Brian Clough and Peter Taylor went to watch Malmo before the final and took the opportunity have a good look at the cosmopolitan city that, incredibly, has 170 nationalities represented in its 300,000 population. Clough also took delight, and a psychological advantage, in beating Houghton at squash.

The Forest manager summed up Malmo as a team that gets results from its defensive strength: 'They place the same importance on clean sheets as we do,' he said. 'I think they have mastered the art of keeping things tight at the back and, in Munich, it might be a case of us trying to break them down.' As he predicted, the 1979 European Cup Final was not an adventurous game. Croydon-born Houghton, then only thirty-two and the youngest coach ever to reach the final, was a shrewd tactician who had masterminded victories over Bayern Munich, Inter Milan, Dynamo Kiev and, in the semi-final, stopped a prolific Austria Vienna from scoring over two legs. World Cup midfielder Herbert Prohaska warned, 'Our attackers could hardly get a glimpse of the ball against such a destructive side. Nottingham Forest will find it hard to break them down in Munich.'

Inevitably, it was John Robertson who unlocked the stubborn Malmo defence. 'We tried to mark him man for man but he needed only three or four yards to get the killer cross in,' Houghton reflected. And, inevitably, it was Trevor Francis, in his first-ever European game, who met the ball beyond the far post and headed home the only goal. 'I really thought we could win,' said Houghton. 'But Forest had so many good players in that team. If I had to pick just one for my team it would have to be John Robertson. Then they had Trevor Francis, Tony Woodcock and Garry Birtles. Their centre-backs, Lloyd and Burns, were very strong and, of course, there was Peter Shilton in goal.'

Nottingham remains the smallest city ever to provide European champions. And, remarkably, all eleven of the Malmo players came from the local region – another feat never repeated by any other finalist.

16

'Everyone a Hero'

A £2-million cantilever stand to seat 10,000 was being built at the City Ground as the 1979/80 season got underway and its funding would lead to the 200-member club becoming a limited company in April 1982. The structure towered over Trentside but only the lower tier was in use when Stoke City came for the first home match on 22 August. The attendance was just over 26,000 and O'Neill scored the only goal.

Frank Clark had told his teammates after Munich, 'it doesn't get any better than this'. And, in fact, the final proved to be his last game as a player – he left Nottingham to become assistant manager at Sunderland. With Barrett still struggling with injury, the need for a left-back was urgent and Forest paid Leeds £500,000 for Frank Gray. Archie Gemmill's was another notable departure. He left to join Birmingham City for £150,000. Peter Taylor said it was too good an offer to refuse for a thirty-two-year-old but Brian Clough later regretted letting the player go – especially after paying £500,000 to Manchester City for another Scottish international, Asa Hartford, but then offloading him to Everton for £400,000 after only three games, oddly all of them victories. Young goalkeeper Chris Woods, frustrated by the lack of opportunity as deputy to Peter Shilton, was allowed to join Queen's Park Rangers for £250,000 and Jim Montgomery, then thirty-five, was signed from Birmingham to replace him. Trevor Francis was tied to his summer contract in the United States with Detroit for the first couple of months.

The season marked the Silver Jubilee of the European Cup with holders Forest and league champions Liverpool representing England. Coincidentally, Oesters Vaxjo, who had succeeded to Malmo's Swedish league crown, were Forest's first European Cup opponents. Two goals in the last half-hour by Ian Bowyer gave the Reds victory in the home leg and a Tony Woodcock equaliser in Sweden assured progress to round two. Much to the surprise of most, Liverpool fell at the first hurdle to Dinamo Tbilisi. Forest were First Division leaders when they met Arges Pitesti in the first leg of the second round at the City Ground. Woodcock and Birtles gave them a two-goal advantage to take to Romania. Pitesti had come from behind to beat AEK Athens in the first round, winning 3-0 at home to overcome a two-goal deficit from the away leg. There was no comeback for them this time though as Bowyer and Birtles scored to give the Reds a 2-1 victory and a 4-1 winning aggregate.

A 5-2 win against Bolton Wanderers in front of a crowd 24,564 on 20 October was Forest's fiftieth successive undefeated league game at the City Ground. Lloyd, Woodcock, Francis, Anderson and Robertson (penalty) were the scorers. Then Francis got both goals in a 2-0 home win against Ipswich but the run came to an end with a shock 1-0 defeat by Alan Mullery's bottom-of-the-table Brighton. Gerry Ryan scored for the Seagulls after twelve minutes and just before half-time, goalkeeper Graham Moseley saved a John Robertson penalty. The result sparked a turnaround in fortunes for Albion who were pulling away from the relegation zone by Christmas.

Worse than the result so far as Forest fans were concerned was the news that it was Tony Woodcock's last game for the Reds and he was being transferred to Cologne for £650,000, a bargain for the Germans but the maximum fee allowed under European rules at the time. Woodcock remains one of the few Englishmen to have forged a successful career in Germany, scoring thirty-nine goals in 131 Bundesliga appearances over two spells with Cologne before finishing playing with Fortuna Cologne, where he later took over as manager.

A friendly in Cologne on 18 December was agreed by the two clubs as part of the Woodcock transaction and in the Forest side was a surprise replacement. Clough gambled on one of the game's cult characters by recruiting thirty-year-old Stan Bowles from Queen's Park Rangers for £225,000. Bowles made his First Division debut at Old Trafford, where Forest were beaten 3-0, but scored in his first home match, a 2-1 victory over Aston Villa on Boxing Day. He played nineteen First Division games for the Reds, scoring just one more goal. Next to arrive was former Arsenal star Charlie George, who had been on the manager's wanted list for a year but his club, Derby County, had refused to sell him to their East Midlands rivals. Instead George went to Southampton, much to Clough's fury, for £400,000. In January, however, the player came to the City Ground from the Saints on loan with a view to a permanent transfer.

The scene was set for the introduction of a brilliant ball-playing inside-forward partnership. In some respects it was reminiscent of Billy Walker's inspired pairing of former London favourites Doug Lishman (Arsenal) and Eddie Baily (ex-Spurs) in the successful 1956/57 campaign for promotion to the First Division – except Clough's initiative was doomed to disappoint. Bowles and George had the talent but not the stomach for the challenge. Clough's domineering style offended. They played together only three times yet both left with European Super Cup winners' medals.

A Manchester City apprentice, local boy Bowles showed early signs of a fiery temper when he upset coach Malcolm Allison and, after a series of off-the-field incidents, was released in 1970 with just seventeen first-team appearances. In two years he had three different clubs – Bury, Crewe Alexandra and Carlisle United. But his undoubted natural ability caught the eye of QPR and in September 1972 the Londoners bought him for £112,000 as a replacement for a previous Rangers' folk hero Rodney Marsh, who had been transferred, incidentally, to Manchester City. Bowles had no qualms taking over Marsh's No. 10 shirt. He spent just over seven years at Loftus Road and played a central role in arguably Rangers' greatest ever team, which finished as First Division runners-up in 1975/76 under Dave Sexton.

In 1979 he fell out with new manager Tommy Docherty. The Scot supposedly told Bowles, 'You can trust me, Stan.' To which the player allegedly replied, 'I'd rather trust my chickens with Colonel Sanders.' Docherty made Bowles train with the reserves, though still playing him in the first team for nearly six months before selling him to Clough. He remains a favourite with the Shepherd's Bush club's fans who, in 2004, voted him Rangers' all-time greatest player.

Bowles missed the home leg of the European Super Cup competition against Barcelona on 30 January, when George scored the winning goal; he did play in the second leg five days later when Burns scored after the Spaniards had taken the lead from the penalty spot. Forest might have won but Robertson missed a penalty in the second half after Bowles had been tripped. There was a crowd of 23,807 at the City Ground and 90,000 at Camp Nou. After playing in the City Ground leg of the European Cup third round against Dynamo Berlin, which Forest lost 1-0, Bowles missed the return match, apparently because of a fear of flying. Teenager Gary Mills deputised and the Reds won 3-1 with two goals from an outstanding Trevor Francis and a Robertson penalty. Bowles was back in the side when Forest beat Ajax 2-0 in the first semi-final at the City Ground on 9 April but Clough left him out for Mills in the Amsterdam leg, which was won 1-0 by the home side. His Forest career came to a controversial end when he went absent without leave and refused to play in the final against Hamburg in Madrid at the end of May.

Skipper McGovern recalls one occasion when Clough, in full flow, was interrupted by a cocky Stan, who told him, 'No Boss, you're wrong.' McGovern groaned. He knew what was coming. The player was subjected to a lengthy lecture on his past demeanours, his present weaknesses and how he must improve in the future. It was perhaps this incident that inspired the often-quoted Clough remark, 'We talk about it for twenty minutes and then we decide I was right.' On Clough, Bowles commented:

> He couldn't coach. Him and Peter Taylor just used to walk their dogs down by the Trent, where we trained in the park. Jimmy Gordon, a little Scots fella, he took the training. Cloughie must have had something but I haven't a clue what it was. I never saw it. I liked Peter Taylor. He was a gambler like me. We could relate.

Charlie George, still idolised by the Arsenal fans, was a key player in the 1970/71 double-winning team, scoring a superb goal in the FA Cup Final victory over Liverpool. He had three decent seasons at the Baseball Ground and memorably scored a hat-trick for Derby against Real Madrid in the European Cup, although the Rams eventually lost the tie 5-6 on aggregate. He must have been a great disappointment to Clough, who admired his swagger and exceptional talent, for he played only four games for Forest – two of them in the Super Cup – and was at the City Ground for less than a month. Bowles and George, for Forest they were the odd couple – moody but sometimes dazzling mavericks.

Forest's inconsistent form was a problem in the league but the cup competitions were a different matter. The Reds began their defence of the League Cup with a 1-1 draw at Blackburn but won the replay 6-1; Bowyer scoring twice, Robertson also got two, including a penalty, and the other goals came from Woodcock and Frank Gray. Woodcock hit a hat-trick to knock out Middlesbrough 3-1 at Ayrsome Park but Forest needed a replay to overcome Bristol City. The quarter-final against West Ham finished goalless at Upton Park and still neither side had scored after ninety minutes in the replay but O'Hare, Birtles and O'Neill lifted the spirits of a rain-drenched 25,000 City Ground crowd with extra-time goals to set up a two-leg semi-final against Liverpool. A crowd of 32,000 at the City Ground on 22 January saw a late John Robertson penalty give Forest a slender lead to take to Anfield. O'Neill, playing up front with Birtles in the absence of Francis, was brought down by goalkeeper Ray Clemence and Robertson put away the penalty. Substitute David Fairclough scored an equaliser in the dying seconds but Forest were through for an unprecedented third successive League Cup Final trip to Wembley.

In the FA Cup, the Reds had a comfortable 4-1 third-round victory at Elland Road, where Frank Gray scored in the first minute against his former club, but Liverpool returned to the City Ground a week after their League Cup defeat to gain revenge with a 2-0 FA Cup fourth-round knockout blow. Francis marked his comeback with a hat-trick in a 4-0 home league win against Manchester City and then scored two more as Tottenham Hotspur were beaten by the same scoreline.

Forest were in fine fettle for Wembley and the League Cup Final against Wolves, who were managed by former Forest player John Barnwell. Both were mid-table in the league but Barnwell had strengthened his team by bringing in former Liverpool and England captain Emlyn Hughes and striker Andy Gray, a £1.5-million record signing from Aston Villa. Forest were without suspended Larry Lloyd, who was replaced by David Needham. Clough had led the side out of the Wembley tunnel for the 1978 final against Liverpool, Peter Taylor was given the honour a year later against Southampton and this time trainer Jimmy Gordon was at the head of the team alongside Barnwell. Gordon was as surprised as anyone. He wasn't told of the manager's decision until just before kick-off and didn't have time to change out of his tracksuit. The game is remembered chiefly for its only goal and the collision on the edge of the box as centre-half Needham and goalkeeper Shilton both tried to deal with a long punt from Wolves' right-back Peter Daniel. The ball broke for Gray to tap into an empty net.

With the League Cup route to Europe now closed and Liverpool fighting out the championship with Manchester United, winning the European Cup became of even greater importance – it was no longer a fight for the trophy, but also for the right to compete on the Continent in 1980/81. But at the City Ground on 3 May, the Reds suffered a severe blow. The visitors were Crystal Palace, managed by Terry Venables and featuring Gerry Francis as an effective playmaker from midfield. But they were being taken apart by a Forest side playing some of the most attractive attacking football of the season. Trevor Francis, in particular, was on fire. Playing in his favoured central striker role, he had scored two goals and was chasing a hat-trick as the Reds led 4-0 with twenty minutes left. Sprinting towards the Palace goal on the heavy pitch, he suddenly pulled up and stumbled, clutching his ankle. He had snapped his Achilles tendon and would miss not only the final but would be out for seven or eight months.

Clough and Taylor took the players to Majorca to relax their mood before Madrid. There was no training but McGovern ran 3 miles each morning and Shilton found a patch of grass on a traffic island in Calla Millor, where Gordon put down two tracksuit tops as goalposts and goalkeeper and trainer set to work. A fitness obsessive, as a youngster Shilton hung from a banister at the top of the stairs in his parents' shop with weights attached to his feet trying to add inches to his height. No wonder some later commented that his arms were extraordinarily long.

With Francis injured and Bowles missing, Forest had only one recognised striker, Garry Birtles, so the management pair opted for a five-man midfield and brought in seventeen-year-old Gary Mills to initially partner the front man but then drop back. As Robertson said, 'It was a case of anyone who was fit would figure.' There were only four instead of the allowed five substitutes on the bench. Forest wore an all-red strip and Hamburg, now firm favourites, wore white. German internationals Manny Kaltz and Felix Magath were Hamburg's defensive stars and England's Kevin Keegan was their main attacking threat, though they also had Horst Hrubesch, nicknamed 'the Heading Monster', on the bench. Lloyd and Burns made it their business to unnerve Keegan but the Germans forced Forest on the backfoot for most of the game and Shilton had to be at his magnificent best.

However, soon enough McGovern won the ball and began a well-constructed move with a pass to Bowyer. He found O'Neill, who drifted infield to send Gray charging at the heart of the Hamburg defence. Mills took over and worked the ball left to Robertson. The winger jinked between two defenders and played a one-two with Birtles before hitting a right-foot shot from the edge of the penalty area and the ball went in off the inside of the post. After twenty minutes Forest were ahead and now they had to absorb intense Hamburg pressure. Having failed to pass their way through the Reds' resolute defence, the Germans sent on Hrubesch and tried to unsettle Burns and Lloyd with 'route one' long-ball tactics. Jack Charlton, sitting alongside Brian Moore in the commentary box, assured his anxious colleague that the defenders were too good for this to work. Clough sent John O'Hare on for young Mills for the last half-hour with instructions to 'calm things down'. Then Gray had to come off injured and was replaced by Bryn Gunn.

Birtles had followed instructions in his lone-ranger role and throughout the game repeated to himself the mantra, 'Hold it and wait for help. Hold it and wait for help.' He had run himself into the ground but might have made it 2-0 in the final minute. One-on-one with Peter Nogly, he nutmegged the defender but, exhausted, stumbled slightly, allowing Kaltz to get back and block him. Clough was appreciative. 'I've never seen a lad cover as much ground, willingly and unselfishly, as Birtles did that night,' he said. It was all over. In his excitement, Moore told ITV viewers, 'Hamburg are champions of Europe again!' John McGovern was presented with the trophy at the side of the pitch and the Forest players carried it together in a lap of honour as Keegan led away his dejected teammates. Trevor Francis watched it all on television in a Cannes hotel. He would have liked to have been there but the manager wanted him out of the way. 'Everyone was a hero,' Clough commented. 'We had application, tenacity, dedication and pride. We did everything right.'

John McGovern thought this win overshadowed that at Munich, retaining the trophy against a quality side like Hamburg. 'We tackled, blocked, hustled and harried until we dropped,' he said. 'We did drop but only after the final whistle.' Sharing the glory with the players and fans in the Bernabeu stadium, and then showing the trophy to thousands more from the top of an open bus back in Nottingham, made the captain reflect, 'Against all the odds, little old Nottingham Forest had matched and bettered the achievements of some of the giants in European football.' That season Forest had won the European Cup, the European Super Cup, finished fifth in the First Division and reached the final of the League Cup. 'We had probably reached a peak on that magical night in Madrid,' McGovern concluded. 'A massive bonus, which added to the club's respect throughout the world of football, was the conduct of our supporters during the two European campaigns. We won like champions while they had conducted themselves like champions.'

On a family holiday in Lloret de Mar on the Costa Brava, I discovered the impact that the name of Brian Clough was having in Spain – indeed, throughout Europe. We had decided to travel on a local bus to the provincial capital, Gerona. A group of Basque pensioners, who were staying at our hotel as government-subsided guests, also caught the bus. They were with us again on the return journey and I decided to try out my basic Spanish. I learned they had been to the city to collect their pensions. I said we were from the Nottingham and Sherwood Forest area, the home of Robin Hood. But 'Brian Clough, Brian Clough!' they chanted in reply. We'd also become friendly with a young German couple and arranged to watch the final with them. The 'crowd' in front of the television set in the hotel lounge included British, German and neutral holidaymakers. Then the pensioners came in and when Robbo scored they resumed their chorus: 'Brian Clough, Brian Clough!'

17

After Taylor

Sitting on the bench with Brian Clough for the First Division match against Tottenham Hotspur at the City Ground in mid-November 1980, substitute John McGovern was suddenly asked, 'Do you know what's wrong with Ponte?' The deposed skipper was too stunned to reply. He'd been dropped in favour of Swiss midfielder Raimondo Ponte, a summer signing from Grasshoppers for £180,000. 'I'll tell you,' Clough said. 'I bloody signed him, that's what's wrong with him.' Ponte made way for O'Neill but Forest still lost 3-0. The open admission seemed significant to McGovern. Not only was a great team being dismantled, perhaps prematurely, but the management partnership was breaking down. 'Brian was a great manager and Peter was the best judge of a player I have ever known,' McGovern said. Now it seemed Clough no longer trusted Taylor's judgment and neither was he confident of his own.

After a string of friendlies in North America and in Europe, the league season began at Tottenham Hotspur with Ponte and £1.3-million striker Ian Wallace from Coventry City making their First Division debuts for the Reds, who lost 2-0. There had been a dispute on the eve of the match between the players and management over win bonuses. Clough gave them a 'take it or leave it' ultimatum and McGovern, who had tried to get agreement, signed up for the slight increase. 'I didn't think the issue should have been argued so close to the start of the season,' he explained. 'You have to be your own man and stand by your own judgment.' The first home game was won 2-1 against Birmingham City on 20 August, when Brian Clough performed the official opening of the Executive Stand with 26,561 in attendance. O'Neill was sent off.

Forest's hopes of a European Cup treble were dashed in the first round by unfancied Bulgarian champions CSKA Sofia, who won both legs 1-0.

This shock early exit may have influenced Clough and Taylor in their decision to remodel the side. The biggest surprise was that the first to go was Chilwell-born Garry Birtles, a Forest fan since boyhood of whom his teammate Viv Anderson, another international and local from Clifton, said, 'He could do everything – hold the ball up, turn and run at defenders, score goals. Birtles was the best centre-forward I have ever seen. A fabulous, fabulous footballer.' The next home match after the European Cup tie was his final appearance before manager Dave Sexton broke the Manchester United transfer record to take him to Old Trafford for £1.25 million. Nearly 30,000 saw the game against United, who won 2-1, where Wallace scored the Forest goal.

There were only 12,248 at the City Ground at the end of November when Ian Bowyer scored twice to give the Reds a 2-1 lead against Valencia in the first leg of the European Super Cup. Uruguayan striker Fernando Moreno scored the only goal in the return leg in December to make the aggregate score 2-2 and give the Spanish side the Super Cup on away goals. Having lost out on European glory, Forest could still become World Club Champions if they defeated the leading South Americans Nacional Montevideo of Uruguay. The match took place before a 70,000 crowd in Tokyo on 11 February. Injured skipper McGovern watched frustrated from the sidelines as his teammates outplayed the opposition but were beaten by a goal from Waldemar Victorino, who was voted man-of-the-match by sponsors Toyota and was rewarded with a brand new car. It turned out to be Larry Lloyd's Forest finale. Three days later he was Wigan Athletic's player-manager and losing 1-0 to Rochdale. Bowyer had moved on a month earlier to Sunderland but came back to the City Ground at the beginning of 1982 for a five-year second spell. Lloyd returned to Nottingham to manage Notts County, then took over the Stage Door pub in the city centre and became an outspoken local radio broadcaster.

Ten days after Lloyd, Martin O'Neill bade farewell to the City Ground. He joined Norwich City for £250,000 and later returned to Nottingham with Notts County. It was against Norwich on 28 March that Ponte played his last match for Forest before joining Corsican club SC Bastia. Lloyd's replacement, Norwegian Einar Jan Aas, signed from Bayern Munich, made his debut for the Reds and Trevor Francis, recovered from his lengthy Achilles injury, scored both goals in a 2-1 victory. Aas, a popular and stylish centre-half, was limited by injury and in November left to join his home town club Moss. Forest went out of the League Cup with a 4-1 defeat at Watford but had a good run in the FA Cup. Francis scored twice in a 3-3 third-round draw with Bolton at the City Ground and then the only goal in the replay. He continued in prolific form with another winner against Manchester United at the City Ground in round four. Bristol City were beaten 2-1 at home in the fifth round and then Francis was again on target as Forest drew 3-3 with Ipswich in the sixth. Ipswich were 1-0 winners in the replay at Portman Road. The Reds ended the season seventh in the First Division.

In June Frank Gray returned to Leeds United for £300,000 but £1-million centre-forward Justin Fashanu, bought from Norwich, and England Under-21 midfielder Mark Proctor from Middlesbrough, bought for £425,000, made their debuts in the league opener against Southampton at the City Ground on 29 August, when Francis scored twice in a 2-1 win. He played his last game for Forest two days later in a goalless draw with Manchester United at Old Trafford and was transferred to United's neighbours, Manchester City, for £1.2 million. In early October Kenny Burns departed to Leeds for £400,000.

The 1981/82 season would be the first without European football at the City Ground since 1978. Forest lost at home to Wrexham in the third round of the FA Cup but reached the fifth round of the League Cup before going out 1-0 to Tottenham Hotspur at White Hart Lane. Their final league position was twelfth. Willie Young had been signed from Arsenal to replace Lloyd, winger Jurgen Roeber had arrived from Chicago Sting and striker Peter Ward for £400,000 from Brighton, but neither provided long-term answers. More encouraging was the emergence of youngsters Peter Davenport, Steve Hodge, Colin Walsh, Chris Fairclough, Stuart Gray and Calvin Plummer.

If the Ponte business had given John McGovern some concern about the Clough-Taylor partnership, he had further reason to worry as the season neared its end. With the manager away on a short break with his family, Peter Taylor told McGovern he was on the transfer list with Wallace and Fashanu. Then Brian Clough returned and asked, 'Who told you that? You're going nowhere.' McGovern wrote in his autobiography that the next day he was summoned to see 'a somewhat agitated' Peter Taylor. 'Look, I told you that you were going and you're going,' the player was told. 'It's over, finished.' The indecision continued with Clough telling him, 'I decide who stays or leaves this club.' Finally, McGovern sat in the manager's office and was informed, 'I have had ten enquires regarding the names on our transfer list and, considering Wallace cost over a million and a quarter and Fashanu cost a million, you'll be pleased to hear all the enquiries are about you but I see no reason why you shouldn't play at least twenty games for me next season.' That was not a wholehearted endorsement and when McGovern heard Bolton Wanderers wanted him as their player-manager, he decided to leave.

'At the end of fourteen years there wasn't even a handshake from Brian or Peter,' wrote their captain. 'No sentiment. They paid me my wages. I did my stuff on the field. End of story.' To those supporters who would say to him 'Brian Clough and Peter Taylor loved you' or 'you were Cloughie's blue-eyed boy', McGovern says please replace the word 'loved' with 'respected'. This worked both ways 'for them and me', he adds. 'Every time Brian Clough walked towards me, I didn't know whether he'd shake my hand or bite my head off.' John McGovern's last game for Forest was a friendly in Morocco against the Kuwait national team and it ended as a 1-1 draw. In 2014 he returned to a Kuwaiti-owned Forest as club 'ambassador' – an honour and a job he relished as much as being captain.

Peter Shilton's five seasons at the City Ground also came to a close. With the Reds he had won a League Championship medal, a League Cup winners' medal, two European Cup winners' medals, European Super Cup winners' and losers' medals, a medal as a World Club Championship runner-up and nineteen England caps. He had reserved probably his greatest individual performance for the final of the 25 European Cup final. Clough's trademark green sweater, usually worn over a red shirt, was supposedly inspired by Shilton's number one goalkeeper's top. 'There's only one number one round here,' the manager told him. 'And it's not you.' Shilton won little with his other clubs, who included Leicester, Stoke, Southampton and Derby, but he holds a record number of 125 England caps. His replacement at the City Ground was Johannes Franciscus Van Breukelen, known to all on Trentside as Hans, a Dutch international when Brian Clough paid £200,000 for him to FC Utrecht. Six-foot-tall Hans played superbly for Forest between 1982 and 1984 and was immensely popular with the fans before returning to Holland with PSV Eindhoven. Van Breukelen's debut at the City Ground on 4 September coincided with the return of Garry Birtles but there were only 13,709 fans to see a 4-0 victory over Brighton.

All of McGovern's fears for the Clough-Taylor relationship were justified when Peter Taylor said he had 'shot it' and would have to retire. He would not be persuaded to stay but then accepted an offer from Derby County, who were struggling in Division Two, to take charge at the Baseball Ground. As fate would have it, the FA Cup third round paired Clough's Reds with Taylor's Rams in Derby and it was the second division side who triumphed 2-0 in front of a crowd of 28,494. Forest finished a respectable fifth in the First Division but the only silverware they had to show for the season was the County Cup as Notts were beaten 4-3. In May, they played a couple of friendlies in Canada, beating Montreal Manic 4-3 but losing 2-1 to Toronto Blizzard in a televised game.

The zenith of the Clough-Taylor relationship came during the summer when Peter Taylor signed out-of-contract John Robertson for Derby while Brian Clough was away on a charity walk. Clough went to the transfer tribunal with evidence of offers for the player from Luton and Southampton. The tribunal was persuaded to set a transfer fee of £135,000, which was higher than Derby expected and one they could scarcely afford. Robertson's style did not suit the second division. Derby were relegated and Taylor was sacked. Birtles and Davenport scored fifteen goals each as Forest finished third in the First Division. Paul Hart had been signed from Leeds United and the thirty-year-old centre-back formed a solid central defensive partnership with the equally experienced Colin Todd for the first part of the season, and young Chris Fairclough from November.

The Reds went out of both the FA Cup and the League Cup in the early stages but had a fine run back in European competition, having qualified for the UEFA Cup. Vorwaerts were beaten 2-0 at the City Ground and 1-0 in East Germany in the first round and then PSV Eindhoven were beaten in both legs of the second, Davenport hitting the target in each game. The third-round tie with Glasgow Celtic was played in icy conditions in front of a City Ground crowd of over 34,000 and ended goalless. Goals by Hodge and Walsh earned Forest a 2-1 second-leg victory watched by nearly 67,000 at Celtic Park. Sturm Graz were the quarter-final opposition and a rare goal from Paul Hart earned Forest a 1-0 win in the home leg. Both sides scored from the penalty spot in the second leg in Austria, Colin Walsh equalising for Forest with just six minutes of extra time left to ensure a 2-1 aggregate win.

Semi-final opponents were the defending champions Anderlecht, who had beaten Forest 4-2 in Belgium on the pre-season tour. Without the injured Birtles, the Reds were unconvincing in the first leg at the City Ground until the final five minutes when Steve Hodge scored twice, turning in a Gary Mills cross at the far post and then profiting from a fine delivery by Steve Wigley. After making his First Division debut in a 3-0 defeat of Arsenal at the City Ground in October 1982, Wigley gave one of the most dazzling displays of his Forest career in that high-scoring County Cup final in May 1983. There were only 5,000 fans on Trentside to see it. He had made his reputation as a tricky, ball-playing winger for his home town club Curzon Ashton at Ashton-under-Lyme, where he was spotted and promptly signed by Brian Clough. But, unusually, he was at inside-right when he jinked his way through the Magpies' defence to lay on goals for Viv Anderson, Peter Davenport, Steve Hodge and John Robertson. Both sides were in Division One and, in the league, Notts had beaten Forest 3-2 at Meadow Lane with the Reds winning the return match 2-1. That season, Wigley made only four First Division appearances, all from the substitutes' bench, and played twice in cup ties. His best season at the City Ground was in 1984/85 when he played thirty-five times in Division One and in nine cup ties. Steve was a maker rather than a scorer of goals and hit only three in over 100 games for Forest before joining Sheffield United in October 1985.

That was the season Stuart Pearce joined Forest. It seems incredible now but the player who was to become the second of Clough's great captains was viewed as the makeweight in a £450,000 summer deal that also brought centre-half Ian Butterworth to Nottingham from Coventry City. Butterworth did not last two years and made only thirty-three appearances. Pearce stayed twelve seasons, during which he played 522 games for the club (only Bob McKinlay with 685 and Ian Bowyer 564 have played more), won seventy-six of his seventy-eight England caps and scored eighty-eight of his career total of ninety-nine goals. Pearce and Wigley were Forest teammates on ten occasions, eight times in the First Division and twice in the League Cup. Wigley returned to the City Ground as assistant academy director to Paul Hart and later joined up as coach with Stuart Pearce when he managed first Manchester City and then the England Under-21 squad. Wigley also had successful spells coaching the young players at Southampton, Bolton Wanderers, Bristol City, Hull and Fulham. The pair teamed up again on Trentside with Stuart as the Forest manager and Steve his assistant at the start of the 2014/15 season.

With a two-goal advantage, the Reds eagerly anticipated the away leg in Anderlecht and the strong possibility of taking part in an all-English European final against Tottenham Hotspur, who faced Hajduk Split in the other semi-final. John Robertson confesses in his book that he knew within a week of pre-season training that he had made a terrible mistake in joining Derby. 'I was in a relegation battle and could have been in a side that reached the UEFA Cup semi-final,' he lamented. But the Anderlecht encounter was to prove one of the most controversial games Forest have ever played. It was 1-0 at half-time, a low drive from twenty-five yards by Enzio Scifo putting the home side ahead in the 20th minute. 'We were still confident,' said Paul Hart. 'We'd won every away game in Europe that year and we were used to grinding it out.' Spanish referee Carlos Guruceta awarded Anderlecht a disputed penalty after deciding that full-back Kenny Swain had tripped Kenneth Brylle. Hart said it was a disgrace, 'Ken was two yards from him'. Birtles, sitting on the bench, was equally convinced of the injustice of the decision. 'Kenny was nowhere near the guy,' he wrote in his autobiography. There was 'complete daylight' between them. Erwin Vandenbergh made it

3-0 with two minutes remaining but then Forest won a corner and Paul Hart headed the ball powerfully into the net for what seemed to be a vital away goal. The referee disallowed it for an alleged push on a defender. 'We were diddled out of it,' Hart said. 'I never won a medal, ever.' Van Breukelen, who had made a number of fine saves, insisted that Forest had been playing against 'twelve men'.

Anderlecht lost the final to Spurs in a penalty shoot-out. Some years later Birtles, Van Breukelen and Ian Bowyer, on behalf of the players, unsuccessfully sued Anderlecht in the Belgian courts. In 1997 Roger Vanden Stock revealed that his father, Constant, Anderlecht's president at the time of the tie, had paid referee Guruceta £18,000 and the club was punished with a season's ban from UEFA competition. Guruceta could not defend himself. He had been killed in a car crash ten years before. But he had form in Belgium having sent off two Italians and being awarded a controversial penalty to Standard Liege when they beat Napoli 2-1 in the first leg of the 1979/80 EUFA Cup second round. The second leg in Naples ended 1-1. Liege went out in the third round.

Forest ended the season in fine form, beating Watford 5-1 at the City Ground, West Ham 2-1 away and Manchester United 2-0 at home. After retaining the County Cup with a 3-0 victory over Mansfield Town, the Reds went on an Australian tour, playing matches in Perth, Adelaide, Brisbane and Sydney and losing only one – to Manchester United in Melbourne. The tour party met up with Nottingham's world ice-dance champions Jane Torvill and Christopher Dean when they were in Brisbane. Colin Griffin, discussing modern perceptions of Nottingham in John Beckett's *A Centenary History of Nottingham* (1997), credits the ice-dancers and Clough's footballers with projecting a 'glamorous and vibrant' image of the city, contrasting sharply with the unflattering picture painted by its most acclaimed twentieth-century writers, D. H. Lawrence and Alan Sillitoe.

18

The Hillsborough Effect

Intense rivalry, thrilling matches, great goals, controversy and unimaginable tragedy marked clashes between Liverpool and Nottingham Forest during the Clough years. When Labour MP and Celtic season-ticket holder Jim Murphy wrote *The 10 Football Matches That Changed the World* in 2014, he chose to feature two games between the Reds of Merseyside and Nottingham. One kicked off at 4 p.m. on 16 August 1992, when a Forest team that included Stuart Pearce, Nigel Clough, Scot Gemmill, Steve Chettle and Ian Woan outplayed Liverpool in the first-ever Premier League broadcast on Sky television. Commentator Martin Tyler welcomed viewers with, 'Good afternoon, everyone. A new league, alterations and amendments to the very laws of the game, even a different button to push on your television set.' Riches generated by Sky's involvement opened up the great divide between Premiership clubs and the rest. Teddy Sheringham scored the only goal with a right-foot drive beyond goalkeeper David James's outstretched left hand high into the net. In sixty-two appearances for Forest, England international marksman Sheringham scored twenty-three goals and this was his last. Before the end of the month he had been transferred to Terry Venables' Spurs for £2.1 million in a deal that later gave rise to 'bungs' allegations.

'Good afternoon. Welcome back,' was the message from Sheffield Wednesday's chairman to the visiting fans from Liverpool and Nottingham in the programme for the FA Cup semi-final on 18 April 1989 that would be abandoned and forever known as the Hillsborough Disaster. 'As you look around Hillsborough you will appreciate why it has been regarded for so long as the perfect venue for all kinds of important matches,' the article, unfortunately, continued. His 'welcome back' was because this was the second consecutive semi-final contested by the two clubs at Wednesday's stadium. In 1988 Liverpool had won 2-1, reversing a league scoreline at the City Ground a week earlier. Arrangements for accommodating the two sets of supporters had been identical to those a year later with Forest occupying the Kop end and Liverpool Leppings Lane, simply because the police wanted them at the ends of the ground nearest their arrival points.

Inevitably, this match was Murphy's other selection. Also inevitably, the Hillsborough chapter concentrates on the long fight for justice for the ninety-six blameless Liverpool fans who were crushed to death and their families. In the House of Commons in October 2011, a motion calling for all documents – including cabinet notes and briefings – to be handed to an independent panel set up to review the papers for public release was passed unopposed and with the support of Home Secretary Theresa May. There are many thousands of official documents but the key facts were already known, including that the stadium's safety certificate was out of date. Some 24,000 Liverpool fans had to be funnelled through just twenty-three turnstiles in the north and west sides of the ground. They could not cope before kick-off and when a crush developed outside police ordered an exit gate to be opened to admit hundreds of fans together. Undirected, they tried to get into the central Leppings Lane 'pens', which were already full.

Those at the front of the pens tried to climb out onto the pitch to escape and I have a memory of Bruce Grobbelaar, the Liverpool goalkeeper, gesticulating to persuade police these were not hooligans but potential victims. The game was stopped after only six minutes and the players were sent back to the dressing rooms. It did not restart. I and many others hoped that the season's FA Cup competition would be abandoned but the clubs were ordered to replay the match at Old Trafford, Manchester. Their performance showed the Forest players had no heart for it. Liverpool went through to beat Merseyside neighbours Everton 3-2 at Wembley on 20 May. On 12 September 2012, Prime Minister David Cameron stood up in the Commons to apologise to the nation for the mistakes and deceit that had taken place at the time and over the years since. An inquest verdict in 2016 exonerated fans of any blame and recorded a verdict of unlawful killing.

There is a side of the story that is unconsidered, unacknowledged, rarely heard: the Forest side. In his autobiography *The Man with Maradona's Shirt*, Steve Hodge recalled the team coach going down the hill to the stadium on a beautiful spring day. 'When we went out for a warm-up I noticed that their end behind the goal was quiet but our end, the big kop, was packed and really loud.' he wrote. A couple of lads said to him, 'Where are their fans?' The game kicked off and it was end to end. Peter Beardsley hit the bar in the opening seconds and then Forest broke away to win a corner. 'There was some disturbance among their fans behind the goal,' Hodge continued. His mind went back to the pitch invasion at Newcastle in 1974. 'I was half expecting the whole lot would come spilling out onto the pitch. I just thought, "Jeez, we've only just started."' Then someone shouted 'There's people dying in there!' He was only about fifty feet from the barrier and could hear the screams. Hodge said the FA's Graham Kelly came into the dressing room and told them, 'Whatever happens, the game has to be completed today.' But Brian Clough, having heard that people had died, replied, 'Graham, we're going home,' and then, turning to his players, added, 'Lads get changed, we're off.' That was my view, too, and I said to my sons as we sat in the paddock in front of the main stand, 'Let's go, this game won't restart and we should let mum know we're on our way home.'

The Forest team for Sheffield and Manchester was Steve Sutton, Brian Laws, Stuart Pearce, Des Walker, Terry Wilson, Steve Hodge, Tommy Gaynor, Neil Webb, Nigel Clough, Lee Chapman and Garry Parker. According to Chapman, the players did not want to replay the semi-final. 'We thought, what's the point?' he said. The whole country away from Trentside demanded an Everton-Liverpool final. 'We were in a no-win situation. We didn't get any counselling or anything and I don't think others realised how it affected the people of Nottingham.' John Aldridge gave Liverpool an early lead but, almost relunctantly, Neil Webb equalised. Aldridge restored his side's lead after the break but then to the disgust of Forest players and supporters alike mockingly celebrated a Forest own-goal by ruffling the unfortunate culprit Brian Laws's hair. 'I would have chinned him,' Pearce years later told *Guardian* sports writer and Forest fan Daniel Taylor.

Ten years later Forest and Liverpool set up a junior challenge contest for the Hillsborough Memorial Cup. It was won by a Liverpool Under-10 representative side. Arnold Boys brought the trophy to Nottingham in 1999/00 but it was not competed for again. That seems such a shame.

The manner of the FA Cup exit disguised what had been an outstanding season for the Reds. The League Cup and the Simod Cup had been won at Wembley, they were FA Cup semi-finalists and were third in the First Division for the second successive season, behind Liverpool and champions Arsenal. Forest began the league season with a defeat at Norwich followed by five successive draws before registering a 2-1 victory at Queen's Park Rangers on 8 October after a 6-0 morale-boosting defeat of Chester City in the League Cup first leg. Tommy Gaynor hit a hat-trick in the second leg at Chester, where Forest won 4-0. Lee Chapman joined Forest from Niort, France, for £350,000 in October and for fifteen months was a superb partner for Nigel Clough before moving on to Leeds for £400,000. Chapman, who had been born in Lincoln when his father, Roy, a former Aston Villa star, was with City, made his home debut in an impressive 2-1 defeat of Liverpool and then scored his first goal for the Reds at the end of the month as Newcastle were beaten away 1-0. Coventry and Leicester, after a replay, were dismissed in the League Cup and in the fifth round, Chapman scored four goals as Queen's Park Rangers were crushed 5-2.

Garry Parker was switched from midfield to the left-wing against Sheffield Wednesday on New Year's Eve and the move coincided with Forest striking a rich vein of form with ten wins in a row including the FA Cup defeats of Ipswich and Leeds. QPR earned a goalless draw in the league to end the run but a Parker goal at Ashton Gate disposed of Bristol City in the League Cup semi-final and he scored again in the sixth round of the FA Cup to knock out Manchester United. It was the first goal scored by a visiting team at Old Trafford for three and a half months and was a tap-in for Parker after speedy Franz Carr had left Lee Sharpe in his wake and put the ball across the six-yard box.

A tenth successive away win came at the Baseball Ground where Hodge and Chapman scored as Derby went down 2-0 and next Manchester United were beaten by the same scoreline at the City Ground with goals by Pearce and Chapman again. Pearce got another with Clough also scoring as Norwich lost 2-0 on Trentside four days before the League Cup final. The holders, Luton Town, who had beaten Arsenal 3-2 in the 1988 final, were Forest's Wembley opponents. Brian Laws declared himself fit enough to play despite having thirty-six stitches in his hand after an accident at home with a couple of wine glasses. He had been in hospital for forty-eight hours. Clough threw a ball at him and when he caught it, said, 'If you can take a throw in, you can play.' There was disquiet in the camp when Lee Glover, viewed as a manager's favourite, was named as substitute instead of Brian Rice, who had played in five games on the way to the final and would now miss out on a £10,000 bonus if Forest won.

More than 76,000 were at a Wembley bathed in early spring sunshine and there was a live television audience of millions. Forest began nervously. Lee Chapman got the ball in the net and that might have settled them but the goal was disallowed for offside. The Reds fell behind after thirty-six minutes when Mick Harford headed in a Danny Wilson cross. At half-time, Clough told his players, 'Now, my wife's in the stand, so are yours, so are your relations and friends and all those lovely people from Nottingham. So please, go out there and show them what you can really do.' The Reds dominated the second half. Luton goalkeeper Les Sealey upended Steve Hodge as he ran on to a pass from Neil Webb and Nigel Clough equalised from the penalty spot. Webb scored the second himself after Clough had spread the ball wide for Tommy Gaynor, who made a great run and cross for midfielder to flick the ball over the advancing 'keeper. There was no way back for Luton. Pearce found Gaynor, who squared the ball for Clough to stab the ball past Sealey to make it 3-1. Stuart Pearce wore a red and white scarf and a red-trimmed white woolly hat as he led the Forest players up the steps to the royal box to collect the League Cup, the seventh major trophy at club level won by Brian Clough, overtaking the six Don Revie had achieved.

After wins in the league at home to Southampton and away at Middlesbrough, the Reds returned to Wembley for the final of the FA Full Members' Cup, sponsored by Italian sportswear company Simod. Forest had beaten Chelsea 4-1, Ipswich 3-1 and Crystal Palace 3-1 en route and faced Everton, who had eliminated Millwall, Wimbledon and Queen's Park Rangers, in front of a 50,000 crowd. The Blues were desperate for a trophy after a disappointing league campaign, and they took the lead in the 8th minute with Tony Cottee finishing well after beating two defenders and even getting ahead of Des Walker. Garry Parker equalised from close range after Lee Chapman had flicked on a corner and it became an exciting end-to-end game. Five minutes into the second half, Graeme Sharp lobbed Steve Sutton to restore Everton's lead but a superb individual effort by Parker, who ran 60 yards after receiving the ball from Nigel Clough before driving it past Neville Southall, forced extra time. Forest went in front for the first time two minutes after the restart through Chapman, but Cottee put the Toffees back on level terms and the game seemed to be heading for penalties. Then Webb released substitute Franz Carr down the right and his cross was toe-poked home by Chapman to make it 4-3. Forest had become the first side ever to win two Wembley finals in the same season and what a great day out it had been.

Steve Hodge reckoned his decision to return to Trentside had been fully justified. 'In three seasons away I hadn't won anything at Villa or Spurs,' he said. 'Cloughie had proved that he could produce a new young team of high quality and he'd done it without Peter Taylor.' Forest's reserve side won the Central League and their Under-18s won the Midland Youth Cup. Unfortunately, because of another stadium disaster, the new Reds were not allowed to test themselves in Europe. On 29 May 1985, Liverpool met Juventus at Heysel Stadium, Brussels, in the European Cup Final. There was provocation and fighting on the terraces, a wall collapsed and thirty-two Italians, four Belgians, two people from France and one from Northern Ireland died. Not just Liverpool but all English clubs were banned from European competition for five years.

Brian Clough's take on the season was:

I don't think I have ever been involved with a side who have been applauded so much having won away from home. Supporters have appreciated us, referees are glowing in their praise about our discipline and my fellow managers have been unstinting in their praise for the manner in which we go about our work. We've always tried to play the game in the way it was intended. We don't argue, we don't moan, we don't spoil. We have no negative thought. It's a collector's item if we catch the opposition offside.

19

Final Heartbreak

During Brian Clough's last five seasons – 1988/89 to 1992/93 – Wembley, the national stadium, almost became Nottingham Forest's second home. The Reds played three League Cup finals, winning two of them, won the Simod and Zenith Data Systems (Full Members) Cups and were beaten in the FA Cup Final. The manager had assembled an exciting young squad with home-grown talents like Des Walker, Steve Chettle, Gary Charles, Nigel Clough, Scot Gemmill, Terry Wilson, Steve Sutton and Mark Crossley supplemented by astute signings such as Stuart Pearce, Brian Laws, Franz Carr, Garry Parker, Ian Woan, Gary Crosby, Brian Rice, Nigel Jemson, Roy Keane and the returning Steve Hodge and Neil Webb.

The final payment on the Executive Stand (later renamed the Brian Clough Stand) was made during the summer to add to the optimism on Trentside, but Neil Webb opted to join Manchester United for £1.2 million. His replacement, John Sheridan, who had been signed from Leeds for £650,000, featured in the pre-season tour in France and in the 3-1 County Cup victory over Notts County but missed the opening league game against Aston Villa at the City Ground, which was drawn 1-1 thanks to a Garry Parker equaliser. Parker switched to the left wing to allow Sheridan to take his place in midfield for the League Cup second-round first leg at home to Huddersfield. The newcomer laid on the opening goal for Gary Crosby but the match was drawn 1-1. He wasn't picked again and moved on to Sheffield Wednesday for £500,000. At Huddersfield in the second leg, Forest seemed comfortable with goals by Crosby, Clough and Gaynor putting them 3-1 ahead, but after conceding twice late on went through only on the away-goals rule.

League form was erratic and again it was the League Cup campaign that would rescue the Reds' season. After a goalless third-round draw at

Crystal Palace, Forest romped to a 5-0 victory in the replay. Steve Hodge scored in the first minute, then Nigel Clough caught the goalkeeper going walkabout and Stuart Pearce made it 3-0 after only eighteen minutes. Pearce forced an own-goal before half-time and Hodge completed the scoring after the interval from the full-back's free-kick. In the fourth-round clash with Everton at the City Ground, Lee Chapman got the only goal seven minutes from the end after an indirect free-kick had been awarded against goalkeeper Neville Southall for time-wasting. Aston Villa knocked Forest out of the ZDS Cup and in the third round of the FA Cup, substitute Mark Robins got the only goal for Manchester United in the game at the City Ground that famously saved Alex Ferguson from the sack. Terry Wilson had a late equaliser ruled out.

After First Division defeats at Aston Villa and at home to Norwich, Forest dipped into the transfer market to sign Danish-born Icelandic international Thorvaldur Orlyggson for £175,000. He made his debut in a 2-0 home win against Southampton. One of his shots was turned in by Chapman in what turned out to be his last goal and final game for the club.. Nineteen-year-old Nigel Jemson was signed for £150,000 from Preston and made his debut at Luton on Boxing Day as Chapman's replacement. Jemson would go on to play an important role in the League Cup run.

A crowd of 30,044, the best of the season at the City Ground, saw Forest go two goals in front through Crosby and Parker against Spurs in the fifth round but Gary Lineker and Steve Sedgeley scored to force a replay. Going back with the Reds to White Hart Lane after his transfer eighteen months before, Steve Hodge scored twice, including the winner, as they triumphed 3-2. Forest gave 'a marvelous display of passing, tackling and finishing' wrote David Lacey in the *Guardian*. 'It was the old Spurs push-and-run set in a modern context and given extra speed and vision.' Nayim had scored first for the home side, but Crosby and Clough combined for Hodge to slide in for an equaliser. Then Jemson skipped past Sedgeley to hit a right-footer high into the top corner of the net for a 2-1 half-time lead. Paul Stewart levelled but, within two minutes, Hodge restored Forest's lead and put them in the semi-finals for the second year running. Des Walker, against the club who had not wanted him as a youngster, gave a man-of-the-match performance to deny Lineker a chance. During January, Clough signed a more experienced striker, David Currie, from Barnsley for £700,000 but Jemson's form was such that Currie would make few appearances before being sold in April to Oldham Athletic.

Forest faced Coventry City in the semi-final. Both legs were televised and kicked off at 3.30 p.m. The first at the City Ground was played in driving rain before a crowd of 26,153 on 11 February. Nigel Clough put the Reds ahead with a first-half penalty after Cyrille Regis had handled the ball. With the pitch deteriorating badly, a mistake by Orlygsson let in Steve Livingstone for a 73rd-minute equaliser. Seven minutes later, Forest won a free-kick and Stuart Pearce smashed in the winner off the underside of the crossbar from 20 yards out. Pearce's fearsome free-kicks were as celebrated by supporters as those of Johannes Antonius Bernardus Metgod. 'Johnny' had joined Forest as a twenty-six-year-old Dutch international midfielder from Real Madrid in August 1984, and soon became a crowd favourite. He scored only fifteen goals in 116 appearances for the Reds but most of them were special and he was a cultured giant towering over midfield. After three seasons as a regular, he moved with Chris Fairclough to Tottenham Hotspur, where he made only twelve appearances before rejoining Feyenoord. After 164 games in six years, he retired as a player and became the club's youth director. Metgod came back to England as Portsmouth's coach in 2008 and then joined Nigel Clough at Derby as coach until both were dismissed in 2013.

The weather was equally bad two weeks later when a goalless draw at Highfields Road was enough to see Forest through to Wembley. It also secured a twenty-second Manager of the Month award for Brian Clough, equalling Bob Paisley's record with Liverpool. But League form collapsed and the Reds won only two of their eleven First Division games before the final. They did win the first match at home to Manchester City by a single and controversial goal. City goalkeeper Andy Dibble had the ball in the palm of his hand as he calmly considered his next move. He was too relaxed as he looked downfield and failed to notice Gary Crosby, who cheekily nipped in to head the loosely held ball to the ground and tap it into the net.

Second Division Oldham Athletic, who had also reached the semi-final stage of the FA Cup, were Forest's Wembley opponents. It wasn't a great game and was decided by a scrappy goal two minutes into the second half, Jemson forcing home the rebound after his first attempt had been blocked. Forest fans were happy. The League Cup had been retained and they'd had another day out at Wembley. Forest ended the season in ninth place in the First Division after finishing with a flourish. Manchester United's visit three days after the final became a City Ground celebration as Forest scored four goals in the first half-hour to win the game. Garry Parker struck a 20-yard volley for the first, Stuart Pearce slotted a free-kick inside the near post, Nigel Clough had a shot deflected over goalkeeper Jim Leighton and Steve Chettle headed in the rebound after an overhead kick by Tommy Gaynor had come off the bar. The last league match was at Hillsborough, where Sheffield Wednesday had to win to survive in the First Division. The Reds were merciless. Stuart Pearce scored first from one of his trademark free-kicks and then again after a rampaging run from the back, and Nigel Jemson made it 3-0.

Winger Ian Woan made his debut in the County Cup final against Mansfield Town at Field Mill on 8 May, when Carr (2), Parker and Crosby gave the Reds a 4-0 victory and their second trophy. A few days earlier, the manager had made one of his best-ever signings after being alerted by Noel McCabe, his Irish scout, to the potential of a nineteen-year-old lad from Cork named Roy Keane. Clough picked him up from Cobh Ramblers for around £50,000.

Forest went on a pre-season tour to Sweden, scoring twenty-one goals against two in five matches and helping Karlsunds open their new stadium. They then played three matches in Italy without defeat before retaining the County Cup with a 5-0 defeat of Mansfield Town at the City Ground on 22 August. The league season began on Saturday 25 August, and Forest drew 1-1 with Queen's Park Rangers, thanks to a Jemson penalty. On the Monday, Forest travelled to Liverpool, where it became apparent that Hodge had fallen victim of flu and was unfit to play at Anfield the next night. Clough took a gamble and got his assistant, Ron Fenton, to bring Keane from Nottingham on the morning of the match. The youngster was helping the kit-man lay out the shirts when he was told to put on the No. 6 jersey because he was playing. Forest lost 2-0 but the Irishman was so impressive he went on to play thirty-five First Division games and make thirteen appearances in Cup competitions that season. In his first home game against Southampton, the City Ground crowd gave him a standing ovation when he was substituted, with the Reds leading 3-1. Jemson scored two goals in a minute to become the First Division's top scorer with five goals from four games, but this had been the side's only win.

That September Brian Clough signed a three-year contract and, at the end of the month, a Pearce thunderbolt from a free-kick almost 40 yards out hit the net at the Stretford End to silence 46,000 Manchester United fans and inflict a first home defeat on their club. The players wore black armbands for the home game with Everton on 7 October as Peter Taylor had died suddenly, aged sixty-two, while on holiday in Majorca. The Reds won a decisive 3-1 victory, with Jemson's eighth goal of the season and two from Steve Hodge. However, form dipped, and when Derby won 2-1 on 24 November it was Forest's first league defeat at the Baseball Ground in a decade. Again it was cup competitions that captured the attention. Keane scored his first goal for the club in a 4-1 League Cup victory at Burnley, who were eliminated 5-1 over two legs. A 2-1 win at Plymouth gave Forest a twenty-two-match unbeaten run in the competition and set up a fourth-round clash with Coventry City at Highfield Road.

A Kevin Gallagher hat-trick helped Coventry to a 4-0 lead after only half an hour. There seemed no way back but before half-time Nigel Clough scored a hat-trick and eight minutes into the second half Garry Parker drilled an equaliser. A scramble in the six-yard box led to Steve Livingstone knocking the holders out. After winning 2-1 at home against Newcastle United, Forest went to Barnsley and were beaten by the same scoreline in the ZDS second round, leaving them with just the FA Cup to play for. An away tie with Crystal Palace, third in the First Division, was a tough assignment but with Des Walker keeping star striker Ian Wright quiet, Forest managed a first clean sheet in ten starts to earn a replay. A freezing cold spell caused two postponements before the teams could meet again. It was again a cold Nottingham evening as Palace led through an Ian Wright goal going into the last fifteen minutes but Terry Wilson's shot went in off defender Richard Shaw to force extra time. Stuart Pearce charged forward and volleyed a return ball into the Trent End goal but there was another twist of fortunes as Keane's underhit back-pass made goalkeeper Mark Crossley rush his clearance and John Salako lobbed him from long range for 2-2.

Forest won the draw to host the second replay and the game was scheduled for the following Saturday. This time, however, fog caused a cancellation. The game finally kicked off on Wednesday 28 February when three goals in eleven minutes in the second half saw the Reds go through. Garry Parker got the crucial first, side-footing home a pass from Hodge, and then he blasted number two with an unstoppable shot that went in off the underside of the bar. Gary Crosby killed off Palace with the third from Terry Wilson's pass.

The fourth round was another tough one away at Newcastle, and their opponents built up a 2-0 lead in the first twelve minutes. In the second half, Pearce volleyed home a cross from Keane and, with time pressing, Nigel Clough fired a low shot into the net after Keane and Wilson had combined to put him through. Yet another replay to face but it proved no problem as Hodge, Clough and Parker made it 3-0. Forest were on the road again for the fifth round with another difficult trip, this time to meet Southampton at the Dell. Neil Ruddock put the home side in front with a goal after two minutes and the Saints held on for seventy-eight minutes before, in descending fog, a Pearce shot came back off the post, Keane got hold of the rebound and Hodge turned in his cross to equalise and take the tie to the City Ground. The replay began well for the Saints, with Rod Wallace pouncing on a headed back-pass by Walker that fell short to give them the lead, but a Jemson hat-trick, his first, took Forest to the quarter-finals. For the fourth successive round, Forest were drawn away and on 9 March faced Norwich City on a Carrow Road surface of mud and sand. After withstanding first-half pressure, the Reds gained control and this time no replay was needed as Roy Keane drove in the only goal of the game from the edge of the box.

Three London sides joined Forest in the semi-finals. It was the third time in four years that the penultimate stage of the competition had been reached and, as Tottenham Hotspur met close rivals Arsenal, the Reds went to Villa Park,where their opponents would be Second Division West Ham United. Speculation in the press was that 1991 could be Brian Clough's year for the FA Cup glory that had always eluded him. Fate, too, seemed on his side when, after twenty-five inconclusive minutes, referee Keith Hackett showed the red card to Tony Gale for pulling down Gary Crosby. It was the first time a directive to send off the last defender for a professional foul had been applied. Down to ten men, the Hammers were destroyed by Forest's clinical passing on yet another heavy pitch and conceded four second-half goals, scored by Crosby, Roy Keane and both raiding full-backs, Gary Charles and Stuart Pearce.

Centre-back Steve Chettle said that getting to the final for the manager was like lifting 'a monkey off our backs' and, certainly, the side immediately struck a rich seam of goalscoring form in the league. Chelsea came to Trentside six days after the semi-final and the floodgates opened for Stuart Pearce and Roy Keane to hit two goals each as the Blues were thrashed 7-0. Four days later, Norwich City were given a 5-0 beating. There were birthday celebratory goals for both twenty-one-year-old Lee Glover and twenty-nine-year-old Stuart Pearce. Spurs were held 1-1 in a Cup Final dress rehearsal at White Hart Lane. Then Liverpool were in Nottingham hoping for a victory that would keep them in the running for the First Division title. A 26,000 City Ground crowd saw Crosby shoot as he was brought down by Steve Staunton and the ball hit the back of the net. The referee awarded Forest a penalty instead of a goal. It was calmly converted by Nigel Clough for his fourth goal in four games. Liverpool were given a penalty after the break when Chettle was judged to have fouled Ronnie Rosenthal. It looked a dubious decision and TV replays showed the Forest centre-back had played the ball. Liverpool weren't on level terms for long as Ian Woan chested down a cross and neatly volleyed the winner. 'You're not champions anymore!' chanted the Forest fans. The championship would be Arsenal's. The league season ended with a thrilling 4-3 home win against Leeds, for whom former Forester Lee Chapman scored twice to become the top goalscorer with a tally of thirty-one. Parker and Clough got two each for the Reds.

The FA Cup final at Wembley on 18 May was the last game of the season and Forest's sixty-fifth, including ten friendlies. Fourteen league games had been won and twelve lost, earning eighth place. On the day before the final, the manager gave his captain his team sheet. Pearce's reaction, he revealed in his autobiography, was that Brian Clough had picked his favourites rather than the strongest team. Left out were Nigel Jemson, Steve Hodge, Franz Carr and Brian Laws. Jemson, who was in tears when he heard, and Carr didn't even make the substitutes' bench.

Clough wore a rosette proclaiming himself 'the world's greatest grandad' and grabbed Spurs manager Terry Venables by the hand as the squads stepped out of the tunnel together and into the arena. Venables later said Brian had asked to hold his hand because he felt so nervous. This had been Hodge's impression in the dressing room. But when the teams were presented to the Princess of Wales before kick-off, Clough chatted to her for almost a minute. Later he said he couldn't get Princess Diana out of his mind for the first twenty minutes of the game. That seems incredible, since before fifteen minutes had passed a hyped-up Paul Gascoigne had committed what the Forest boss described as 'two despicable fouls'.

Just a couple of minutes after the start, the England star flew into a chest-high tackle on Garry Parker, who went down in a heap. It deserved a red card but referee Roger Milford didn't even produce a yellow when awarding a free-kick. Ten minutes later Gary Charles was the victim of a lunge at the knee. Again Gascoigne escaped punishment apart from giving away another free-kick. Stuart Pearce, though, from twenty-five yards blasted the ball into the top corner of the Tottenham net and turned to the Forest fans with his arms outstretched. It was the captain's sixteenth goal of the season, all from left-back and none from the penalty spot. As Forest celebrated, Gascoigne collapsed in the middle of the field and it became clear that he had hurt himself making the challenge. He was stretchered off and substituted. Clough thought that despite the damage he did to himself Gascoigne should have been red-carded and said that but for the referee 'copping out of his responsibility', the second incident might not have taken place.

Before half-time, Forest goalkeeper Mark Crossley brought down Gary Lineker, who was attempting to go around him. He then dived to his left to push the Spurs and England striker's penalty away for a corner. Ten minutes into the second-half, Paul Allen put Paul Stewart through to equalise with an angled shot past Crossley. It was 1-1 after ninety minutes and while Venables went to encourage his players Clough stayed on the bench, his arms folded. Early in extra time, the influential

Stewart flicked on a Nayam corner from the right and, as Mabbut came charging in on the far post, Des Walker got there first but headed the ball into his own net. It was all over. Forest were like 'the boxer who leaves his hardest punches in the gym', the *Nottingham Evening Post* reported. 'The overwhelming favourites were unrecognizable as the team that had scorched its way through the First Division fixture list over the last month.'

20

Cup Fighters

Four Forest players – Des Walker, Nigel Clough, Gary Charles and Stuart Pearce – went on England's summer tour of Australia, New Zealand and the Far East. Pearce was given the honour of captaining his country for the first time. Back home, Brian Clough was pursuing Welsh international striker Dean Saunders, but when he decided to join Liverpool instead Clough turned to Millwall's Teddy Sheringham and sealed the deal with a £2-million bid. The newcomer found Forest's training methods of a warm-up and some five-a-sides unusual but went along with his manager's ideas. On a pre-season tour to Sweden, he scored five in one game but he would become much more than a stereotypical target man. Clough thought the Reds could mount a reasonable title challenge.

Despite a 4-0 victory against Notts County at Meadow Lane, early results were inconsistent. Jemson was signed by Trevor Francis for Sheffield Wednesday for £800,000 and helped them finish third in Division One. Parker joined Aston Villa for £650,000. Forest fell to fourth from bottom by the end of October but victories at home to Coventry and away at Villa were followed by a 5-1 thrashing of Crystal Palace at the City Ground with Sheringham getting a brace. The striker was on the scoresheet with Gemmill and Woan as Arsenal were beaten 3-2 in Nottingham but had a barren spell, failing to get a goal in the next eleven games. He was dropped and Clough sat him on the bench beside him. It was an education, Sheringham acknowledged later. He learned why it was so important for a centre-forward to hold the ball up under pressure rather than trying to flick it on and risk losing possession.

Forest were at their best in cup competitions. Bolton were beaten 4-0 at home and 5-2 away in the two-leg second round of the League Cup and Bristol Rovers succumbed 2-0 at the City Ground in the third. It took a replay to dispose of Southampton and another to settle the quarter-final against Crystal Palace but a Sheringham hat-trick in a 5-2 home win took the Reds through to the semi-finals. Wolves, Hereford United and Bristol City were beaten in the FA Cup but Forest fell to Portsmouth of the Second Division in the sixth round after Crossley dropped a cross from a free-kick to gift the home team the winner.

The first leg of the League Cup semi-final against Tottenham Hotspur was played in driving rain at the City Ground just four days after the quarter-final, and Gary Lineker gave the away side the lead from the penalty spot. That award had been disputed and Forest felt they were being robbed when the referee denied them two goals before Sheringham hit the equaliser on the hour. Conditions were no better for the second leg at White Hart Lane and a bomb scare that delayed kick-off did not improve the mood. An early goal by Lee Glover did, however, until Spurs drew level. A Roy Keane header in front of the Forest support from a Crosby cross took Forest back to Wembley, where Manchester United would provide the opposition. It turned out to be a dull final. Forest missed the injured Pearce and Brian McClair scored the only goal to give United the trophy.

There was Wembley success for the Reds in the ZDS Cup Final, which they had reached with wins over Leeds, Aston Villa and Tranmere Rovers before a two-legged triumph against Leicester in the semi-final. Alan Shearer, Matt Le Tissier and Iain Dowie were in the Southampton line-up for the final but, in front of a 68,000 crowd, Forest went 2-0 ahead through spectacular goals from Scot Gemmill and Kingsley Black. The Saints stormed back to take the game into extra time but Gemmill volleyed the winner past Tim Flowers. Brian Clough had gained a twenty-fifth Manager of the Month award but this was to be his last piece of silverware.

Forest, who again finished eighth in the league, gained a sort of revenge when they dented Manchester United's championship hopes with a 2-1 win at Old Trafford with goals by Woan and Gemmill.

On 27 May 1992, the First Division clubs who had resigned en masse from the Football League formed the FA Premier League, a limited company administered in an office at Lancaster Gate, then the headquarters of the Football Association. It was viewed by the FA as an opportunity to steal a march over the 104-year-old Football League and by the breakaway clubs as the key to greater television and sponsorship income. Promotion and relegation between the Premier League and the First Division would be unchanged. With the involvement of Sky TV, football's elite generated the wealth they dreamed of, but to many observers the game lost its soul. And, quite soon, the Football

Association lost its influence as in 2007 the FA appellation was dropped and the Premier League became a corporation owned by its twenty member clubs.

Des Walker departed during the summer for Sampdoria, Genoa, in the Italian Serie A. The England star was never adequately replaced. Both Keane and Nigel Clough were drafted into central defence for spells during the season. Despite the lack of signings, optimism abounded and the *Evening Post* envisaged the prospect of the inaugural Premier League title landing on Trentside. It didn't seem so far-fetched when football's brave new world began with Sky TV cameras and a 20,000 crowd at the City Ground to see Forest humble mighty Liverpool and play like potential champions, especially in the first half. A Teddy Sheringham stunner ensured the Merseysiders first opening-day defeat for eleven years and another team in red, Manchester United, eventually became the Premiership's first champions – their first title for twenty-five years.

Sheringham played only two more games for Forest before getting his wish to return to London where his young son, Charlie, was living. He joined Tottenham Hotspur for £2.1 million. It was a controversial move on two levels: Forest could ill afford to lose a marksman of his quality – he ended the season as the Premier League's top scorer with twenty-two goals – and the deal was investigated by an independent inquiry into bungs. The case against Clough collapsed for lack of evidence but his assistant, Ron Fenton, was banned from working with an English club again.

At first, it appeared the impact of the striker's departure would not be shattering as Gary Bannister, a thirty-two-year-old acquired on a free transfer from West Brom, scored twice on his league debut, a 5-3 defeat at Oldham, after coming on as substitute for Sheringham. He added to his tally at Blackburn Rovers but a 4-1 defeat at Ewood Park was Forest's fifth in a row and left them bottom of the table. 'For the second time in less than a week Forest conceded an early goal, fought their way back to take control of the match and then, in the space of ten crazy second-half minutes, committed defensive suicide,' reported Ian Edwards in the *Evening Post*. Selling their top striker and best central defender was proving destabilising. Chairman Fred Reacher blamed the construction of the Bridgford Road Stand at a cost of £4 million, a measure to comply with the post-Hillsborough Taylor Report, for lack of spending on players. The stand was opened on 17 October, when nearly 25,000 saw Arsenal win 1-0. Four days later, Forest registered their second league win in their twelfth Premiership game when a deflected shot by Kingsley Black saw off Middlesbrough. There were fewer than 18,000 at the City Ground to watch it and Forest remained stuck at the bottom.

Still anchored in the depths, the squad was in need of a boost and at the end of November, Clough bought back foraging midfielder Neil Webb from Manchester United for £750,000. He played in the 2-1 home defeat by Southampton, a game notable chiefly for a rare penalty miss by Stuart Pearce saved in the last minute by Tim Flowers. In his second game, Webb dictated midfield at Elland Road and prompted Forest to a 4-1 victory against the reigning champions, ending Leeds' thirty-one-game unbeaten home record. Roy Keane scored twice, with Nigel Clough and Kingsley Black adding the others. 'We thumped them,' Webb recalled. 'And we thought that would be the end of our struggles.' It began to look as though he was right, as five wins and two draws were taken from the next ten league games, including a 3-0 thrashing of Chelsea.

For all their problems, the Reds were proving doughty cup fighters. They reached the fifth rounds of both the FA Cup and the League Cup before losing both to Arsenal at Highbury by 2-0 scorelines. It was the FA Cup defeat on 13 February that was to prove disastrous. Webb, who had snapped his right Achilles while with Manchester United, now had trouble with his left and had to be substituted. He needed an operation and his season was over. It was also all over for Stuart Pearce, who finished the game but then needed surgery on his groin. Back to back wins against Middlesbrough 2-1 away, with goals by Nigel Clough and Steve Stone on his debut, and Queen's Park Rangers 1-0 at home gave hope briefly, but then the Reds won only twice in the last fourteen League games.

On 23 March, two days after his fifty-eighth birthday, Brian Clough was made a Freeman of the City of Nottingham. His decision that month to sign journeyman striker Robert Rosario from Coventry for £400,000, and then to pull out of a £1.75-million deal to take the much fancied Stan Collymore from Southend, was enough to convince many Forest fans that the game was up for the club among the elite. They had serenaded him with 'Happy Birthday' at the Leeds game on 21 March and 26,000 hailed him with the chant 'Brian Clough's a football genius' at the City Ground finale on 1 May against Dave Bassett's Sheffield United, who were also relegation threatened. United won 2-0, condemning their hosts to the drop, and also won their next two games to ensure their own survival.

At the final whistle, Forest fans demonstrated their gratitude to the great man for the good times he brought and the visiting Sheffield fans joined in the acclaim. A distraught young girl approached and presented him with a flower. Taking it from her, he said tenderly, 'Hey, beauty, no tears today please.' To a television reporter who asked, 'Brian, can I have a word?' he replied, 'Goodbye.'

In an interview with Duncan Hamilton of the *Post*, he admitted that not replacing Sheringham adequately 'was stupid'. He had the money to sign Collymore but, no longer sure about players, 'not the inclination'. Clough also dismissed the prospect of becoming a director or life president of the club. This was not because the club tactlessly precipitated an announcement of his intention to retire at the end of the season but because he did not want to inhibit a successor. In his memoir of twenty years with Brian Clough, *Provided You Don't Kiss Me*, Hamilton recalls Clough saying he tried to line up Archie Gemmill for the vacancy. It was also commonly thought that he had recommended Frank Clark, who was given the job. Judging by comments in *Walking on Water*, Clough's final autobiography, that seems unlikely. He admired the work done by Martin O'Neill like 'a young Clough' at Leicester with John Robertson as his assistant – 'Martin O'Neill and John Robertson, the academic and the scruff, chalk and cheese, just like Peter Taylor and me.' O'Neill turned down an opportunity to replace his mentor. Of Clark, Clough wrote, 'Team management just wasn't in him as far as I could see.'

Family resentment about the abrupt disclosure of Brian Clough's departure led to Nigel Clough leaving Nottingham for Liverpool in June for £2 million. Despite this, they remained on good terms with Chairman Reacher and Christmas cards continued to be exchanged even after Brian Clough's death. Nigel, the 'number nine', was one of the best Forest centre-forwards, making 412 appearances and scoring 131 goals. He gained fourteen senior England caps and played in fifteen Under-21 matches. Speed of thought made up for lack of pace and he soaked up any number of physical challenges from behind as he received and shielded the ball before setting up teammates. Showing such courage, the fact that he was the manager's son mattered not a scrap. Brian said of his son:

I was secretly chuffed that our Nige signed with Forest. I constructed the team around him to get the best out of him and it worked, not only for the team but for individuals within it. Stuart Pearce said to me on one of those occasions when he was accusing me of being too hard on the lad, 'I wouldn't be half the player I am without your Nige in the side – and I play left-back.' Even Teddy Sheringham, with whom I didn't get on that well, told me after that one full season of his, 'I've scored twenty-odd goals this year but without your Nige in the side, I wouldn't have got ten.' Oh yes, the players knew he had talent.

Clough the Younger also played for Manchester City and became first player-manager and then manager of Burton Albion before taking over at Derby. Defeat by Forest in front of 28,000 on Trentside at the end of September 2013, thanks to Jack Hobbs heading in a wicked inswinging corner from the brilliant Andy Reid, led to a sacking that evening that shocked both sets of supporters. Before the weekend was out a short-lived manager of the Reds, Steve McClaren, had replaced him. Nigel was soon back at work in charge of Sheffield United. Then he again took charge of Burton.

Another Forest favourite to leave during the summer of 1993 was the redoubtable Roy Keane, who cost Manchester United £3.75 million and proved a bargain at that. 'Roy Keane is – and was for me – the genuine article,' Brian Clough wrote in *Walking on Water*, 'I never remember him giving an ounce less than his utmost, his absolute maximum, in a Forest shirt.' Keane 'shone like a beacon through all the gloom' of his manager's last 'desolate season'. He played forty games and scored six goals although 'the way we performed, he had to spend most of his time defending'. Sir Alex Ferguson couldn't have made a better signing at Old Trafford than Keano, Clough declared.

On one occasion after training, the manager burst into the dressing room and shouted insults at his players in turn; even Pearce was told, 'You've been crap since you got that new contract.' Jemson was told to 'stop rabbiting to refs'. There was a different put-down for each player until, finally, he got to Keane. 'I love you, Irishman,' he said. The affection was mutual. In his latest autobiography, *The Second Half*, written with award-winning author Roddy Doyle, Keane says he worked under two great managers, Brian Clough and Alex Ferguson, and he puts his Forest manager ahead of the United boss because 'his warmth was genuine'. He also comments, 'He hit me once, and I thought, "I know why you punched me." I got him – I just got him.' Clough was denied the opportunity to manage at international level. What would he have thought when O'Neill, as manager of the Republic of Ireland, appointed Keane as his assistant?

David Goldblatt, in his social history *The Game of Our Lives*, published in 2014, comments:

> Clough never created an empire in the same way (as Bill Shankly at Liverpool) but winning consecutive European Cups with Nottingham Forest – a club from perhaps England's eighth largest city – was an unrepeatable, demograph-defying achievement. Shankly and Clough were linguistically brilliant. Shankly was more gnomic but sardonic,

sharp and funny. Clough, who helped invent the very notion of a television football pundit, was garrulous and could be cruel and arrogant. In the end, they were killed by the same slow horrors that took so many men of their class and generation; Shankly by the pointless empty boredom of life after work, Clough by the bottle.

Clough was a larger-than-life character, Shakespearian in complexity, who in turn could be comic, dramatic and, ultimately, tragic.

21

Forest Feet

Forest's longest serving and most successful managers – Billy Walker, twenty-one years from 1939, and Brian Clough, eighteen years from 1975 – had much more than job longevity in common. They shared the same football philosophy. It all boiled down to keeping possession by passing the ball on the ground to feet and picking players willing to take responsibility and knocks. No one in a shirt of Garibaldi red embodied those qualities more than Brian's son Nigel, his No. 9. Neither Walker nor Clough had time for coaching theories. They would agree that football's a simple game, so why complicate things? Players knew what was expected of them and were instructed to concentrate on their own game whoever the opposition.

Clough said,

My players didn't need to be told what to do – they did it as a matter of course. They did the things they knew they could do when we bought them. You don't spend a fortune on a player and then expect to have to teach him how to play, do you? All I asked of players was that they did their jobs – and that's not an over-simplification. A winger has to be able to cross a ball. If he can't, then the next best thing is to have a bit of pace. A centre-forward's job is to score goals and if he's none too clever at that, the next best thing is the ability to create them. As for the midfield player – I don't care what other attributes he possesses but he must have the ability to pass the ball.

We had all those things in our side. A keeper who knew what he was doing, defenders who could head, tackle and scare people, a midfield with pace and know-how and a wonderful talent for delivering the ball where we wanted it, and men up front who would run and work and, hopefully, get us a goal. We were to lose only four matches in the 1978/79 season and the one that brought the most disappointment ended that incredible run of forty-two unbeaten matches in the League. The more I think of those forty-two games, the more I glance at that silver salver showing every one of them, the more convinced I am that it was an absolutely phenomenal achievement. I suppose it had to be Liverpool who brought it to an end – a 2-0 defeat at Anfield didn't it?

The beliefs shared by Walker, Clough and Taylor were shaped by the ideas of perhaps the finest coaching genius of the twentieth century – Jimmy Hogan, born in a terrace house in Victoria Street, Nelson, Lancashire, in 1882. An inside-forward, he played for a number of Football League clubs, including Rochdale, Burnley, Fulham and Bolton Wanderers, but it is as a coach that he is remembered, even revered on the Continent. Austria, Hungary, Germany, France, Switzerland and the Netherlands all based their playing styles on Hogan's brand of quick, short, incisive passing football. His favoured tactics demanded versatility and the ability to pass the ball on what he always called 'the carpet' – anticipating what would become known in the 1970s as 'Total Football'.

It was England's humiliating 6-3 defeat by Hungary's 'Magical Magyars' at Wembley in 1953 that so impressed Clough and Taylor but Walker had captained England against Austria's legendary 'Wunderteam', coached by Hogan, in 1932. Four years later he had also attended the first FA coaching course at which the Lancastrian had been 'chief instructor'. Other 'pupils' included such luminaries as Alex James, Arthur Rowe, Joe Mercer, Peter Doherty and Walker's former captain at Villa, Frank Barson. Despite earlier reservations, Walker was persuaded that not all coaching was 'moonshine'.

Hungarian Football Federation president Sandor Barcs dedicated their Wembley victory to Hogan. 'Jimmy Hogan taught us everything we know about football,' he said. Len Shackleton was among those who, in the aftermath of England's defeat, urged the FA to give him a national role. Sir Stanley Rous, the schoolmasterly secretary of the Football Association, was unimpressed by Hogan's coaching skills, believing his methods depended too much on demonstration with insufficient explanation. He was more sympathetic to the blackboard expositions of another Lancastrian, Walter Winterbottom, England's first manager, who became the FA's director of coaching and was later knighted. Rous, a former sports master and international referee, was president of FIFA when Sir Alf Ramsey's England won the World Cup in 1966.

Tommy Docherty, who came under Hogan's influence as a teenaged midfielder at Glasgow Celtic, was inspired by the coach's passing philosophy. 'He used to say football was like a Viennese waltz,' said 'the Doc'. 'One-two-three, one-two three, pass-move-pass. We were entranced. His arrival at Celtic Park was the best thing that ever happened to me.'

As youth team coach at Aston Villa, Hogan made a similar impression on apprentice Ron Atkinson:

When Jimmy came to Villa, he was revolutionary. Everything was geared around ball control and passing. He would have you on the stadium carpark and you would be told to play the ball with the inside of your right foot, outside of your right foot, inside again and then turn to come back playing the ball on the inside and outside of your left foot. He would get you doing step-overs, little turns and twists on the ball. Everything you did was to make you comfortable with the ball.'

Brian Clough said it was Alan Brown at Sunderland who taught him about discipline and the value of decent behaviour that, years later, was to become a hallmark of Clough teams and 'the reason why we were the favourites among referees'. He wrote in his autobiography:

The Sunderland manager's approach was a shock to my system. He stood straight as a Buckingham Palace guardsman and when he delivered a bollocking you knew it. There were occasions when I was downright scared of the man. He detested shabby clothing and insisted his players always had a regular trim. There was never a sign of long hair at Roker Park. He made an immense impression on me. I hope –indeed, I know – that I carried his influence and sprinkled it through the game for a long time. He ran Sunderland from top to bottom. I recognised that from the start. What he said mattered and people responded. He was *the boss* in every sense of the word and I said to myself, even then: 'If ever I become a manager, this is the way the job should be done.' You can have your chairmen, chief executives, secretaries and the blokes who run the development funds, they are nothing, nobodies, and have no chance of succeeding unless *the* most important figure at the football club gets things right in the first place. The manager in charge of the team is the key. Unless the manager has sound judgment, all the other football club employees might as well stay at home. And although the game has changed down the years, I remain convinced that the manager has to be the boss.

This conviction was reinforced when Peter Taylor introduced Clough to Harry Storer, then manager at the Baseball Ground.

I remember his square jaw that looked as if it had been sculpted from a block of granite. He had a reputation for toughness and I was in awe of him. He wasn't large physically but he was the rugged, tenacious type – the classic wing-half of his day. I listened and I learned.

The first subject he discussed was football club directors. 'Don't ever forget – directors never say thank you.'

Storer's pet subject was courage – the need for moral as well as physical courage in football. He once literally dragged one of his players back onto the pitch after a game and demanded, 'Show me where it is?' The player was dumbfounded. 'Where what is, boss?' 'The hole,' Storer roared. 'The hole you've been hiding in all afternoon.' Storer also advised, 'When you are leaving for an away game, look around the team coach and count the number of hearts. If you're lucky, there will be five. If there aren't, turn the coach round and go back!'

'Everything said by Harry Storer on football management has stood the test of time,' Taylor said. 'He boiled down the job to one sentence: "It's easy to be a good manager; all you do is sign good players." Then he would wink, he knew that was the hardest part of all.'

Storer had been an England international wing-half and a professional cricketer, who opened the batting for Derbyshire. He was scathing about coaches. 'They're telling us we should copy the Continentals and have retreating defences,' he said. 'When an opponent has the ball, they say we should fall back until he makes a mistake – but they have no answer when I ask them, "Suppose he doesn't make a mistake?".' Coaches, a word that Harry almost spat out, had no answer, either, to his stock challenge, 'There are hundreds of coaches and miles of film showing exactly how Stanley Matthews used to beat a full-back. Yet where is the coach who has taught just one lad how to perform Stan's tricks.'

It was George Hardwick at Middlesbrough who put Clough in charge of the youth team and gave him a taste for management. A rakish moustache and debonair manner disguised the fearsome tackler that was Hardwick the player, a left-back who captained England in all his thirteen international appearances, remarkably including his first. In 1947 he also captained the Great Britain side to a 6-1 victory over the Rest of Europe, led by another left-back, Johnny Carey, then of Manchester United and Ireland, who later managed Forest. Clough described his mentor as an attacking full-back before his time. 'He could get the ball and play it – normally they'd just kick it but George used it brilliantly,' he said. Hardwick went on to work as a coach with the Dutch FA and PSV Eindhoven.

Clough said:

> The Sunderland youth side responded to me immediately because I scrubbed those dreadful, monotonous laps from the training routine. I put a ball down and we played football – five-a-side, six-a-side, anything that enabled them to practice the way they were expected to play as a team.

Simply, Clough and Walker believed the game was football, play the ball to feet, Forest feet.

Both managers understood that captaincy was more than calling heads or tails before kick-off and they wanted players they could trust. Brian Clough chose John McGovern, who won a League championship medal and was twice a European Cup winner with Forest. Eventually, McGovern was succeeded by Stuart Pearce, who captained England.

Like Clough, Billy Walker was unimpressed by the graduates of FA coaching courses and theorists of Winterbottom's ilk. As a player and then a manager, he respected above all experienced pros, believing he learned more from them during matches than on the training field. Even as their boss, Walker listened to players and readily accepted their advice. 'When I came into the Villa side as a boy, I had the best coaches in the world in the team right behind and alongside me,' he said. One was hard-as-nails centre-half Frank Barson, who captained Villa and then Manchester United, and the other forward Clem Stephenson, both England internationals.

> As soon as I got the ball – and, mind you, even at the age of seventeen I was a fairly handy, instinctive user of it – I would hear the voice of one or other of these towering personalities shout a direction. It got so that the voices of my tutors, particularly that of Barson, gradually amplified my own instinct and I automatically reacted to their commands. It was all done in actual play, in competitive games. There was no getting away from the genius of these two men and whatever I was able to add to it was a bonus. Nowadays, I am convinced young players are being over-coached at the wrong time and in the wrong place. They are being drilled in mannered moves based on theories about what the opposing team will do in certain circumstances. When they get on the field in a real match they are already bogged down by tactics ill-equipped to react to unexpected opportunities.

Planning moves on the blackboard or with figures on magnetic tables was 'unutterable nonsense' that ignored the fluctuating course of an actual game. Walker went on:

> It is an axiom of football that one man does not make a team. Barson was the exception that proved the rule. His tremendous command on the field made the great Aston Villa side of which I was a young and very proud member. I am unhesitating in saying that he was the greatest captain of them all. His presence on the field was worth all the tactical talks of a dozen coaches off it.

Manager Walker surprised a few people when he promoted Jack Burkitt, a tough twenty-nine-year-old unrelenting half-back, to be his captain when Horace Gager, his stylish, experienced centre-half, retired in 1955. But the manager knew best. Freddie Scott, the next in line, was six months older than Gager, and Burkitt had six good seasons in the League team behind him. Jack more than justified his manager's confidence leading the Reds back to the top flight and showing true leadership at Wembley in 1959, when Forest won the FA Cup despite the handicap of being down to ten men for two-thirds of the final, having lost Roy Dwight with a broken leg.

Some programme notes from early in 1952 indicate that Burkitt had long been groomed for the captaincy. He had given up an apprenticeship as an engineering draughtsman to become a professional as a nineteen-year-old in 1946. In the 1947/48 season he captained the Forest 'A' team to a league and cup double. After a short spell in the reserves, Jack got his big chance against Coventry City on 20 October 1948 and never looked back.

He was described as 'a hard, industrious worker, always giving his best for the team'. Against Bolton Wanderers, he gave 'a classic display'. However, it was difficult to pick out any particular match as being outstanding, so well was he playing. 'Well built, Jack is 5ft. 10ins. and weighs 11st. 5lbs. He is married to a Darlaston girl and is never happier than when he is with his wife and young son in his Nottingham home,' it was noted.

Jack Burkitt, like his manager, was born in Wednesbury, Staffordshire, and both spent their early years in nearby Darlaston, playing in their youth for the town football club. Town won the Birmingham Combination in 1945/46 with Jack, then nineteen, playing a major role as centre-half. His brother, Bill, told Darlaston Town historian Neil Chambers for the club history in 2011 how Jack came to join Forest.

Darlaston were playing Nuneaton away in the FA Cup on 21st September 1946, when a Nottingham Forest scout was watching the Nuneaton centre-forward. Jack had the centre-forward in his pocket and although Darlaston lost 3-1 the scout reported back to Forest manager Billy Walker that he should not pursue the Nuneaton centre-forward but should sign the young Darlaston centre-half.

Walker decided to see for himself. 'Jack was on the verge of signing for Worcester City but Walker came to watch him and decided he wanted to sign him,' Bill said. 'The deal took place in the White Lion pub in Darlaston and the club received £500 and an agreement to a testimonial game for Herbert Hunt, who played for Darlaston for about fourteen years and was a good friend to Jack.'

Burkitt joined the Reds in August 1947 and went on to make 503 senior appearances, captaining the side for six seasons. After his playing career ended in 1962, he stayed on as a coach and gained a full FA coaching badge. It was from Jack that a young Henry Newton learned the basics of solid tackling. In 1966, Burkitt crossed Trent Bridge to manage Notts County for a year and then joined Derby as a trainer under Brian Clough. Jack had already bought a post office in Oakdale Road, Bakersfield, Nottingham, and on leaving the Rams in 1969 he worked there until his retirement. He died on 12 September 2003 in Brighouse, Yorkshire.

He had been given a testimonial in 1961 against Swedish side Malmo, who eighteen years later were to meet Forest in the European Cup Final in Munich. On a cold, foggy November weeknight 7,800 hardy City Ground diehards (I was among them) turned up to support Jack but the game was abandoned after seventy-nine minutes with the Reds leading 5-1 through Colin Addison, Johnny Quigley, Geoff Vowden, 'Flip' Le Flem and Colin Booth.

When schoolboy John McGovern came home with fresh cuts and bruises on his knees and shins, his mum would say to him, 'Don't complain. They're medals you've won.' It gave him the winning mentality that so impressed Brian Clough, then the new manager of Hartlepool United when he started a youth team at the club and included the slight fifteen-year-old who needed to 'stand up straight, shoulders back and get a haircut'. Clough was not to know that the teenager was deeply embarrassed by a badly rounded left shoulder that caused him to run 'with a funny waddle'. It was not until he went for a medical examination at Nottingham Forest that McGovern learned that he had been born with a back muscle missing, making him throw his left arm across his body when he ran.

The handicap slowed him down but he compensated by having the stamina to run all day. And it did not stop him winning two European Cups, two league championships, one Super Cup, a League Cup and the FA's Charity Shield, a list of honours envied by some of the world's greatest players. One of them, the German international midfielder Gunter Netzer, of Real Madrid fame, saw him play against Cologne in the 1979 European Cup semi-final and commented in the newspapers, 'Who is this McGovern? I've never heard of him yet he ran midfield.'

Burkitt was the Derby County trainer when McGovern signed for the Rams in September 1968 but, oddly, the two great Forest captains did not get on together.

22

New Direction

Billy Walker, Brian Clough, Sir Matt Busby, Jock Stein, Don Revie, Bill Shankly and Alex Ferguson ran their clubs from top to bottom. What would be their reaction to the new frontier of football, to the age of data collection and analysis, performance measurement, breaking down the beautiful game into mere statistics? Revie, who had a fondness for having dossiers compiled on opponents, might be unfazed by this modern trend but he would have demanded to be the top man. The others, I suspect, would be torn between responding with ridicule or rage.

Match day programmes these days contain pages of facts supplied by data companies like Prozone and Opta. Televised games also show stats recording possession percentages, pass completion, goals to shots ratio, assists and even metres run by individual player.

One Saturday morning John McGovern, racked by pain, struggled to get out of bed. He got to his car and drove to the City Ground. In the dressing room he quietly told Brian Clough, 'Sorry boss, I'm not going to be able to play. I can hardly walk, let alone run.' 'John, you never could run,' Clough replied. 'Get your boots on, pick up the ball and lead the team out, skipper.'

First the deflating 'you never could run' and then the morale-boosting 'lead the team out, skipper'. That was great psychology, never mind good management. It wasn't the distance a player ran that mattered to Clough. It was the purpose behind covering the ground that did.

So far as this country is concerned, the ghost of the Wing Commander Charles Reep, hailed by the *Journal of Sports Sciences* on his death in 2002 as 'the first professional performance analyst of football', haunts this particular house of cards. He concluded that most goals were scored from fewer than three passes; therefore, he proposed, the quicker the ball was propelled forward with the least number of passes, the more goals would be scored. His theory became known as the long-ball game and, later, was derided as hoofball. The basic principle appealed to Stan Cullis, manager of Wolverhampton Wanderers, in the aftermath of Hungary's shattering victory over England in 1953. The Cullis-Reep collaboration led to a period of success for Wolves, who won the League championship three times in the 1950s.

For Cullis in the modern game, think 'Big Sam' Allardyce, another former rugged centre-half who has been labelled (wrongly, he claims) a long-ball manager. Certainly, he has a technological and statistical approach to tactics and coaching. Reep wrote treatises asking *Are We Getting Too Clever? Or Declaring Pattern-Weaving Talk Is All Bunk.* His quasi-academic philosophy attracted the attention of Clough's arch nemesis Charles Hughes, and for a time was implanted into the FA's coaching manuals. Brian Glanville, three years my senior and one of the greatest of football writers, wrote that Reep tried to make the long-ball option respectable and Hughes, 'with his computers, fanatical credo and insistence that Brazil had got it wrong, appeared to be preaching a pseudo-religion'.

Analytics – 'the discovery and communication of meaningful patterns in data' – has crossed the Atlantic to our shores. Baseball, basketball and American gridiron football have long embraced statistical analysis and performance measurement. It must work for them. But soccer (if we must call it that) is so different to those games. The ball is a free spirit during play – not imprisoned by the hands. The game flows. Gridiron and baseball are episodic. Even basketball has its time-out calls and its court is small so that the action takes place at the two baskets with little build-up play. Unlike the other games, soccer is low-scoring. The pulse quickens and tension heightens during an attack and emotions explode when the goalkeeper is beaten and the ball hits the back of the net. Scoring in basketball, by contrast, comes with monotonous machine-gun-fire rapidity – the teams seemingly taking turns to drop the ball through their opponents' hoops. A typical American pro-basketball scoreline would be Warriors 90 Cavaliers 120. Where's the passion in that?

Association football is only true football game. The rugby and American codes are more about carrying and throwing than kicking and, to facilitate this emphasis, the ball is distorted – not round but oval. Muscle is more important than skill and, consequently, play can be controlled (the Americans even have 'playbooks' with moves worked out in advance by coaches to be implemented robotically by the players). Because the ball cannot be contained, our football is a fluid, open game, limiting the effectiveness of planning.

There is a story about Walter Winterbottom's theoretical scheming. 'Alf,' he said to full-back Ramsey. 'When you win the ball, bring it out of defence and pass it to Tom on the wing.' Turning to Finney, he went on: 'Tom you let Billy (Wright) have the ball and make your run to take a return pass near the goal line. Cross the ball to the far post.' Next he spoke to centre-forward Tommy Lawton. 'Tommy,' he said. 'Leave your marker and put a header into the net.' Addressing the team, Winterbottom asked, 'Any questions.' Lawton put his hand up. Winterbottom: 'Yes, Tommy.' Lawton: 'Walter, which side of the goal do you want me to aim at?'

The fact is that ours, with twenty-two players and a ball in almost constant motion, is the most unpredictable of all team sports. There are no certain winners and few no-hopers: Iceland, with a population of 333,000, beat England, with 54 million, 2-1 in the 2016 European Championships in France. Nottingham, incidentally, has a city population of 315,000 and a suburban area large enough to take it over the million mark. The Icelanders, it was reported, played the type football seen in the 1980s, but they deserved their victory. Randomness defines the sport. In football, miracles do happen.

One statistic worth recording is that the likelihood of the underdog winning at soccer is 45 per cent. A football game is made up of hundreds of small actions dependent on speed of ball and brain, little pieces of skill but also luck. So can players be judged by reference to performance indicators informed by mathematical modelling as the sports scientists suggest? Imagine Brian Clough and Billy Walker being asked this question in the football Heaven. Clough, exploding with mirth, would request a brandy. Walker would light a cigarette and quietly chuckle to himself.

A development that is of enormous benefit is the advances in sports medicine. It is worrying, for instance, that so many great players of the past suffered from memory loss that has been identified by a comprehensive medical study as the result of constantly heading the ball. Former Notts County and West Bromwich Albion centre-forward Jeff Astle, an England international who died in 2002, is a case in point. I must admit to avoiding heading the ball whenever possible in my playing days.

Forest legend Tinsley Lindley, described by all-round athlete and scholar C. B. Fry in *Annals of the Corinthian Football Club*, published in 1906, as 'one of the greatest centre-forwards ever known', was another reluctant header. But, wrote Fry, Lindley was 'very good at taking the ball on the full volley from a centre; it was just eye and timing, like a Ranji glance to leg'. However, a Forester who helped form Arsenal in the 1880s, Morris Bates, was one of the earliest headers of a ball and was nicknamed 'Iron Head'. Appalling as they are, the statistics for soccer head injuries do not approach those of American gridiron football. And some of the greatest British headers of the ball like Dixie Dean of Everton and John Charles of Leeds United and Juventus, are not recorded as having any later problems. One in twenty of those aged over sixty-five suffer from dementia and the disease affects all types and classes. Distinguished author Iris Murdoch, who died aged seventy-nine in 1999, was diagnosed with Alzheimer's three years earlier. She was not noted for heading a ball. More investigation is necessary if football is to find a way forward.

Neither Clough nor Walker were seen as coaches. FA Cup-winning centre-half Bobby McKinlay saw Walker as a father figure rather than a tactician. The late, great McKinlay is remembered for the manner in which he played the game. A stopper with style, he played nearly 700 games and was never sent off, receiving just two cautions. 'That's one every ten years,' he told me, with a smile, when I interviewed him for a football magazine after his retirement. He had become a prison officer at Lowdham Grange near Nottingham, then an institution for young offenders, and lived with his wife Pauline at a house in the grounds, where his neighbour and a colleague was former Notts County wing-half Gerry Carver. The Lowdham boys could not have had better role models.

Uncle Billy had introduced the sixteen-year-old Bob to Forest in 1948. Billy had been a wing-half for the Reds when they had one of the finest half-back lines in the country. The famous trio was made up of an Englishman, a Welshman and a Scotsman: centre-half Tommy Graham, Bob Pugh and Billy McKinlay. Recognised as one of the most creative players in the game, Billy played 357 senior games for Forest in ten years and later became a club scout. The McKinlay family in Lochgelly, Fife, was steeped in football tradition. Bob's father, Rab, had been a semi-professional centre-half with Cowdenheath. Bobby was playing for Fife junior side Bowhill Rovers as a right-winger and it was in that position that he had a week's trial in Nottingham. At the City Ground, coach Bob Davies, a former Welsh international centre-half, switched him to the middle of the defence.

Bobby returned home to his job with a local garage wondering whether he would get the chance of a football career in England. Seven days later came the good news that he was to be signed as soon as he was seventeen. Rab and Billy McKinlay were at the signing ceremony on 15 October 1949. Bobby was still not convinced that he would make the grade and decided to look upon his move over the border (coming to Nottingham was the first time he had been out of Scotland) as probably 'a year's paid holiday'. In fact, he stayed with Forest twice as long as Uncle Billy had done and played in double the number of matches. Walker decided the tall but slim youngster needed to work on his strength and got him a summer job as a farm labourer. That was fine, Bob told me, except that the manager wanted an agent's percentage of his wage.

He had just turned nineteen when he made his first-team debut in a Second Division game at Coventry on 27 October 1951, replacing veteran captain Horace Gager at centre-half. Billy Walker said,

> There is only one way, in my opinion, to bring on a young player and that is by gradual experience. He will be in for one game and the next time for two or three games. The chief consideration for all young players is the physical side. They must not overtax their strength. Bobby will learn this vital lesson. He must at all times give 100 per cent concentration to his game, must think and act that fraction quicker than an opponent and, above all, keep cool and calm. He must not let himself be rattled by the talkative, experienced adversary that he will meet. He alone can accomplish this. I can only assist him.

It was not an auspicious start for young Bobby. Peter Taylor was in goal for Coventry and the home centre-forward Ted Roberts scored a hat-trick in a 3-3 draw. After the match, Walker commented,

> I am quite satisfied with Bobby's display. Roberts, a tough centre-forward, took the three chances that he had but he never once had Bobby rattled. I realised that it would be a big ordeal for this boy but was certain he would rise to it and I am sure you are going to hear about this lad for a number of years.

Those two sets of quotes speak volumes for Walker's management style. In my interview with him, McKinlay had this to say about his old boss:

> Billy Walker was never a tracksuit manager. Team talks were brief and to the point. There was virtually no coaching but we knew to play the passing game. He always said that if we were good enough for him to pick us for the team, we were good enough to know how he wanted us to play and to recognise the strengths and weaknesses of the opposition. There is no doubt, however, that Walker knew how to build a team. He had a fair eye for a player.

Talking to Bobby reinforced my impression of the similarities in the football philosophies of Billy Walker and Brian Clough.

The game is football, play to feet – Walker

If God had wanted us to play football in the clouds, he'd have put grass up there – Clough

England international left-winger Alf Spouncer was an FA Cup winner with Forest in 1898 as a twenty-year-old and was with the club for thirteen years. He had a season managing Barcelona in 1923/24, when the Catalans won the ten-match provincial championship with a 100 per cent record. His players were given 'ten commandments'. The most important were: attack is the best form of defence, football is a team game and no individual player, however talented, is more important than the team, pass the ball accurately to retain possession, keep it on the ground – *we don't play football in the air.* Sounds familiar, doesn't it? Another former Forest winger, incidentally, guided Real Madrid to the Spanish championship in 1932/33. He was Bob Firth, who was at the City Ground before and after the First World War.

Clough advocated building from the back and emphasised keeping the ball with accurate passing using the full width of the pitch and making opposing sides use up energy chasing it. The priority for defenders was defence, heading and tackling. For midfielders, it was possession – opponents couldn't score if they didn't have the ball. Forwards had to receive the ball under pressure and not release it until support arrived. Get the ball, he said, and enjoy its company. Away from home, his tactic was dropping back and counter-attacking, which has now become commonplace.

At Anfield, there is a 'This is Anfield' sign above the stairs in the tunnel leading to the pitch. It was originally erected on the orders of legendary manager Bill Shankly to strike fear into the opposition as they left the away dressing room to take on Liverpool. Great psychology. But Clough trumped this when Forest went to Merseyside to defend a two-goal lead in the second leg of the European Cup in September 1978. First, he took the now retired Shankly to the match in the Forest team bus astounding but also relaxing his players. Then, in the dressing room, he gave a succinct team talk. 'Gentlemen,' he said without concern. 'You'll see a sign out there that tells you "This is Anfield". Let's show them we're not bothered.'

Neither Clough nor Walker had much time for coaching theory but, in practice, they could get their instructions across clearly and concisely.

Much was made of Clough's absences from the training ground but his match day demeanor was decisive. Walker respected his senior professionals and liked them to become leaders. He also listened to their views when recruiting new players. Walker forked out £4,500 on the recommendation of 'Sailor' Brown for winger Freddie Scott from York City, a record fee for the selling club. 'Sailor' had partnered him in wartime football at York and Charlton and knew his worth. He acted on the advice of centre-forward Wally Ardron to buy left-wing pair Tommy Capel and Colin Collindridge.

Forest's scouting network during Walker's management included Warrant Officer Danny Long, who spotted wing-half Calvin Palmer at Skegness and goalkeeper Peter Grummitt from Bourne, Lincolnshire. And thanks to the talent-spotting of former physiotherapist Ted Malpass, who had played with Billy Walker at Aston Villa and lived in Guernsey, Forest had a string of Channel Islanders recommended to the club from the late 1940s to the early sixties.

They included right-back Bill Whare, who could break opposing wingers' hearts by, when they thought he was left behind, winning the ball with recovering sliding tackles that left them flat on their faces. Their feelings were hurt but never their limbs. Whare always played fairly. He was born in Guernsey in 1925 and made his debut for Forest a few weeks before his twenty-fourth birthday in a 2-2 draw in front of a 27,000 crowd for a Division Two match at the City Ground on 23 April 1949. It was his only first-team appearance in a relegation season. And he was at left-half. Whare got back into the side at the end of October in his preferred full-back position. There was competition from veteran Jack Hutchinson but he chalked up 298 first-team appearances before ending his League career against Burnley at Turf Moor on 21 November 1959. It was not the send-off he would have wanted. Forest lost 8-0 with Jimmy Robson scoring five goals for the home side.

During Bill's decade in the Garibaldi red shirt, Forest rose from Division Three South to the First Division but the highlight was playing his part in the Wembley triumph of 1959. Whare's Cup Final partner at full-back was Joe McDonald but the best-remembered pairing was with Geoff Thomas, who had been signed from a Derby youth club. They played together through three divisions of the Football League and for a total of 204 games.

The Guernsey-born Farmer brothers were recruited from Jersey side St Aubins. Goalkeeper Bill Farmer made his debut in a 2-0 win against Hull City in a Second Division match at the City Ground on 16 September

1953. He made forty-four Division Two appearances in his three seasons on Trentside and played six games in the FA Cup in 1954/55 including the fifth-round tie against Newcastle United, which went to two replays. Bill had left for Loughborough Brush Sports before his brother Ron, a wing-half, made his Forest debut against Gillingham in the FA Cup third round on 4 January 1958.

Although born in Barnsley, Geoff Vowden was brought up in Jersey and came to Forest as a teenager. He scored two goals in his first-team debut in a friendly against Scottish Cup winners St Mirren at the City Ground on 23 September 1959. Three days later, as an eighteen-year-old, he made his First Division debut at inside-right in a 2-0 home win against Bolton Wanderers. Geoff scored thirty-eight top-flight goals in ninety games for Forest and also got eight goals in seventeen FA Cup and Football League cup-ties. He scored in his last game for the Reds on 19 September 1964, a 3-2 defeat at the City Ground by Fulham, for whom full-back Jim Langley struck a 50-yard free-kick past goalkeeper Peter Grummitt. Vowden was at centre-forward and scored in a 3-1 victory at Cardiff when Forest's fifth Channel Islander eighteen-year-old Richard 'Flip' Le Flem made his debut.

Le Flem delighted supporters and frustrated opponents in the manner of his predecessors on the Forest left-wing Colin Collindridge and Stewart Imlach, establishing a tradition of individual brilliance in that position that was to be carried on by Ian Storey-Moore, Duncan McKenzie and John Robertson. And he scored one of the greatest goals ever seen at the City Ground. In their pre-match pub debates, many Reds fans would put the 7-0 defeat of Burnley on 18 September 1957, as a newly promoted Division One side as the best of all home performances. Manager Walker described that display as 'one of the most sparkling exhibitions of team football I have had the pleasure of witnessing for a long time – all played their parts to perfection'.

The match against Burnley four seasons later when Le Flem scored his 'wonder goal' was much tighter but a stirring struggle seen by 34,000 fans at the City Ground on 1 December 1962. Burnley were unable to take advantage when Forest went down to ten men for twenty minutes during the first half after right-winger Trevor Hockey damaged his arm and shoulder in a heavy fall. A big factor in this was the way Jeff Whitefoot, normally known for his creativity at wing-half, shackled the great Irish inside-forward Jimmy McIlroy. Then, with the team back to full strength, just before the interval young, blond centre-forward David Wilson met a cross and headed the ball down for inside-left Johnny Quigley to drive Forest ahead. From a 52nd-minute corner, conceded after a period of heavy pressure, the visitors equalised through Ray Pointer, another blond centre-forward England international.

From then on, it was a tremendous battle settled by Le Flem's brilliant individual goal. He received Wilson's pass on the left flank just inside the Burnley half and set off on an amazing dribble, leaving five defenders in his wake, including England internationals John Angus and Brian Miller as well as the visitors' captain, Jimmy Adamson. It was finished off by a superbly struck right-foot shot past Adam Blacklaw, Scotland's goalkeeper. The crowd rose as one to acclaim 'Flip' and the applause went on for minutes afterwards. The goal shattered the visitors and jolted their championship hopes. Burnley finished third and Forest ninth in Division One.

Richard 'Flip' Le Flem was born in Bradford on Avon, Wiltshire, in July 1942, his parents having left the islands during the German wartime occupation. A successful schoolboy athlete and footballer, he arrived from Jersey with Vowden to sign apprentice forms just a month after the 1959 Cup Final. Word soon got round Nottingham about this tricky young ball player Forest had signed and numbers of supporters went down to the Victoria Embankment pitches specially to see Le Flem play for Forest Colts in the Notts Thursday League. It was a competition that pitched the young pros against physically stronger amateurs determined to make the most of their afternoons off from work. His exceptional talent was soon apparent but not always appreciated by some teammates who, like their opponents, could not anticipate what 'Flip' would do next and who berated him for hogging the ball.

Le Flem made the left-wing spot his own after his First Division debut in a 3-1 victory at Cardiff on 10 September, 1960. During his three and a half seasons in Nottingham, 'Flip' made 151 appearances and scored twenty goals. He also played in an England Under-23 victory over Holland in Rotterdam with Bobby Moore as captain. In January 1964, Le Flem was controversially swapped by manager Johnny Carey for Wolves' winger Alan Hinton.

Some of the soccer modernisers are telling scouts 'distrust your eyes' watching live matches and study a bigger sample on video. How Peter Taylor would laugh! He would recall a match against Hull City, watched by a 15,000 crowd at the City Ground on 12 March, and notable not just for goals by Withe and Woodcock in a 2-0 win but for the debut of twenty-year-old local lad Garry Birtles who went on to become Nottingham's best-known carpet fitter and Clough's preferred squash partner as well as the scorer of Forest's first-ever goal in the European Cup. Birtles had been recommended by scout Maurice Edwards and championed by Taylor, who had admired his ability to wrong-foot a defender by dummying to go one way then dragging the ball back and swivelling away with it. Clough had reservations, favouring another young striker Steve Elliott, and reportedly remarked after first seeing Birtles in action, 'The half-time Bovril was better than he was.' Yet the manager was impressed when after being carried off on a stretcher Birtles returned to the action despite having a huge gash on his shin.

In his autobiography, *My Magic Carpet Ride*, the player wrote,

> He must have spotted something in me. Maybe it was just my sheer bravery to come back on to the pitch after getting smashed like that. He was a striker, too. He would have killed to score a goal and even tried to get up and play on when he had his cruciate knee ligament severed playing for Middlesbrough.

In fact, Birtles was used as a midfielder, wearing the No. 7 shirt, against Hull and found himself facing the tigerish ex-Leeds captain Billy Bremner. It was a position he did not like but had played for the reserves 'to build up my strength and stamina'. Before the match, he travelled to the City Ground in John McGovern's car. McGovern was driving in with John O'Hare from Derby and diverted off the A52 to give him a lift. 'It always stuck with me that our captain would go out of his way to pick up some young kid,' Birtles said. Apparently, he did not play particularly well. Clough said to him after the game, 'If I ever play you in midfield again, tell the chairman to give me the sack.'

He had to wait eighteen months for another league chance and to make the No. 9 shirt his own. Birtles' character and talent, I suspect, would have been beneath the radar of performance analysts.

23

Always To Be Here

The Erewash Valley is D. H. Lawrence country. From Eastwood, where he was born in 1885, he would have looked across the valley landscape he loved and which he described in the opening paragraph of the first chapter of *The Rainbow*, chosen by the *Guardian* a couple of years ago as one of the 100 best novels written in the English language:

> The Brangwens had lived for generations on the Marsh Farm, in the meadows where the Erewash twisted sluggishly through alder trees, separating Derbyshire from Nottinghamshire. Two miles away, a church-tower stood on a hill, the houses of the little country town climbing assiduously up to it. Wherever one of the Brangwens in the fields lifted his head from his work, he saw the church-tower at Ilkeston in the empty sky.

Thirteen years before *Lady Chatterley's Lover*, some 1,011 copies of *The Rainbow* were burned by a hangman outside the Royal Exchange. The book had been seized and suppressed under the 1857 Obscene Publications Act. *Lady Chatterley's Lover* is the more notorious but at least through one of its characters, a middle-aged female nurse, Lawrence, the famous novelist, poet, playwright and painter, showed himself a true son of the Erewash Valley with the comment, 'Even football's not what it was, not by a long chalk.'

If destiny decreed that you were to become a football fanatic then fate couldn't unearth a better time or place for you to grow up than in 1940s' industrial Ilkeston (town motto: *labor omnia vincit* – work above all). The town boasted a community of miners, ironworkers and factory hands settled in the Erewash valley bordering the counties of Nottingham and Derby; the crossing point was a bridge at Gallows Inn.

Ilkeston had two weekly newspapers both established in the Victorian era: the *Pioneer*, founded first – as its title suggests – in the Conservative cause, and the *Advertiser*, easily the most popular, started by a Liberal mayor named William Shakespeare. There were four cinemas. Rugby was unheard of, even at the grammar school; cricket merely a summer diversion. Life revolved around work and football. My love for the round ball was not inherited. My father had little interest in the game. He was a motorcycle enthusiast. In the spring of 1940 the headmistress of Bennerley infants school called me out of the classroom. Dad had got his call-up papers and was to report to the Grenadier Guards barracks at Caterham in Surrey. But first, he'd got permission to take mother and me to Skegness for the day. We went on the back of his motorbike. And, in battledress, he kept on riding – carrying despatches with the Guards Armoured Division.

Back home, a ball was my constant companion. I played football in the backyard by myself and on the street with pals. If Harry Altham, a Winchester public school master who later became president of the MCC, was correct then I had all a young boy needed. Instead of the three Rs (reading, 'riting and 'rithmetic), he advocated the three Bs – a ball, a book and bed. So I played, read (avidly, anything and everything) and slept – sometimes sleeping on a makeshift bed made up in the pantry beneath the stairs, our shelter when the air-raid siren sounded.

Nearby Stanton Ironworks and the Ransome and Marles ball-bearing factory at Newark were targets for German bombers on their way back towards the North Sea after raids on Sheffield and the Midlands. Stanton was so big at that time that if it were to be put down in London's Hyde Park, there would not be enough of the park left over to make a bowling green. The ironworks included a plant, built in cooperation with the Ministry of Supply, and in four years it cast 875,000 bombs – a total weight of 175,000 tons – for the RAF.

As well as school football, I played for Cotmanhay Waverley (formed by a devotee of Sir Walter Scott's *Waverley* novels), Stanton Ironworks Colts in the Ilkeston and District League and, in the Midland Amateur Alliance, for Old Ilkestonians, but I enjoyed watching as well as playing the game.

The Manor Ground had been home to Ilkeston football since 1893. Ilkeston Mechanics, Ilkeston Wanderers, Ilkeston United, Ilkeston Town and Ilkeston FC were all senior clubs that had used the ground but fallen by the wayside. I played there towards the end of the war for Granby Junior School and saw Ilkeston Grammar win the town's senior schools' championship, inspiring me to pass the eleven-plus exam. Grammar played in red shirts and blue shorts, colours I desperately wanted to wear. Much later I read that Forest's 1898 FA Cup winners, who defeated Derby County 3-1 in the final, wore those colours, too.

Ilkeston Town's greatest rivalry was with Heanor Athletic (later renamed Heanor Town) just four miles away. Matches between the two were always played at Christmas, at home on Christmas Day and away on Boxing Day or vice versa. Special trolleybuses ran between the two towns for these games but many supporters chose to walk-off a hearty Christmas meal. When a snowfall halted the buses, hundreds trudged across Shipley common, past Shipley colliery, up Hardy Barn hill and through Marlpool before turning left at Heanor market place to the ground. It didn't stop the football. They used to play on snow.

After two seasons, Town joined the Central Alliance and appointed as player-manager Gibson McNaughton, a veteran inside-left who had played for Scottish clubs Clyde, Dundee and Dunfermline Athletic before joining Forest and making eighty-two appearances, scoring thirteen goals, for the Nottingham Reds. Other former Forest players to manage Ilkeston were Jack Hutchinson, John McGovern, Nigel Jemson and Bill Brindley. Steve Chettle was a Town assistant manager.

Ex-Foresters who have played for Ilkeston include inside-right Ken Faulconbridge, a Forest colt as a sixteen-year-old; right-winger Ken Ledger; centre-half Les Smith; left-half Horace Hackland; centre-forward Jackie Ward, scorer of a club record 139 career goals; full-back Dave Baker; and inside-forward Dennis Alexander, who was in the 1957 First Division promotion squad. Several were products of Walker's wartime youth policy. He had started a Colts team as soon as the war began in September 1939, six months after taking the Forest job. It was an innovative venture and, twelve years later, was recalled in a special tribute by former Arsenal and England star Charles Buchan in the first edition of the world's earliest modern-style football magazine *Charles Buchan's Football Monthly* (September, 1951). Walker, said Buchan, was showing the way forward for the English game.

Hackland, a skilful, attack-minded half-back, had been spotted as a teenager with Basford United and Grove Celtic. He was signed by Walker towards the end of the war and, in 1950, by Ilkeston in the office at Oscroft's car showroom on Castle Boulevard, where he worked. Terms of £4 a week were agreed for the part-timer, who was sought after by a number of non-league clubs, but the clincher in the deal was Ilkeston's willingness to provide the player with a pair of contact lenses, making him one of the very few footballers wearing them in those days.

Hackland won four championship medals and later became a coach and then general secretary of the Town club.

Strangely, although many Town players graduated to Football League clubs, none found their way to the City Ground. Two of the most outstanding among them joined Derby County. Full-back Geoff Barrowcliffe, who played 475 times for the Rams between 1950 and 1966, and centre-forward Ray Straw, joint record-holder with thirty-seven goals in a season, came from the Granby Park area of Ilkeston and it was on the park as youngsters that they learned their football.

Two uncles took me to the first Football League match I saw. We were among a 19,000 crowd at the Baseball Ground in May 1947 when 1946 FA Cup winners Derby lost 1-0 to Arsenal. I took a lasting delight in the drama and spectacle. Centre-forward Ronnie Rooke scored the goal and I added Arsenal, in their red shirts with white sleeves, white shorts and blue-and-white-hooped socks (red, white and blue) to my list of favourite teams with Town and Forest. Oddly, Forest and Notts were also both at home that Saturday. There were 16,000 at the City Ground for the Second Division match against Birmingham City, one of my favourite players 'Sailor' Brown scoring for Forest in a 1-1 draw. Across the river, in the Third Division South, Notts beat Brighton 2-0 in front of a crowd of almost 13,000. That was before Lawton mania, when crowds of 30,000 to 40,000 were drawn to Meadow Lane. Why is Derby supposedly a football town and Nottingham not?

It was not until years later that I learned my home town, Forest and Arsenal were linked – by a goalkeeper named Fred Beardsley. Born at Ilkeston on Christmas Day 1856, Fred became one of the finest goalkeepers in England despite being just 5 feet 7 inches in height. What he lacked in inches, he made up for in agility and anticipation. Beardsley was the first of a long line of great Forest goalkeepers, including England internationals Sam Hardy and Peter Shilton. But it was England Under-23 international Peter Grummitt who was probably the most like him for razor-sharp reflexes.

A key figure in the stories of both Nottingham Forest and Arsenal, Fred was a teammate of Forest legends Sam Weller Widdowson and Tinsley Lindley. He moved to London after being sacked from Chilwell Ordnance Depot for taking time off to play football. He got a job with the Royal Arsenal factory at Dial Square, Woolwich, and was instrumental with three other former Forest players, Morris and Charlie Bates and Bill Parr, in the formation of Royal Arsenal Football Club. It was Fred who agreed to approach his former club for help. Forest responded with a full set of red shirts and a football. In return, they asked that the new club allow Fred to rejoin them for FA Cup ties.

Beardsley's last game for Forest was a cup tie three years after leaving Nottingham. He played a total of fifteen FA Cup ties for Forest and the committee honoured him with the presentation of an inscribed and ornately engraved silver cigarette case. A miniature painting of the player himself decorated the lid and the inscription recognised his 'valuable services as the Forest goalkeeper'.

Fred was elected vice-chairman when Arsenal became a limited company in 1893 and served for the next two decades. He quit when Arsenal moved north of the Thames to Highbury and joined the committee at Charlton Athletic for a time before deciding to concentrate on his tobacconist's business. He died in 1939 aged eighty-two. In 1940 a German bomb flattened his former shop.

Nottingham Forest 'A' were the first champions in 1947/48 but, in the early 1950s, Ilkeston Town dominated the Central Alliance, winning the championship in four successive seasons. Gates in excess of 2,000 were the norm. In April 1953, Sheffield Wednesday visited the Manor Ground for a benefit match and were held to a 2-2 draw before a crowd of 4,000. A fortnight later, another 4,000 gate saw Derby prove too strong for the home side. Straw scored a hat-trick against his former club and Jackie Stamps got one in a 4-1 win. Barrowcliffe was also in the Rams' team. Hackland scored Town's goal.

In his book *Football Year* (1954), Dr Percy Young, a respected chronicler of the game, described a visit to Ilkeston where he saw a notice box attached to the wall of the Rutland Hotel. It contained an Ilkeston Town teamsheet that also advised supporters wishing to travel to an away match (if any, he wrote) to meet at the nearby Barton bus company garage. He couldn't know, of course, that Town had a huge travelling support. I remember seven Barton double-deckers being called out to take fans to Linby for a top-of-the-table Alliance clash.

Phil Bibby, Les 'Snowy' Smith and Hackland, all former Foresters, formed a formidable half-back line for Town in a remarkable game that became part of Ilkeston folklore that (with apologies to novelist Mark Haddon) could have been titled *The Curious Incident of the White Ball in a Tree*. Town had reached the first round proper of the FA Cup for the first time and in November 1951 a crowd of about 10,000 came to the Manor Ground to watch the tie against Football League side Rochdale of the Third Division North.

'Please consider your neighbour and squeeze up those extra few inches which will make all the difference to the comfort of the crowd,' wrote secretary Bernard Shaw in his programme notes. 'If you have a boy and he cannot see properly or is in danger of being crushed, send him to the children's corner just above the dressing rooms. A police officer will be in charge there and he will be safer.'

It rained heavily for hours before kick-off. My game for Stanton Colts was called off so I managed, with the cooperation of a friendly official, to get in to watch the second half. The rain was now coming down in torrents. Former West Ham United left-winger Eric Betts had given Rochdale an interval lead when he had beaten goalkeeper Joe Sharman, who had parried his first shot, from the rebound. Jackie Ward, the other former Red in Town's side, ploughed through the mud early in the second half but was thwarted by the conditions and couldn't force the ball past Jimmy Nicholls in the visitors' goal. Then Betts got a second from the penalty spot. Town pressed strongly with only about seven minutes left and Rochdale's desperation showed when a defender smashed the ball high into an elm tree behind the Bath Street goal.

The club had provided a white ball because of the gloom, but it was the only one they had and it was now stuck at the top of a tree outside the ground on land adjacent to the Rutland Hotel. Committee member Alf Jackson tried valiantly to climb the tree but failed to retrieve the ball. After a lengthy delay, referee Turner of Halifax was forced to allow play to resume with a standard ball. Rochdale cleared the resulting corner but in the hectic closing minutes a player from each side was sent off. An FA inquiry was held into allegations by the referee that club officials had not cooperated fully in trying to rescue the white ball. In mitigation, it was pointed out that the ball had been kicked out of the ground by a panicky Rochdale defender. Town were fully exonerated and the white ball episode intrigued the nation after famous broadcaster Richard Dimbleby interviewed secretary Shaw about it when his *Down Your Way* radio programme visited Ilkeston.

The Ball in a Tree became Town's emblem and was worn on their shirts until 1966, when the club replaced white with red as the dominant colour and became known as the Robins. This was the nickname that had been given to Ilkeston United in the past. A new club badge depicting a robin was adopted.

My first steps in journalism were at the Manor Ground as a schoolboy, taking copy from *Ilkeston Advertiser* chief reporter Bill Beardall and running to phone it through to sub-editors at Nottingham's tabloid *Football Post* and broadsheet *Football News,* as well as the Derby *Football Special.* Sadly, the local council decided to redevelop the site of the Manor Ground. The New Manor Ground was opened on 15 August 1992 on a former waste tip off Awsworth Road between the Erewash canal and the river. It has a 3,000 capacity, a landmark Clocktower Stand, a clubhouse and floodlights. Town FC, however, went the way of its predecessor, being ruled insolvent by the High Court over an unpaid tax bill. A new Ilkeston FC was formed in 2010 and plays in the Northern Premier League.

I went with Bill to the FA Cup Final at Wembley in 1950, when Arsenal, wearing gold shirts, beat the reds of Liverpool 2-0. Veteran Joe Mercer, whose father played for Forest in the years leading up to the First World War, captained the victorious Gunners. High-scoring Forest won promotion to the Second Division in Festival of Britain Year 1951 and, on a school trip, I saw my first Shakespeare production at Stratford-upon-Avon. It was *Henry IV, Part I* with a young Richard Burton as Prince Hal and Michael Redgrave playing Hotspur. I was hooked. My wife and I have been Royal Shakespeare Theatre regulars for most of our married life. We also go to opera and ballet. A friend, John Crudgington, whose father was a draughtsman and had drawn the plans for Forest's East Stand (replaced by the Brian Clough stand), persuaded me to go to the Theatre Royal to see a D'Oyly Carte production of *The Mikado*. We went together to the Royal Opera House and, after leaving Covent Garden, we rushed to St Pancras to catch the midnight newspaper train home. The station was a hive of activity with vans offloading batches of the *Mirror, Express, Mail* and more papers hot from the Fleet Street press to be despatched by rail to Nottingham. It was a thrilling sight for a young journalist and a dramatic finale to a remarkable day. John was a fine pianist whose mother had played the organ at city centre cinemas. His father was the first person I knew who drank tea without milk or sugar. Perhaps, then, it's not so surprising then that, to me, football is like a performance art. With handling in play outlawed – apart from the inspired exception of by the two goalkeepers inside their areas – the action is propelled by the players' artistry and the caprice of the ball. If this sounds fanciful, I call upon a few great names in support.

In the 1800s, Sir Walter Scott observed, 'Life is itself but a game of football.' The twentieth-century writer and broadcaster J. B. Priestley wrote in his novel *The Good Companions* that football supporters passed through the turnstile into an 'altogether more splendid kind of life, hurtling with conflict and yet passionate and beautiful in its art' – which, perhaps, should be regarded as the progenitor of the latter-day sobriquet 'the beautiful game', often attributed to Pelé. The twin passions of Dimitri Shostakovich, the famous Russian composer, were music and football. He was an ardent follower of Lenigrad Zenit (now Zenit St Petersburg) and kept meticulous records of scores, teams, transfers and league standings in a ledger. Shostakovich described football as 'the ballet of the people' and included a referee's whistle in the score of his 1930 ballet *The Golden Age*, about a Soviet team touring the West, anticipating the Moscow Dynamos visit to Britain in 1945. The great English composer of *Pomp and Circumstance* (1901), Sir Edward Elgar, went to the matches of Wolverhampton Wanderers with Miss Dora Penny, seventeen years his junior. On their first meeting, she wrote, he wanted to know if she ever watched the Wolves. He set a football chant to music – and immortalised his match day companion as 'Dorabella' in his celebrated *Enigma Variations*. A plaque commemorating the Elgar connection was unveiled at Wolves' Molineux ground in 1998. Author and illustrator of highly collectable guides to the Lake District, Alfred Wainwright co-founded Blackburn Rovers Supporters Association and found happiness in equal measure from both the quiet of remote landscapes and the tumult of a packed Ewood Park. My final witness, the Austrian philosopher Ludwig Wittgenstein, found inspiration at a football match from the game's ebb and flow, strict rules but ready innovation, to write his major work *Philosophic Investigations*.

The defence rests its case. But if you are still unconvinced, I like to add to my argument a few words written an all-time favourite footballer, Tom Finney, of Preston North End and England. His book *Instructions to Young Footballers* was published in 1955 by the Museum Press as part of the Brompton Library, a series which also included titles for young yachtsmen, young swimmers, young gardeners, young anglers and even young geologists. It keeps its place on my bookshelves. Here's what Finney wrote:

> Football is to me a glorious spectacle when you get eleven craftsmen playing the game. Soccer, even in this twentieth century, is not a machine game. I hope we shall never live to see the game played entirely by a system of numbers, so eliminating all artistry. There are times when football must be a duel of man against man to try to create openings. It is in situations like this that we see beautiful movers with the ball like Stan Matthews, Jimmy Hogan, Ernie Taylor and Len Shackleton, shining in all their glorious poetry of movement. They are Masters of the Ball.

Stanley Matthews had just been knighted when he came to the Manor Ground in 1965 as general manager of Port Vale to watch Ilkeston forward John Froggatt. Then editor of the *Advertiser*, I spoke to the great man after the match to see if he had been impressed enough to sign the player. He replied, 'No, he's short-necked and won't win many headers.' I was tempted to ask the 'Wizard of Dribble', 'But what about his dancing feet?' Froggatt later joined Colchester United, helped them win promotion to the Third Division and was voted their Player of the

Year. Eventually, the Vale did sign him – for a fee of £10,000. He returned to Ilkeston in 1986 as manager.

Our two managers, Walker and Clough, probably wouldn't admit to being influenced by football's aesthetic appeal, but the way their teams played tells a different story. I was drawn to the City Ground by the Walker style. Clough's positive outlook kept me attending and enthused sons David and Stephen. Hence, *my desire is always to be here.*

In his autobiography *Soccer in the Blood*, Billy Walker wrote a chapter headed 'Leave the Boys Alone!', condemning early coaching of schoolboys by games masters who destroy their individuality. A natural ball-player would be told not to be selfish, the big kicker praised. 'Let the boys do what comes naturally,' he urged. 'Leave them free to develop their natural skills. The rest will come if the coaches don't get them first.' Brian Clough's approach to working with youngsters was similar. 'I put the ball down and we have a game,' he said.

Their comments, more than fifty or thirty years ago respectively, chime remarkably with the words of Chris Waddle, the former Spurs, Newcastle and England forward, who, after England's 2016 European Championship humiliation, argued:

I was always a dribbler when I was a youngster. If I was starting off now that would be coached out of me. People would say I give the ball away too much or I need to pass quicker. These are things you learn as you get older – when to try to beat your man and when to release the ball. That was something older players drilled into me once I was sixteen or seventeen.

Walker couldn't have put it better.

As Shostakovich would agree, football is a dance with a ball. I learned the steps all right, no problem, but lacked rhythmicity. The coach, or dancing master, may have an influence, good or bad, but it is talent that counts. Were it otherwise, the Austrians, Russians and Hungarians would have continued to dominate European football.

Despite being overwhelmingly 'the people's choice', Clough wasn't given the opportunity to manage at national level. In his final autobiography, *Walking on Water*, Clough wrote:

It would have been the most relaxed England set-up of all time. We would have had a colourful team, playing the type of football the public wants to see, and it would have been winning football as well. The sense of leadership was in my blood and, from somewhere, I had the knack of making players feel good about themselves.

That is a view endorsed by a lifelong friend from another sport, cricket's Geoffrey Boycott, who had known him from back when Clough was a young footballer with Sunderland and Boycott was a young cricketer for Yorkshire. In his book *The Corridor of Certainty*, published in 2014, Boycott wrote:

When I look back and think about all the people I have met during my life, there is one man who has left a lasting impression: Brian Clough. When he retired from playing and became a football manager, I would travel to watch his teams at Derby County and Nottingham Forest, and he, in return, would come to see me bat. I once had a personal glimpse of his man-management skills.

In June 1974, he came to watch me bat against Derbyshire in a championship match at Chesterfield. I was in really good form but early on I pulled Alan Ward straight to the fielder at midwicket, Brian Bolus, and was out for four. I was beside myself with disappointment and, after a little while, Brian came in to see me and I said I had 'ruined the day.' I will never forget what he said to me: 'Look, you see your colleagues outside. They are not sure if they will make a hundred now or ever again. You will get one, if not tomorrow then the week after. You will get plenty because you are that good.' I had just failed and he made me feel ten feet tall. That was his gift: it must have been unbelievable to play for him as he gave players absolute belief in their abilities. I wish he had been my manager as well as a best friend.

What of Billy Walker? Well, I'm convinced he would have made a successful England manager, too. Captain at club and national level, he was open to new ideas, making a point of meeting Jimmy Hogan and Hugo Meisl, learning from the Austrian 'Wunderteam' of the 1930s, the 1945 visit of Moscow Dynamo and the 1953 Hungarians, and being willing to modify English methods. He believed in giving youth a chance without giving them too much too soon. Perhaps that was the failing of Roy Hodgson's England. 'For me, the ideal balance is achieved by having in the team five young players and six with not only the craft for them to emulate but also the experience young men have still to gain,' wrote Walker. 'I am content for them to continue to play patterned football even if the skies should fall.'

Cool Down

We must embrace new ideas and not fear change. The Forest of Billy Walker and Brian Clough is part of this club's glorious past. With European triumphs, governance by committee was outgrown. Next, a local board of directors was dismissed and the single owner arrived. Now we have foreign owners, a Portuguese director of football, Pedro Pereira, and a French head coach, Philippe Montanier, who cuts a fine figure pitchside with an open-necked white shirt, navy-blue suit and Paul Smith designer trainers. Yet it's still 'our Forest' to supporters. The history belongs to them.

Encouragingly, excellent progress is being made with the Nottingham Forest Supporters Trust, now a legal entity, which aims to safeguard the long term future of the football club and act as an independent, effective and democratically organised means of constructive communication between the club and it supporters.

Also seeking to refresh the way fans support the club, a new independent quarterly magazine *Bandy & Shinty* has been established. An editorial in the first edition, published at the beginning of August 2016, declares,

> We hope that by sharing stories we can remind ourselves why we fell in love with this wonderful football club, whilst also creating a library of shared history that we can collect, cherish, nurture and pass on to those who will follow us into the stands.

Another small group of fans who thought that Forest's 150th anniversary was passing them by got together to organise their own celebration.

In April 2016, they were overwhelmed when hundreds gathered at the Orange Tree, formerly the Clinton Arms pub where the club was formed, and then walked together from the Brian Clough statue in the city centre to a match at the City Ground. 'It was abundantly clear that there was a huge appetite for this type of gathering and we felt that it helped create a positive spirit among the fans despite another season of struggle for the club,' Matthew Oldroyd, one of the organisers, told me. 'In a troubling period of NFFC we want to inject some positivity into matchdays with an overall aim of creating a greater level of enjoyment for supporters and, fundamentally, a greater level of support for the team.'

Now it has grown into a new fan movement, the Forza Garibaldi, which aims to stage events at various locations, home and away, to create a positive pre-match atmosphere that continues into the stands. 'We want a culture at Forest centred on an unwavering, relentless support through the good times and the bad, doing things our own way, being original, and not following the latest trends at other clubs up and down the country,' Matthew said. 'We hope our fellow Reds fans will join us under the Forza Garibaldi banner to try to drive the club forward. In addition, we will focus on support inside the ground with flags and banners to help create the atmosphere.' The first gathering was held before the home Championship game against Leeds United on 27 August. Demand was such that three river cruisers were charted to take fans on a trip on the Trent.

When my wife and I were in Venice some years ago, we saw a flotilla of boats in the lagoon in front of St Mark's Square. They were full of cheering, singing football fans, playing trumpets and waving banners, on their way home to Vicenza after the match against local rivals Venezia, whose ground, the Stadio Pierluigi Penzo, is situated on the island of Sant'Elena and is the second oldest in Italy. Many Italian towns feature a statue of Giuseppe Garibaldi, the Che Guevara of his day, a great popular revolutionary who, with his volunteer army, the Redshirts, unified the country and inspired the Victorian founders of Forest. Quoting Garibaldi, the Forza motto is:

We shall meet again before long to march to new triumphs.

Bibliography

Birtles, Garry, *My Magic Carpet Ride* (2010)
Clough, Brian (with John Sadler), *Clough: The Autobiography* (1994)
Clough, Brian (with John Sadler), *Walking on Water* (2002)
Downing, David, *Passovotchka* (1999)
Finney, Tom, *Instructions to Young Footballers* (1955)
Fox, Norman, *Prophet or Traitor? The Jimmy Hogan Story* (2003)
Giles, Edward, *Once, Twice, Three Times a Winner* (2008)
Hodge, Steve, *The Man With Maradona's Shirt* (2010)
Imlach, Gary, *My Father And Other Working-Class Heroes* (2006)
Keane, Roy (with Roddy Doyle), *The Second Half* (2014)
McGovern, John, *From Bo'ness to the Bernabeu* (2012)
Robertson, John, (with John Lawson), *Super Tramp* (2011)
Smith, Rory, *Mister* (2016)
Taylor, Peter (with Mike Langley), *With Clough By Taylor* (1980)
Walker, Billy, *Soccer in the Blood* (1960)
Wilson, Jonathan, *Nobody Ever Says Thank You* (2011)

Acknowledgements

At Ilkeston Grammar School after the Second World War, I was encouraged to write by Miss Vincent, who taught English, and Mr Bettle, who taught history. Miss Vincent was then a middle-aged Scotswoman and the driver of a battered Morris Minor, who alarmed the local police by absent-mindedly neglecting to give way to main road traffic when she crossed Wharncliffe Road on her way home from the market place to Drummond Road. Mr Bettle was a dashing former Royal Artillery captain, who enthused the class with a graphic explanation of how the English archers helped Henry V win the battle of Agincourt. After I had ignored advice from art master Mr Ripley and gone ahead with a colour wash, failing miserably, he told me, 'One day, Wright, you may become prime minister but you'll never make an artist.' He was not angry but amused because he realised I had taken his warning as a challenge. I owe much to the three of them.

My thanks for help and guidance in the writing of this book go to Alan Murphy, Clare Owen and everyone at Amberley Publishing, to Chris Key, Ben Harris, Harvey Parsons, Ashley Lambell and all at Forest and also to Paul Taylor of the *Nottingham Post*; with gratitude, too, to my wife, Barbara, for putting up with me.